Kings and Conquistadors

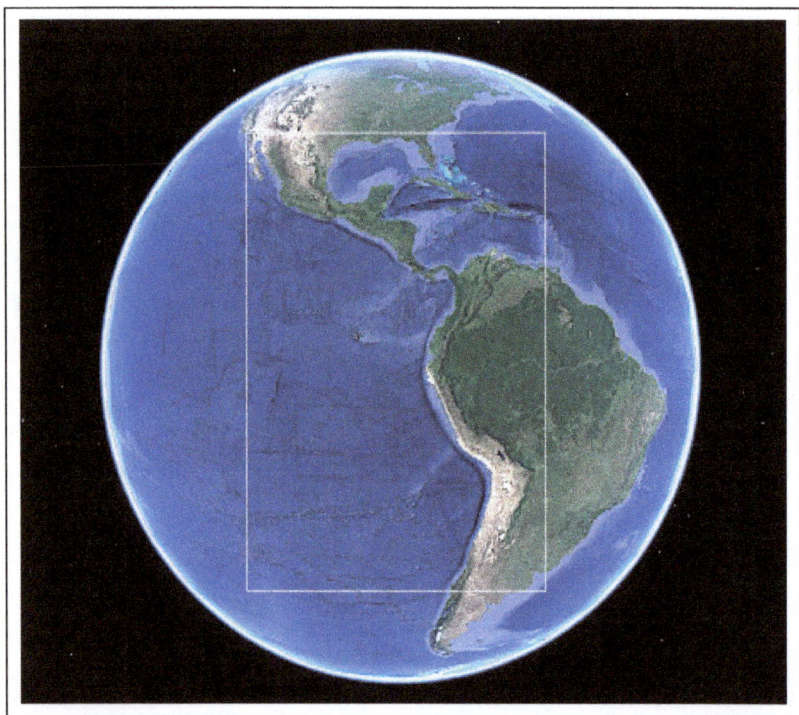

 *Plus Ultra*

Kings and Conquistadors
The Birth of Spain's American Empire

Richard C. Thornton

Academica Press
Washington~London

Library of Congress Cataloging-in-Publication Data

Names: Thornton, Richard C., author. |
Title: Kings and conquistadors: Spain's american empire / Richard C.
Thornton
Description: Washington : Academica Press, 2020. | Includes references.
Identifiers: LCCN 2020942207 | ISBN 9781680531145 (hardcover) |
ISBN 9781680539127 (paperback)

Contents

Preface and Acknowledgements

"History," the poet Theodore Roethke observed, "for all its apparatus, comes to us primarily as a form of intuition. To each his own labyrinth." Roethke's astute insight is particularly relevant to the history of the Spanish conquest of America where, half a millennium removed, the essential facts of the conquest still present a tangled maze, compounded by the paucity of the indigenous record. From the beginning, the Black Legend of anti-Spanish propaganda, court intrigues, and imperial machinations, distorted understanding. Historians ever since have searched the archives in an effort to come to grips with the conquest through the apparatus of historical reimagination, logical extrapolation, and personal intuition. The recent, groundbreaking efforts by Geoffrey Parker, Matthew Restall, and Jared Diamond come to mind.[1] Gaps remain, however, and it is with all due respect and humility that I invite the reader to join me in this adventure through the conquest labyrinth as I attempt to address some of them.

I would like to thank Dr. Thomas LeBlanc, President of The George Washington University, without whose support this book would not have been possible.

I am also indebted to my wife, Joanne, whose research, editing, and map-making skills have enriched this narrative. Her research informs the content, her editing clarifies and sharpens the argument, and her maps provide depth and texture to the history. It goes without saying that all missteps of intuition, extrapolation, or imagination are mine alone.

---

[1] Geoffrey Parker, *Emperor: A New Life of Charles V* (New Haven: Yale University Press, 2019; Matthew Restall, *When Montezuma Met Cortés: The True Story of the Meeting That Changed History* (New York: Ecco, 2018); Jared Diamond, *Guns, Germs, and Steel: The Fates of Human Societies* (New York: Norton, 2017).

Illustrations

Introduction

Spain's American Empire was born in the first half of the sixteenth century, beginning with the voyages of Christopher Columbus. By the middle of the century, a trans-Atlantic structure of islands and colonies stretched from Mexico to Peru and from Nombre de Dios to Seville. How that emerged, and why, is the subject of this history. Initially, the driving force behind exploration was the quest for a new route to China. By the middle of the fifteenth century China had adopted a silver standard, becoming a silver sink as demand outstripped supply. Access to China was severely constricted by the Ottoman Turk seizure of Constantinople in 1453, which prompted a search for an alternate route. The profits to be had from the China trade account for the drive to explore new lands.

The Spanish and Portuguese kings, dividing the world between them in the Treaty of Tordesillas, led the way. King John II of Portugal sent explorers south along the African coast around the Horn of Africa toward Asia. King Ferdinand and Queen Isabella of Spain chose to sail due west. In four voyages, Christopher Columbus stumbled his way to the New World based on completely false premises. Seeking China, he discovered America, believing to his dying day that he had discovered a shortcut to China. Ferdinand, after Isabella's death, attempted to institutionalize the Crown's presence in America, focusing conquistadors' efforts on the acquisition of territory and gold.

In what was a loose, disorderly process marked more by failure than success, the exploration of the New World commenced. The general procedure was for the king to authorize an expedition, partly or wholly finance it, and take a twenty percent share of the profits. Once a territory was conquered, the king would attempt to establish a working government, appointing bureaucrats as governors to administer the new colonies. The conquistadors were generally shunted aside, although there were a few cases of a conquistador becoming a governor, like Pedro de Alvarado in Guatemala.

Although all power came from the king, a dysfunctional triangular tension developed between the king, his governors, and the conquistadors. King Ferdinand, seeking a shortcut to Asia along with gold and territory, encouraged the conquistadors. The governors, seeking power and privilege, sought to bend the conquistadors to their wills. The conquistadors, attempting to evade the restrictions of the governors, sought succor from the king. The press of local circumstances often meant that the king's orders were more honored in the breach than in the observance.

By the time Charles I ascended to the Spanish Throne in 1516, the conquistadors had moved from the offshore islands of Hispaniola, Puerto Rico, Cuba, and Jamaica, onto the mainland of Central America and the north coast of South America—the evolving Spanish Main—but there was little gold and the colonies were foundering. It was already becoming apparent that the native population had declined, afflicted by diseases brought by the Spaniards, and the king sought to augment the labor supply by permitting the importation of slaves from Africa. The conquistadors embarked on forays into neighboring territories to capture slaves on their own. Death from exposure to disease, and from combat, would be a continuing problem for Spanish decisionmakers.

In 1524, King Charles (by then also Emperor Charles V) established the Council of the Indies to provide overall direction of the Spanish enterprise. It was needed, as governors were pursuing personal objectives over those of the monarch. Panamanian Governor Pedrarias, for example, had executed Vasco Núñez de Balboa against the king's wishes and Cuban Governor Diego Velázquez had attempted to thwart Hernán Cortés, but failed to prevent his voyage to the Yucatan. Later, he would send an army after Cortés in Mexico, unbeknownst to the king. Cortés conquered the Aztecs in spite of the governor's interference and the king later displaced him.

The conquistadors were the pathfinders for the Spanish state, whose leaders promised them a share of the discovered wealth. Their success predestined their own eclipse, however, as the king set about to regulate the conquered territories. Throughout, the Crown employed humanitarian policies as a double-edged sword to weaken the *encomienda* system of the conquistadors and to install its representatives as officers to ensure compliance. At this early stage, the Catholic Church was, perhaps, an unwitting co-conspirator in this deception. Policies proclaiming the humanitarian treatment of the natives looked good on paper, but never took precedence over the state's determination to extract American wealth for its imperial designs.

Bureaucratic interference also bedeviled Francisco Pizarro. Yet he built on the efforts of his predecessors to make an unparalleled contribution to the wealth of his country. When he finally landed in Peru after many trials, Pizarro found an Inca regime convulsing in upon itself in a violent succession struggle. He then returned to Spain to seek approval to intervene in the struggle on the side of one of its contenders. That authorization, the *Capitulación de Toledo* signed by the queen, enabled Pizarro to embark upon the conquest of Peru, but it also became the root of the conflict among Spaniards who fought over the spoils.

The conquest of Peru was an awesome feat, considering the challenge of its topography and the ferocity of its people. The Inca Empire, stretching over two thousand five hundred square miles from present-day Ecuador to central Chile and along the western side of the Andes mountains, commanded an estimated population of ten million people. Most of the conquest took place at an altitude between nine and eleven thousand feet, four thousand feet higher than the Mexican plateau, and in extremely rugged terrain. Nevertheless, Pizarro succeeded with the support of disaffected subject tribes and the application of superior Spanish weapons technology.

The main story of post-conquest Peru is that of the struggle of Spaniard against Spaniard, with natives as onlookers and, in a sense, beneficiaries. The king sent an army to regain control of his rebellious colony from Pizarro's brother, Gonzalo, who sought independence. The failure of Gonzalo's war marked the end of the conquistador era, and the entrenchment of the king's rule.

Chapter 1

Searching for China, Discovering America

Trade between China and Europe was established before the Christian era, occurring along the Silk Road since the Han Dynasty (221-206 BC). Land routes through Central Asia between Chang An and Constantinople and sea routes across the Mediterranean and Red Seas took Chinese spices, tea, porcelain, silk, paper and other exotic items to the West. In general, China was the seller in this trade, which the Chinese characterized as a tributary system, supplying quality products of a highly developed culture unavailable in the Europe of that day. But the fall of Constantinople to the Ottoman Turks in 1453 made the land route more difficult, precarious and expensive, and ways were sought to reach China by sea.

Coincidentally, by the mid-fifteenth century during the Ming Dynasty (1368-1644), tumultuous changes were occurring in China that would reverberate throughout the world. As the largest economy in the world with a population of over one hundred million people—more than Europe's combined populations—China was also the first culture to employ paper currency. However, it was not a stable financial system. Based on the woodblock printing process, Chinese paper currency was easily counterfeited, which led to repeated devaluations and inflationary spirals despite vigorous and extreme measures to maintain stability.

During the last of many failed attempts to sustain a paper currency system, there occurred a gradual shift to silver as a medium of exchange. As the value of the paper currency depreciated and inflation roared once again, China's large merchant class increasingly demanded payment in specie, principally in silver. Reluctantly, in 1423, the imperial throne decided to consolidate multiple taxes into one, called the "single whip" or "single lash" tax.

Within a few years, by the middle of the century, the emperor decided to shift entirely to a silver-based monetary system. Suddenly, China had turned from being a seller of goods to the world to a buyer of silver from it, because China's domestic silver production could not come close to satisfying domestic demand. The silverization of the Chinese economy would have far-reaching consequences not only for China, but also for the world, as China became a magnet for the metal. But where would the silver come from, and how would it be transported to the Middle Kingdom?

Word of the monetary transformation spread through China's tributary system to all of Asia, and by caravan along the Silk Road to Europe. No doubt the famous admiral, Zheng Ho, during his seven voyages across the southern oceans to East Africa and places between (1403-1433) was but one of many traders who carried the news of China's growing demand for silver, and her willingness to pay handsomely to get it. The decision to import silver galvanized potential sellers the world over into the search for new routes to China, as well as for the precious metal, because the arbitrage opportunities for profit and wealth accumulation were limitless.

Hypothetically, as Giraldez described it, given the divergent exchange ratio between gold and silver,

> [A merchant] could use an ounce of gold to buy, say, eleven ounces of silver in Amsterdam, transport the silver to China and exchange the eleven ounces there for about two ounces of gold. The two ounces of gold could be brought back to Europe and exchanged for twenty-two ounces of silver, which could again be transported back to China where its value was doubled again. This process of "arbitrage" would continue until China's silver stock rose sufficiently to lower its value there to the value prevailing in the rest of the world.[1]

In other words, as silver flowed into China, gold and other products flowed out. It would in fact take over a century for this process of equilibration to work itself out and for gold and silver ratios to converge in Europe and

---

[1] A. Giraldez Rivero, "Born With a Silver Spoon: China, American Silver and Global Markets During the Early Modern Period," PhD Diss., (University of Amsterdam, 1999), 57.

China and effectively minimize arbitrage opportunities. But until then, it would be the prospect of tremendous arbitrage profits that drove the search for gold and silver in Europe, the Orient, and the Americas, triggering a price revolution and linking together regional economies into a world economy, certainly as far as trade in precious metals was concerned.

Adam Smith, in *Wealth of Nations*, observed the continuing power of the arbitrage effect at the end of the eighteenth century:

> [The] precious metals are a commodity which it always has been, and still continues to be extremely advantageous to carry from Europe to India. There is scarce any commodity which brings a better price there, or which, in proportion to the quantity of labour and commodities which it costs in Europe, will purchase or command a greater quantity of labour and commodities in India. It is more advantageous, too, to carry silver thither than gold; because in China...the proportion between fine silver and fine gold is but as ten, or at most as twelve, to one; whereas in Europe it is as fourteen or fifteen to one. In China, and the greater part of the other markets of India, ten, or at most twelve, ounces of silver will purchase an ounce of gold; in Europe it requires from fourteen to fifteen ounces. In the cargoes, therefore, of the greater part of European ships which sail to India [and China], silver has generally been one of the most valuable articles.... The silver of the new continent seems in this manner to be one of the principal commodities by which the commerce between the two extremities of the old one is carried on, and it is by means of it, in a great measures, that those distant parts of the world are connected with one another.[2]

Spain—Silver, Gold, and Empire

As China's demand for silver grew, multiple supply sources soon emerged, including Hungary and Japan, but the first response came from Spain.[3] Europeans had known of China since the days of Marco Polo's voyages in the late thirteenth century, and travel along the caravan trade route across Central Asia and the Mediterranean was common. But

---

[2] Adam Smith, *An Inquiry into the Nature and Causes of the Wealth of Nations* (London: Strahan and Cadell, 1776; Ann Arbor: Text Creation Partnership, 2011), chap. 11:259, http://name.umdl.umich.edu/004861571.0001.001

[3] Hungary was an important source of silver mining at this time, but its subjection to Ottoman domination limited its role in the emerging global silver market. Japan also became a major silver producer later in the 16th Century.

European interest in the China trade leaped on the news of China's new demand for silver. The Chinese were paying double the price for silver compared to the going rate in Europe. The arbitrage possibility inspired visions of great wealth and power—if only the opportunity could be accessed. Therein lay a problem. By the fifteenth century the Ottomans had taken control of the land route to China, and their fees, added to those of the Venetians commanding the Mediterranean segment of the route, made transit expensive.

Was there a shorter route by sea? The Portuguese thought so. Their intrepid seamen had already explored the west coast of Africa, establishing trading posts and settlements. They believed that once they rounded the Cape of Good Hope at the southern tip of the continent, the way would be open to the Orient.

A young but experienced Genoese seaman and navigator named Christopher Columbus had another idea. Based on his own studies and the charts and records of his deceased father-in-law, who was also a mapmaker and navigator, Columbus advanced the idea of going directly west, instead of south, to reach China more quickly.[4]

In 1484, Columbus presented his idea to King John II of Portugal, who set up a commission to study it. The king's commission rejected Columbus's proposal on logistical grounds, believing that the distances to China were greater than he claimed and that therefore there would be no place to resupply his ships en route. The fact that the king's seamen were succeeding in their voyages sailing along the African coast no doubt was a factor in his decision. The king's rejection combined with the death of his wife, Felipa, left Columbus dejected and despondent, prompting his decision to move to Spain with his five-year-old son Diego the following year.

Gaining an audience in May 1486 with King Ferdinand and Queen Isabella, co-rulers of Spain, Columbus proposed his shortcut to China once again, and once again a king's maritime commission considered and rejected it. But Ferdinand and Isabella believed Columbus's proposal had merit, granting him a retainer and a place at court. They were heavily

---

[4] Arnold K. Garr, "Years in Portugal: Emergence of the Grand Idea," *Christopher Columbus: A Latter Day Saint Perspective* (Provo: BYU Press, 1992) 19-28.

engaged in a long war to expel the Muslims from the Iberian Peninsula and decided to postpone consideration of other projects until the war was over. In the meantime, Columbus accepted an invitation of King John II to return to Portugal, which he did in 1488. Unfortunately for Columbus, the move came at a most inopportune time.

In December 1488, in a major development, Portuguese explorer Bartholomew Diaz returned from his successful circumnavigation of the Cape of Good Hope around the southern tip of Africa. It meant that the Portuguese had found a sea route to India and beyond to the Orient. It also meant that the King now lost interest in Columbus's idea of sailing west. With little hope of finding a sponsor among the Portuguese, who were committed to the southern approach, Columbus repaired once again to Spain. At the same time, he sent his brother Bartholomew to both London and Paris to explore the possibilities there. English King Henry VII showed no interest, but King Charles VIII of France offered him the job of court mapmaker, which he accepted.[5]

Back in Spain once again in 1490, Columbus made yet another pitch for his idea to sail west to China and once again was rejected by the royal commission. This time, however, the king and queen privately advised him to be prepared to present his plan again once the war with the Muslims was over, which appeared imminent. Unfortunately, the battle for Granada, which would decide the outcome, dragged on; and Columbus, losing patience, decided to join his brother in Paris and try his luck at the court of Charles VIII. As luck would have it, he was persuaded at the last moment to make one last presentation to Ferdinand and Isabella.

As the king's commission was considering his proposal, on January 2, 1492, Spain defeated the Muslims at Granada, completing the *Reconquista* and greatly strengthening a newly unified Spain. Ferdinand and Isabella were now favorably disposed to reconsider Columbus's plan, but the admiral overreached. He demanded that, if successful, he be awarded hereditary titles and governorship over all lands discovered in addition to a ten percent finder's fee of all wealth found. Ferdinand and Isabella thought his terms "too extravagant," and declined his proposal.

[5] Garr, "Years in Spain: Columbus Finds a Sponsor," Ibid., 29-37.

Rejected again, Columbus decided once and for all to leave Spain, join his brother in France and try there.

On his way to France, Columbus stopped at Cordoba, and while there, events at court in Santa Fe led to a reversal of fortune. Luis de Santangel, financial adviser to the Crown, persuaded the queen to change her mind. He argued that Columbus's plan offered little risk and great potential reward in terms of imperial glory, religious evangelism, territorial acquisition and national wealth. In the end, after eight years of almost continual frustration and rejection, Columbus received support for his expedition from King Ferdinand and Queen Isabella, who granted everything he demanded—contingent, of course, upon the success of his mission.[6]

Christopher Columbus and the Search for Gold and Cathay

With three ships manned by eighty-seven men, Columbus set off from Palos, Spain on August 3, 1492. Instead of sailing due west to the Azores, which were under Portuguese control, he went south to the Canary Islands off the northwest coast of Africa. After replenishing provisions, he headed west on September 6, under favorable northeast trade winds, arriving off the coast of the Bahamas on October 12.

Columbus thought—and would consistently but erroneously maintain—that he had reached China, but of course he had not. Upon his arrival, the natives all thought he had come from heaven, as their beliefs predicted would occur, and therefore initially treated him with great deference. Moving on, he landed on the southeast coast of Cuba, which he again thought was China, or at least, Japan. Sailing further he arrived at the island that comprises present-day Haiti and the Dominican Republic. He christened it *La Isla Española* (*Insula Hispana* in Latin; subsequently the name was Latinized as *Hispaniola*, which will be used henceforth in this text), and here he at last obtained some gold trinkets but lost one of his ships. Gold and other riches, after all, were what he was after.

---

[6] "Columbus, Queen Isabella and King Ferdinand in Cordoba: The Real Connection," *Infocordoba.com*, History, Articles: Christopher Columbus and Cordoba.

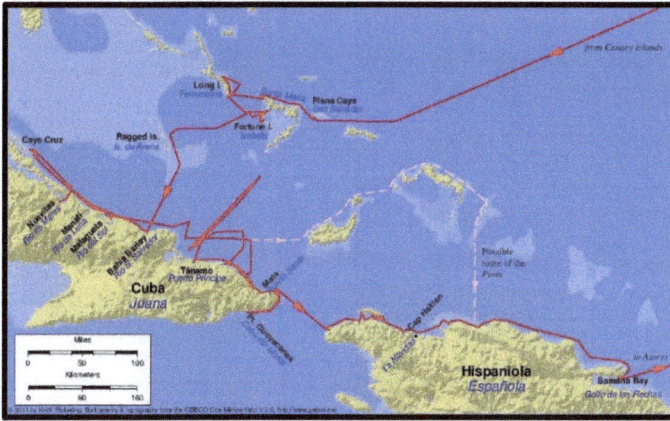

1.1. First voyage of Christopher Columbus, 1492-1493.
Map by Keith Pickering.

After three months exploring the islands, but never actually setting foot on the continent of North America, Columbus departed for Spain on January 16, 1493, leaving behind forty of his men to hold the redoubt they had built, called *La Navidad.* The return voyage turned into a nightmare, as his ships were battered by a severe winter storm in mid-February that forced him to seek safe harbor on the small island of Santa Maria in the Azores. However, unfriendly Portuguese authorities temporarily detained him and his men for ten days (February 18-28) before he was permitted to proceed.[7] Upon approaching the Spanish coast he was beset by yet a second storm that forced him to put in at Lisbon, Portugal. After being "interviewed" by King John II, Columbus straggled back to his point of departure at Palos, Spain, on March 15.

Columbus had not brought back sufficient bounty to pay for the cost of his expedition, but the news of his voyage electrified the courts of Europe. The significance of his undertaking lay not in his failure to reach China, but in its promise of vast new lands to be discovered and riches to be obtained. In his report to the king and queen, Columbus continued to assert that he had discovered the shortcut to China and told of being informed of "a greater abundance of gold" on islands that he had not visited. He maintained that if his sovereigns would support another

---

[7] Rebecca Catz, "Columbus in the Azores," *Portuguese Studies* 6 (1990): 17–23. http://www.jstor.org/stable/41104900

expedition "I will give them as much gold as they have need of, and in addition spices, cotton and mastic…and as much aloes-wood, and as many heathen slaves as their majesties may choose to demand."[8]

News of Columbus's discoveries was, perhaps, of greatest concern to King John II of Portugal. No doubt alerted in advance as the result of his earlier interview with Columbus, the king declared that according to the 1484 Papal Bull of Pope Sixtus IV, which granted to Portugal all of the lands south of the Cape Verde Islands, Columbus's discovery was Portugal's. Ferdinand and Isabella countered his claim with an appeal to the new Pope, the Spanish-born Alexander VI, whom they had helped gain the papacy. Pope Alexander obliged, establishing a demarcation line that ruled in favor of Columbus, thus legitimizing Spain's claim.

Armed with competing Papal Bulls, the sovereigns decided to compromise. The Treaty of Tordesillas, June 7, 1494, divided the unknown world between them. Portugal was awarded rights to all yet undiscovered territory east of a longitudinal line roughly 1,185 miles west of the Cape Verde Islands, and Spain was awarded rights to all yet undiscovered territory west of it. This gave Portugal claim to the eastern portion of Brazil that juts into the Atlantic. Despite the fact that no other country ever recognized the treaty, it served to roughly denote the boundaries of future exploration by the two powers.[9]

Meanwhile, King Ferdinand and Queen Isabella were persuaded by Columbus's promises and agreed to support a larger expedition. Their objectives were to establish a permanent settlement in the "new world," use it as a base from which to find China, and to search for gold and silver to finance their dreams of empire. "Gold fever" had consumed Spain, so there was no dearth of investors to fund Columbus's second trip. This expedition would be nearly six times the size of the first, with seventeen ships and over fourteen times the number of passengers and crew. Twelve hundred adventurers—soldiers of fortune, farmers, carpenters and other

---

[8] "Columbus reports on his first voyage, 1493," *History Now*, The Gilder Lehrman Institute of American History, www.gilderlehrman.org.

[9] "Treaty of Tordesillas," *Encyclopedia Britannica*, www.britannica.com, updated December 10, 2018.

workmen—had signed on for the prospect of enrichment, including priests determined to convert the heathens. They brought with them horses, sheep, cattle, dogs, and various food plants they hoped to cultivate on the islands. They also brought disease.

Columbus set out on his second voyage to America on September 24, 1493, arriving first at the island he named *Dominica*, which lay roughly at the mid-point of the West Indies island chain, on November 3. He sailed north and west from there passing through the Virgin Islands and reaching Puerto Rico on November 19. Three days later he arrived at Hispaniola, the island he had discovered on his first trip. Seeking the forty men he had left to maintain the settlement at La Navidad, he found that they had all been killed and the settlement burned to the ground. Upon investigation he learned that the settlers had begun seizing native women, prompting outraged natives to rise up against them in revenge.

Columbus decided to establish a new settlement on the north coast where he had found some gold nuggets on his first trip. He named this place *La Isabella*. Exploring inland and finding some gold mines, he also

1.2. Second voyage of Christopher Columbus, 1493-1496.
Map by Keith Pickering.

established a fort in the interior. Conditions were difficult and many of the settlers perished from an undetermined sickness. Farming was unsuccessful as crops withered. Many settlers tried to barter with the natives for gold, but pickings were slim, and they became restive. Columbus sought to use force to maintain order against settlers and natives alike, including the use of fierce dogs that he had brought with him, but these tactics only inflamed sentiment against him.[10] Finally, on February 2, 1494, he sent twelve of his ships back to Spain with several hundred disgruntled settlers who had endured enough.

When the ships arrived at Cadiz on March 9, the settlers disembarked along with some thirty thousand pesos worth of gold dust obtained from the mines and from panning the rivers. Despite its paucity, it was enough to arouse ideas of a gold rush to the Indies. Complaints about Columbus's governorship by those who had returned, however, prompted Ferdinand and Isabella to send the papal legate Bernard Buyl to the colony "to check on Columbus." Buyl's report to Ferdinand and Isabella recounted "how Columbus brutalized the natives, how the colony was almost in a state of anarchy, and how the island did not seem to be anywhere near India."[11]

Meanwhile, unaware of the growing concerns of the throne, on April 24, 1494, Columbus set out from Hispaniola on an exploratory trip, searching for China. Instead, he rediscovered Cuba. For the next four months he explored it and nearby islands, returning to Hispaniola on August 20. Again, mistakenly, he believed that Cuba was a peninsula of China. What he found upon his return to Hispaniola was that conditions had deteriorated. Nine months had passed and the settlers who had decided to stay were greatly disillusioned. Worse, there was little prospect of finding enough gold to repay the investors who had funded his expedition.

Desperate to find gold, Columbus's first scheme was to set up a tribute system whereby native men were coerced to deliver a specific quota of gold and silver every three months or face severe punishment. That only drove natives away. Those who did not die from the diseases brought by the Spanish, especially smallpox against which they had no immunity, simply vanished into the forests, or fled the islands entirely. Columbus enslaved those who remained, forcing them to labor in the mines and

---

[10] John and Jeannette Varner, *Dogs of the Conquest* (Norman: University of Oklahoma Press, 1983), 4.

[11] Mary Ames Mitchell, "Christopher Columbus' Second Voyage," *Crossing The Ocean Sea* (Online: Mary Ames Mitchell, 2015), http://www.crossingtheoceansea.com/OceanSeaPages/OS-65-Columbus2ndVoyage.html.

farms. He employed his superior weapons power and war dogs to attack and subdue the natives in the surrounding islands, among them *Caribes* who were said to be cannibals. His brutal policies, along with disease, were responsible for the population decline that began in the islands.[12]

Early in 1495 Columbus hit upon a second scheme whereby he thought he could obtain funds to repay his investors—the slave trade. He knew that the Portuguese had been engaged in a profitable slave trade in Africa and that some of the native tribes he had encountered in the islands enslaved their enemies. He sent a letter to the king and queen aboard one of the ships that periodically returned to Spain proposing that he send natives back to Europe as slaves. Columbus did not wait for an answer, seizing some 1,600 natives and shipping 560 to Spain. Two hundred perished en route, many others were ill by the time they arrived.

Columbus had not shipped these slaves to the king and queen, but to one of his investors, the Florentine venture capitalist Gianatto Berardi, who was in the African slave trade. Ferdinand and Isabella were outraged when they learned that Berardi was attempting to auction off slaves obtained from Columbus. Although they had sent Columbus a reply rejecting his proposal, he had pre-empted them. They had no intention of following in the footsteps of the Portuguese slavers, even though they had enslaved Muslims captured in battle. As Catholics, they were opposed to enslavement, so they released most, sent those who wished back to the islands, and used some to work in galleys. As long as Isabella was alive the throne refused to countenance the slave trade. That would change after her death when the population decline of the indigenous Indians prompted a reversal and Ferdinand authorized the shipment of slaves to the Indies.

Disappointment with Columbus and a New Plan

What Ferdinand and Isabella learned about Columbus's governorship and explorations of the islands convinced them that he had exaggerated about the "riches of the Indies." His promises had been empty. There was no discovery of China, no huge deposits of gold, and no spices or other valuable objects, only slaves. They decided to open the field of

---

[12] See Jared Diamond, *Guns, Germs, and Steel: The Fates of Human Societies* (New York: Norton, 2017), chap.11.

exploration to all comers, while taking back some of the promises they made to Columbus. On April 10, the monarchs issued new rules for colonization of the Indies. Under the so-called *New Permissions*, Columbus's writ was now limited to Hispaniola. Everywhere else was open for exploration and claim by any Spanish subject, as long as they acted in the name of Spain. Henceforth, new expeditions would require the Crown's formal assent, and those that received it would be supported for a full year. The conquistadors were promised one third of the proceeds from their booty and ninety percent of the goods seized. They would be free from taxes although the Crown would expect to receive its "royal fifth." [13]

When Columbus learned of the Crown's decision to change policy, he decided to return to Spain. However, in the islands the hurricane season of 1495 wreaked havoc with Columbus's ships as well as others that had come as part of the new policy, delaying his return. Constructing a new ship from the debris of sunken craft, Columbus set off for Spain on March 10, 1496 with over two hundred unhappy colonists to determine his fate, arriving in Cadiz on June 11. Although it would take over a year for Columbus to clear his name and get back in the good graces of Ferdinand and Isabella, it was apparent that his success in reaching new lands had increased the pace of exploration.

Zuan Chabotto, or John Cabot as we have come to know him, was a Venetian who persuaded England's Henry VII to fund an expedition to find a faster way to China along the North Atlantic route. His first voyage was aborted after he reached Iceland in 1496, but his second was more successful, reaching Newfoundland and Nova Scotia in June 1497. He, too, thought he had discovered the shortcut to China even though the terrain he observed did not match reports about Cathay. Cabot claimed these lands for England and Venice, returning to Bristol in August of the same year. Cabot's voyages were England's first forays into the exploration of the New World, but there would be over a hundred years' hiatus before permanent English settlements were founded in North America.

---

[13] Mitchell, "Christopher Columbus' Second Voyage."

The summer of 1497 saw two more departures. Cabot set out on his third voyage and the Portuguese Vasco de Gama also left on his search for India. His voyage would take over two years to complete, but as far as Ferdinand and Isabella were concerned, pressure was building to continue efforts to find the shortcut to China. Relenting, they once again turned to their proven explorer, the Admiral of the Seas. Two additional factors persuaded them to support Columbus's third trip. These were rumors by some of those who had returned of large gold mines on Hispaniola and Portuguese reports that indicated a large continent lay further to the south of the Indies and west of the Cape Verdes. Could it be the fabled Cathay?

Ferdinand and Isabella commanded Columbus to ameliorate his rule of the island by freeing the enslaved natives and attempting to convert them, instead. He was also directed to relocate his settlement closer to where the gold mines were reportedly located on the south side of the island. (The new settlement would be Santo Domingo, which would shortly become a major portal for entry into the New World.) Most of all, his mission was to look south to determine what was there. Departing with

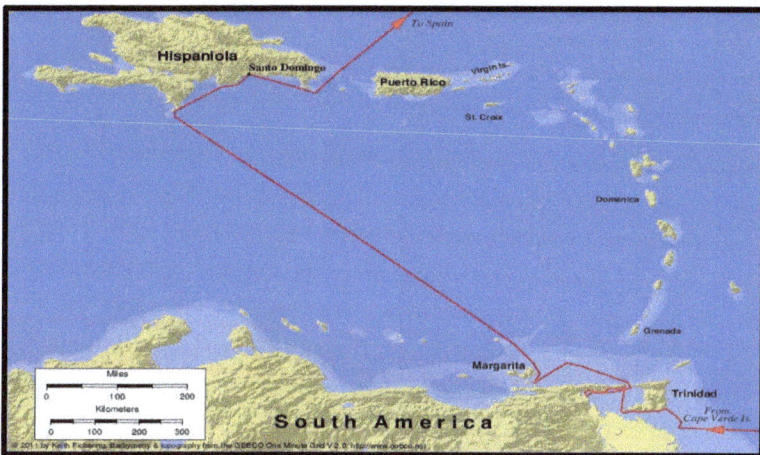

**1.3. Third voyage of Christopher Columbus, 1498-1500.
Map by Keith Pickering.**

six ships at the end of May 1498, he reached the Canary Islands on June 19 where he resupplied his ships. Upon departure he divided his flotilla, sending his brother Bartholomew with three ships directly west to Hispaniola, and sailing the other three southwards to where he thought the rumored continent might be. Columbus found South America, but did not realize it. His ships reached Trinidad, off the northeast coast of South America, and identified the mouth of the Orinoco River before heading to Hispaniola in August. As before, however, he misconceived where he had gone, professing to believe that what he had explored had been the coast of India.[14]

Upon arrival at Hispaniola, Columbus found the colony up in arms against his brother Bartholomew. To restore some semblance of order he employed harsh measures, hanging the rebel leaders and imprisoning others, but animus continued to fester. It would take two years to achieve order, though with lasting resentment. Unable to restore harmony, Columbus requested that Ferdinand and Isabella send a judge to reestablish order. They sent a commissioner, Don Francisco de Bobadilla. When he arrived at Santo Domingo in August 1500, he quickly removed Columbus and his people from power, put them in chains, and sent them back to Spain for trial. In Spain, the admiral was quickly exonerated and compensated for his ordeal but remained under a cloud for several months. It was apparent to Spanish officials that Columbus was a great navigator, but a poor administrator.

Meanwhile, more was being learned about the vast landmass across the Atlantic as Ferdinand and Isabella sent expeditions far and wide. Seamen explored and mapped as far south as the Rio de la Plata in present-day Argentina and as far north as Nova Scotia. Also, Vasco de Gama had returned in the fall of 1499 having reached the west coast of India. It seemed that the dream of bypassing the Turkish grip on the Silk Road to China was in sight—and the Portuguese had done it. All this galvanized Ferdinand and Isabella to make one last effort to discover China—and Columbus was once again called upon to give it a try. The monarchs agreed to finance a fourth voyage, making it clear that their interest was not in further colonization of the Indies, but in finding the way to China and in the acquisition of wealth—gold, silver, spices—to finance their budding empire. Indeed, they forbade him to visit his old island home of

---

[14] Mary Ames Mitchell, "Christopher Columbus' Third Voyage," *Crossing the Ocean Sea* (Online: Mary Ames Mitchell, 2015), http://www.crossingtheoceansea.com/OceanSeaPages/OS-75-Columbus3rdVoyage.html.

Hispaniola, directing him to search for the Strait of Malacca, which was understood to be the gateway to China and Japan.

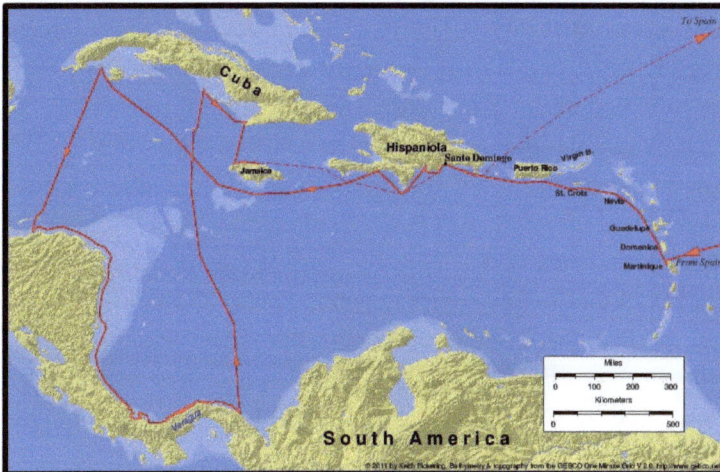

1.4. Fourth voyage of Christopher Columbus, 1502-1504.
Map by Keith Pickering.

Columbus left Cadiz on his fourth voyage with four ships and 140 men at the end of the first week of May 1502, reaching the Indies at the end of June. During the sea passage he discovered that one of his ships had become damaged. Although commanded not to go to Hispaniola where the settlement's feelings were still strong against him, Columbus decided to put in to Santo Domingo anyway to acquire another ship. But the new governor, Nicolás de Ovando, denied him entry, forcing Columbus to drop anchor in a secluded nearby cove. The altercation turned out to be fortuitous because the first of several hurricanes that seemed to dog Columbus hit Santo Domingo destroying nearly all of the treasure ships that had just set out for Spain. Columbus's ships survived the storm with but moderate damage.[15]

Leaving the island, Columbus sailed across the Caribbean, reaching landfall off present-day Honduras at the end of July. He spent the next two months working his way down the coast to present-day Panama. Although beset by storms and hostile natives as well as some friendly ones,

---

[15] Keith A. Pickering, "The Fourth Voyage of Columbus," The Columbus Navigation Homepage, http://columbuslandfall.com/ccnav/index.shtml.

including perhaps some of the Maya tribe, this part of his voyage was truly one of discovery. He found that the natives possessed and were willing to trade away an abundance of gold, and he learned from them that a short distance across the isthmus lay a vast ocean.[16] (This information reinforced what he had learned from fellow Spanish explorer Rodrigo de Bastidas who had discovered Panama a year earlier.)

It was now the New Year, 1503, and Columbus decided to establish a base on the north coast of Panama at the mouth of the Belen River. He sought to use the fort as his headquarters as he searched the area for gold and the south coast. By early April the gold had petered out and he decided to return to Spain with the good news—even though he had not actually reached the Pacific coast. At this point Indians mounted a powerful attack on his fort, which he barely was able to fend off, losing a ship in the process. Columbus abandoned the fort and, cramming his men aboard the remaining three ships, started for home.[17]

No sooner had he set out than he realized his ships were badly weakened by shipworms, the wood-eating mollusks that were the bane of all mariners. In fact, he had to abandon one ship almost immediately, as it was no longer seaworthy. Now with only two ships, overloaded with crew and bounty, Columbus decided to head for Santo Domingo for repairs. He never made it. Another storm hit off Cuba and he was forced to beach his sinking ships on Jamaica, an island that was as yet unsettled by the Spanish. Landing on June 25, 1503, Columbus and his men would be stranded on Jamaica for an entire year, even though two of his men, with help from local Indians, managed to sail a reinforced canoe fitted with a sail to Santo Domingo for help. Governor Ovando, however, no friend of Columbus as we have seen, refused to send a rescue ship. It would not be until mid-June, 1504 that Columbus's men were able to charter a sloop to rescue the marooned expedition. He returned home to Cadiz on November 7, 1504, completing his last voyage.[18]

Columbus had stumbled his way into the new world, an epic achievement based on completely false premises, fervently believing with

---

[16] Ibid.
[17] Ibid.
[18] Ibid.

each voyage that he was only a step away from China. He never reached China, or Japan, or the Malacca Strait, but he did establish that a vast, new unexplored land existed between Europe and Asia. His exploits over a dozen years opened the floodgates to other European adventurers who dared to explore the New World, which would be named after one of them—Amerigo Vespucci—in 1507, a year after Columbus passed away. Columbus enjoyed the legacy of discovery, but it would be his compatriots, whom he inspired, who would establish the financial basis of Spain's empire.[19]

Death of Isabella and Dawn of Ferdinand's Machiavellianism

Christopher Columbus's return to Spain had come less than three weeks before the death of his beloved queen Isabella, November 24, 1504. Her death would mark a major turn in Ferdinand's approach to foreign affairs once issues of succession had been surmounted. In July 1505, Ferdinand struck an alliance with France by marrying Germaine de Foix, niece of Louis XII. Two years later when named Regent to his six-year-old grandson Charles, the future Charles V, Ferdinand's plans to expand the realm became more Machiavellian. Indeed, Machiavelli's *Prince* was said to have been modeled after him. He built a coalition with France, Pope Julius II, and the Holy Roman Emperor Maximillian to defeat the Republic of Venice in 1508. Two years later, however, he turned against France, allying with the pope, the emperor, and Henry VIII to seize the duchy of Navarre on the northwest border between Spain and France.

It soon became apparent to Ferdinand that sustaining armies in combat required more wealth than he had at his disposal. His need for greater wealth to fund his quest for empire soon turned his attention to the Indies. As the king noted the steady increase in gold being imported from the islands, he directed further exploration of the mainland. (Between 1503 and 1505 nearly half a million pesos had been imported and between 1505

---

[19] For a concise account of Columbus's misunderstandings, see Edmund S. Morgan, "Columbus' Confusion About the New World," *Smithsonian Magazine* (online), October 2009, https://www.smithsonianmag.com/travel/columbus-confusion-about-the-new-world-140132422/.

and 1510 the figure nearly doubled, but there were clear signs that they were reaching the limits of what more could be extracted.)[20] On July 25, 1511, Ferdinand exhorted his conquistadors: "get gold, humanely, if you can, but at all hazards, get gold."[21] He would not live to see his charge fulfilled, dying January 23, 1516, but his successors would get gold, in full measure, and not by any means humanely.

In other words, Ferdinand shifted emphasis from a search for a shortcut to China to a search for gold and other wealth in the New World that would support his ambitious dreams for empire in Europe. Yet, Spanish discovery and conquest was not an orderly process. In fact, much the reverse was true. In 1508 King Ferdinand had put in place an administrative structure for exploration of the mainland beyond the islands which he called *Tierra Firme*, or what would be referred to as the Spanish Main(land). The people put in charge, however, were venal officials with connections to the Crown; and they were more interested in consolidating their hold on power than exploring new territories. Much like Columbus, all three of the later conquistadors who became renowned figures in Spanish history—Vasco Núñez de Balboa, Hernán Cortés, and Francisco Pizarro—undertook exploration and discovery in spite of rather than because of the king's men in the Indies.

Triumph and Tragedy of Vasco Núñez de Balboa

During his ten years on the Panamanian isthmus from 1509 to 1519, Balboa rose through the ranks from stowaway to governor of the province of Panama, part of present-day Panama, based on his fighting and leadership skills. He would forever be remembered as the discoverer of the Pacific. His emergence began in a most unassuming manner, in the summer of 1510 as he fled debt collectors by stowing away aboard a ship captained by Martín Fernández de Enciso, partner of Alonso de Ojeda. The ship was bound with supplies for San Sebastián, a newly settled colony on

---

[20] Hugh Thomas, *Rivers of Gold: The Rise of the Spanish Empire From Columbus to Magellan* (New York: Random House, 2003), 291.

[21] Jade Davenport, "Spanish Conquistadors and the Looting of Mexican, Peruvian Gold Treasures," *Mining Weekly,* September 7, 2012. The author estimates that the Spanish extracted an average of one ton of gold a year from the islands from 1503 to 1530.

the Gulf of Urabá in Nueva Andalucía (a Spanish governate that included the northern coastlines of present-day Colombia and Venezuela). When Balboa emerged in mid-voyage from a large barrel in which he had hidden, Enciso at first thought to drop him off on a deserted island but was persuaded to allow him to stay. The crew would refer to him as *el hombre del casco*, the man from the barrel.[22]

On entering the Gulf of Urabá, Enciso encountered an outbound ship of settlers, led by Francisco Pizarro, who had decided to abandon San Sebastián and return to Santo Domingo, Hispaniola. Undeterred, Enciso proceeded to San Sebastián; but upon arriving and seeing that hostile Indians had destroyed the settlement, he was persuaded by Balboa to relocate to the other side of the Gulf. There they established the settlement of *Santa Maria de la Antigua del Darién*, or simply, Darién.

After establishing Darién, a dispute arose over Enciso's leadership. Enciso sought to commandeer the lion's share of all gold accumulated by the settlers. Led by Balboa, the settlers overthrew Enciso and elected Balboa and Martín Samudio as joint mayors of Darién. They then put Enciso on trial, charging him with illegal usurpation of power. He was found guilty and placed in irons. Later, Balboa would exile him to Spain. For the next three years, the settlement thrived under Balboa's leadership. Ably supported by Francisco Pizarro, he explored surrounding territory, defeating hostile Indian tribes, befriending others, but also coming across indications of gold among the tribesman. Most important, Balboa learned from them of a land of great wealth across the Southern Sea where gold was so plentiful it was used as tableware.

Following demonstrable success at Darién, Balboa attempted to legitimize his dubious rise to leadership, petitioning the king to authorize, if not also finance, further exploration. He decided to send Enciso back to Spain in exile, accompanied by two of his own supporters whose charge would be to reinforce his explanation of events. As was frequently the case, when conquistadors came into conflict with the king's appointed officials, the explorers in the field sought direct contact with the king to overrule his island administrators. Thus, Balboa sent two letters to

---

[22] Charles Anderson, *Old Panama and Castilla Del Oro: A Narrative History* [...](Boston: Page, 1914), 158.

Ferdinand explaining his actions regarding Enciso and presenting information he had obtained from friendly tribesmen about vast riches that lay within reach beyond the sea.

Balboa's letters of January 20 and March 4, 1513 spoke of the existence of a land beyond "the other sea," meaning the sea on the south side of the Panamanian isthmus, whose rivers flowed with gold. Wealth was so commonplace, he said, that people used gold plates and goblets in their daily lives. To reach this land he proposed that the king send sufficient men and supplies to build a shipyard to construct enough ships to move a large expeditionary force to conquer the land and seize its riches. He asked for "one great favor," which was for the king to forbid the passage of all lawyers to Tierra Firme because "not only are they themselves bad, but they make others bad" with their "litigations and villainies."[23] Unfortunately for Balboa, it would be the litigations and villainies of the very men the king would send that would lead to Balboa's untimely demise.

Receiving this news, however, King Ferdinand was elated by his conquistador's discovery, yet at the same time deeply concerned about the legality of his methods, for Enciso had managed to persuade him that Balboa had usurped power. To resolve his dilemma, in August, the king made three fundamental decisions. First, he reorganized Tierra Firme, and renamed it *Castilla del Oro*, "Castile of Gold," based on Balboa's news. Then, responding affirmatively to Balboa's entreaties, he authorized the largest expedition to the Indies since Columbus's second voyage and only the second ever financed entirely by the king himself. All other expeditions were financed either by private companies, or as joint ventures with investors. Third, he named the old court favorite Pedro Arias Dávila, known as Pedrarias, to head the expedition. The king also named him governor of the newly designated lands as he was familiar with gold mining and tasked him with resolving the dispute between Balboa and Enciso. He named Balboa *adelantado* (explorer and royal representative) of the South Sea, but relieved him of the dubious governorship of Darién. Presumably, he would be free to continue exploration of new lands to the south.

---

[23] Ibid., 168n8.

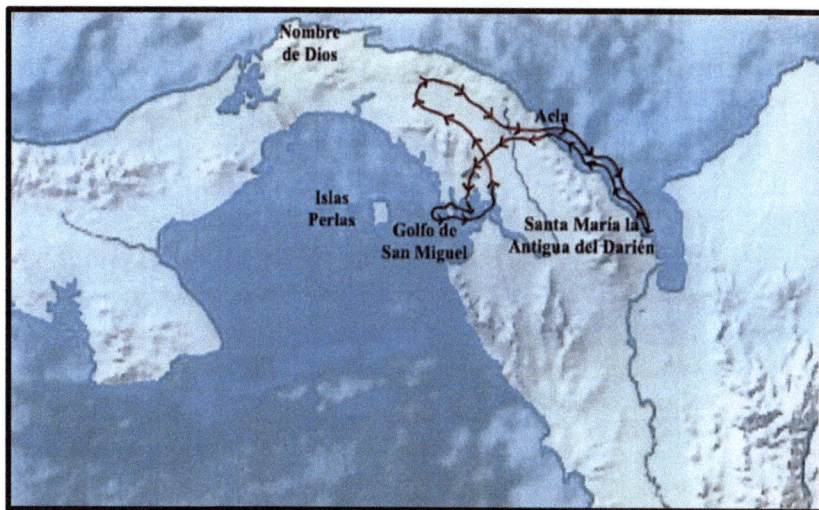

1.5. Balboa's expedition to the "South Sea," 1513.

It would be more than a year before Pedrarias's expedition was properly outfitted, departing on April 11, 1514, but the result would not be what the king hoped.[24] In the meantime, Balboa, learning of the king's decision, and fearful of what it might mean for him, decided to press forward with his explorations. Based on the limited resources at hand, he set off to find the South Sea on September 1, 1513. With only 190 men, but several ferocious war dogs, and by augmenting his forces with natives befriended along the way, he managed to hack through the dense jungle and past hostile tribes to the southern coast of Panama. On September 25, he ascended to the top of a mountain, from which he could see what he named the South Sea (but which would be renamed The Pacific by Magellan seven years later). He named it the South Sea because it was directly south of the Panamanian isthmus, which lies on an east-west axis. He also promptly claimed the sea and all adjoining lands for the king of Spain. It was a moment of triumph for the intrepid explorer for he now knew the fabled land of gold and riches was within reach, once he received the men and materials he requested from the king.[25]

---

[24] Ibid., 184-87.
[25] Ibid., 169-74.

The following June 30, 1514, Governor Pedrarias arrived at Darién with a flotilla of seventeen ships and 2,000 men and women, and all the materials Balboa had requested. On board were Pedrarias's wife, Doña Isabel and Balboa's friend the Bishop Juan de Quevedo, along with magistrates and church officials who were to fill out a full administration in the new land. In what must have come as a shock to Balboa, however, also on board was the same Martín Fernández de Enciso, whom he had exiled, but who was now appointed the chief constable for Pedrarias. Nevertheless, Balboa reported fully on his expeditions, the acquisition of gold holdings, but most importantly of his discovery of the South Sea.

Pedrarias quickly installed his new administration, relieving Balboa and those who had been in charge at Darién, even while congratulating him for the work he had done. Then, he began his investigation of Balboa's performance in Darién. The *residencia,* or formal inquiry, conducted by jurist Gaspar de Espinoza, reluctantly found that he was innocent of serious charges made against him by Enciso, but nevertheless levied a large fine to repair the damage done to him, depriving Balboa of a significant portion of his wealth. Pedrarias, clearly perceiving Balboa as a political threat, had wanted to send him back to Spain in chains and was only thwarted in this by the intercession of his own wife, Doña Isabel, and Bishop Quevedo.

Balboa was free, but relations with Pedrarias became strained to the utmost. Moreover, the governor's concern to establish his dominance over the settlement, rather than promote the welfare of its inhabitants, sent the settlers roiling in discontent, both those who had just arrived as well as those who were already there. Indeed, one hundred of those who had come with Pedrarias decided to leave Darién for Cuba, because they had not been given the land and natives that had been promised to them, a part of the story that will be picked up in the next section.

Seeking the fabled temples of gold described by Balboa, Pedrarias sent out several expeditions to find them. All failed. At the same time, contrary to the king's intention, the governor denied Balboa's request to lead an expedition to the South Sea. Stymied, Balboa decided to proceed on his own, recruit his own men secretly in Cuba, and head off for the South Sea. Unfortunately for Balboa, Pedrarias discovered his plan, arrested him a second time, and once again, Balboa's friend Bishop Quevedo persuaded the governor to show leniency and Balboa was freed. But news of the latest confrontation between the two men reached the king, who finally realized he must intervene.

King Ferdinand, attempting to protect Balboa, sent orders adding to his title of *adelantado* of the South Sea, by naming him governor of Panama.[26] Although Pedrarias would remain in overall command of Castilla del Oro, the king specifically ordered him to release Balboa and dismiss all charges relating to his presumed attempt to mount a clandestine expedition. In an effort to bring about reconciliation, Balboa's friend, Bishop Quevedo proposed the marriage of Balboa to Pedrarias's daughter, who resided in Spain. It would be a proxy marriage—husband and wife would never meet—but it would serve to heal the breach between Balboa and Pedrarias, at least on paper. Balboa agreed; the marriage was performed in absentia in April 1516, and for two years there was a semblance of peace between the two men.

Balboa, now not only *adelantado* of the South Sea, but also governor of a province, and son-in-law of Pedrarias, was free to act more independently. With authority to mount an expedition, in April 1517 Balboa entered into a partnership with Pascual de Andagoya and Hernando de Soto to establish the South Sea company to finance it. De Soto was Pedrarias's man reporting on Balboa's progress.[27] Balboa set up a shipyard in Acla, an outpost some forty miles to the west and up the coast from Darién and began to build four ships with which he hoped to move his expedition. He would build in Acla, which he believed free of shipworm; then transport the components for assembly on the Pacific coast, but the project met one misfortune after another. Balboa was wrong about Acla being immune from shipworm and a major flood washed away much of his materials. Finally, in the fall of 1517 he managed to complete two of the four ships he planned, got them to the Bay of San Miguel on the Pacific coast, and explored the Pearl Islands nearby before turning back.

---

[26] Roscoe Hill, "The Office of Adelantado," *Political Science Quarterly* 28, no. 4, (December 1913): 653. The king's order was dated September 23, 1514 but did not reach Balboa until the following year.

[27] Paul M. Kochis, *God, Glory and Gold: Journey to The Conquest of The Incas,* vol. 2, *The Quest* (Minneapolis: Mill City Press, 2013), 73-74.

Meanwhile, developments in Spain dramatically affected events in the Indies once again. Bishop Quevedo had returned to Spain with some disgruntled settlers and informed the new King Charles I, who had succeeded King Ferdinand after his death on January 23, 1516, that Pedrarias had failed in every aspect of his mission. Persuaded, King Charles decided to replace Pedrarias with the governor of the Canary Islands, Lope de Sosa. When Pedrarias learned of the king's decision, he decided to destroy Balboa, fearful of his fame, of his own disgrace, if not eclipse, and of what Balboa could say against him during the inevitable *residencia*.

When Balboa heard about the king's plan, he resolved to set out for the fabulous land beyond the South Sea as soon as his last two ships were completed and before de Sosa could arrive to prohibit it. Discovery of new land and especially the establishment of a settlement were the legal bases in those days for governorship and political independence of men such as Pedrarias. All claims, indeed all actions, of course, would be undertaken in the name of the king. For Balboa, it would be a repeat performance, but on a grander scale, of his preemptive move to discover the South Sea just prior to Pedrarias's arrival four years before in 1514.

Pedrarias, however, learned of Balboa's intentions—either from de Soto, or from one of Balboa's men, Andres Garabito, who claimed that he intended to "throw off allegiance to him as soon as he reached the ocean." Garabito's motive, it seems, was romantic. He longed for Balboa's Indian companion and set out to thwart him by revealing to Pedrarias that he had not cast her off as he had promised when he agreed to marry his daughter. In Pedrarias's mind, Balboa's presumed faithlessness was the last straw. He now had grounds to believe that Balboa was planning to act without authority to set up an independent settlement.[28]

Pedrarias set a trap to draw Balboa away from his base and followers at San Miguel on the South coast to Acla. He sent a letter to him requesting a meeting to confer about his planned expedition. Unsuspecting, the conquistador agreed to meet. To disguise his intent, the governor sent Francisco Pizarro, one of his loyal lieutenants, who was a friend of Balboa—indeed had been second in command of the expedition

---

[28] Anderson, *Old Panama and Castilla del Oro*, 204-05.

that discovered the Pacific—with a group of men to meet him en route. Taking Balboa by surprise, Pizarro arrested him and brought him before Pedrarias. In a show trial held in Acla, Pedrarias accused Balboa of treason, of planning to usurp power in Castilla del Oro and set up an independent settlement on the South Sea. The governor, supported by Chief Constable Enciso (!) found Balboa guilty as charged and, denying him any appeal, sentenced him and four compatriots to execution by beheading. In Pedrarias's view "since [Balboa] has sinned, let him die for it" (*pues se peco, muera por ello*). The sentence was carried out on January 12, 1519.[29]

The irony was that Governor Lope de Sosa would never live to replace Pedrarias, dying the day he arrived at Darién, May 20, 1520. Pedrarias himself would formally establish the city of Panama on August 15, 1519 as a port on the south side of the isthmus, but the king would reassign him to the post of governor of Nicaragua where he would continue to serve the Crown for eleven more years. As an administrator and agent of the Crown, however, Pedrarias would be a failure as it would be under his aegis that Castilla del Oro would dwindle and limp along with little success. Murder, rape, and pillage could only continue for so long before exhausting the native resources.

Pedrarias is universally reviled by historians of this period, though he was but a metaphor for the contentious dynamic of bureaucrat versus conquistador that defined this early period of the Spanish conquest of the Americas. In all cases during these early years, the impulse of the Crown was to direct governors to gain control and thus to squeeze profits from the activities of the conquistadors, and for the conquistadors to elude constraints of the governors by appealing to the Crown.

Discovery of Yucatan: The Expedition of Córdoba

The factors of production—land, labor, and capital—in the Indies were distorted by the Spanish concept of exploration, conquest, and settlement. Those who signed on for the voyage to the New World were assured land and native Indian slaves to work it, the amount of land and number of slaves being a function of the rank and role of the settler. This

---

[29] Ibid., 206-07.

was the *repartimiento*, or later the *encomienda* system.[30] Even though the natives were slaves, the Spanish justified this arrangement by the euphemism that they were paid workers. The settlers themselves were universally motivated by the lure of gold and other riches and their slaves were there to help them get it.

But everywhere the Spanish went, the native population declined—if not by slaughter during conquest, then by disease to which the Spanish exposed them; if not by disease, then by overwork. Native labor was essential to sustain their settlements and towns, work the fields, and search for gold using placer mining methods in the rivers and shallow mines. Increasingly, the island natives simply melted away. In less than twenty years since Columbus, Spanish leaders began to realize that the population of the main islands of the Indies—Hispaniola, Cuba, Jamaica, and Puerto Rico—was declining. There was a growing labor shortage. Without labor the land was valueless and the capital (gold) could not be obtained.

Spanish leaders came up with three answers to this growing dilemma. The first came from the Catholic Church, whose leaders argued for a more humane treatment of the native population, thinking that religious conversion would persuade more to remain in place. This was a course that was more honored in the breach than in the observance. King Ferdinand made two additional decisions to alleviate the labor shortage. Claiming that "I need [gold] for the war in Africa" against the Barbary pirates, on February 10, 1510 he signed a decree permitting the importation of African slaves to work in the gold mines. He also authorized governors of the settlements to bring slaves in from nearby islands.[31] All three decisions would significantly shape Spanish exploration, conquest, and settlement of the Americas. But it was the demand for gold, its dwindling supply in the islands, and the lure of the rumors of "rivers of gold" on the mainland that drove all else.

Chronicler Bernal Díaz del Castillo provided a first-hand account of this dilemma. Having signed onto the expedition that brought Pedrarias

---

[30] J. H. Elliott, *Empires of the Atlantic World: Britain and Spain in America, 1492-1830* (New Haven: Yale University Press, 2006), 39.
[31] Thomas, *Rivers of Gold*, 290-91.

to Darién in 1514, he and about a hundred other settlers quickly decided to leave because there was neither sufficient land nor native slaves for them. They decided to go to Cuba, which had recently been settled. Upon their arrival, Governor Diego Velázquez allocated them land, but could only promise to give them natives "as soon as there were any to spare."[32] After three years and still no slaves, the men as a group decided to take matters into their own hands and acquire some of their own.

They reached agreement with a wealthy landowner, Francisco Hernández de Córdoba, to mount an expedition. Their goal was to explore new lands, being ever on the lookout for gold, and to acquire slaves to alleviate the labor shortage. Financing the expedition out of their own pockets, they purchased three ships, one from the governor himself, who, in return for granting permission for the expedition was to receive his profit in the form of additional slaves, too. Setting off on February 8, 1517, their crew of 110 men included a priest and an accountant—the priest to provide the usual blessing and opportunity to proselytize, and the accountant to mark out the "royal fifth" the Crown claimed of any treasure found.[33]

Sailing due west of Cuba toward the setting sun, in early March they approached the tip of the Yucatan peninsula, at a place they called Cape Catoche. What they saw amazed them. From the ship they saw a large settlement a few miles off the coast of homes built of stone and mortar, large temples, stone idols, and large fields of cultivated crops. As it was larger than any town in the islands, they named it Great Cairo, for it indicated the existence of an advanced civilization comparable to that of Egypt.[34]

[32] Bernal Díaz del Castillo, *The True History of the Conquest of New Spain*, trans. Alfred Percival Maudslay, vol. 1(London: The Hakluyt Society, 1908), 9-11.
[33] Ibid., 12.
[34] Arthur Helps, *The Spanish Conquest in America, and Its Relation to the History of Slavery and to the Government of Colonies,* vol. 2 (New York: Harper and Bros., 1856), 215.

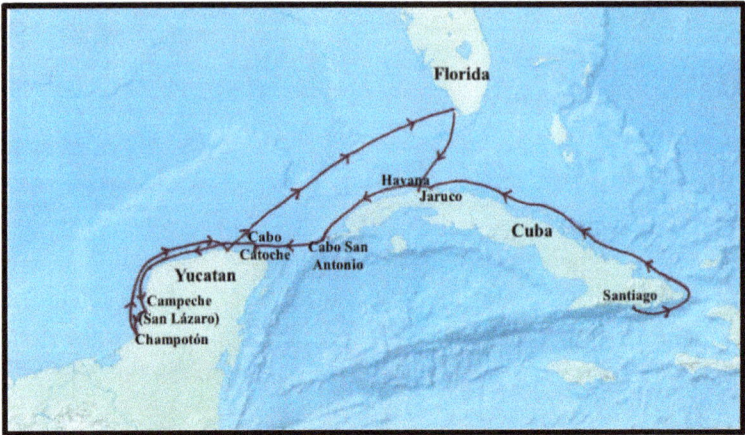

1.6. Córdoba´s Expedition to Yucatan, 1517

Córdoba did not know it, but each stop he made during his voyage took him to a different Mayan province in what was a loosely federated and declining civilization. The Maya had long since been eclipsed by the Aztecs as the dominant force in the Yucatan, but vestiges of their former civilization remained. Indeed, the Spaniards were struck by the disparity between the sophistication of the art and architecture and the relative crudity of the Indians, their tools and weapons.

As they prepared to disembark, they were met by a band of native Indians who rowed out to meet them in canoes. An initial friendly encounter involving an exchange of gifts led to an agreement that the Indians would return the next day to escort them to the town. Next day, as promised a large contingent of Indians appeared, welcoming them ashore. But on the way to the settlement the Indians led the Spaniards into an ambush resulting in a furious battle in which thirteen Spaniards were wounded. Two later died of their wounds. Having driven off the Indians and captured two (whom they would train as interpreters), the men explored the settlement, which was deserted. They found some gold artifacts and marveled at the sophisticated architecture of the temples and stone carvings. Recovering back to their ships, the expedition sailed westward along the coast for two weeks before putting in at a cove they named Campeche.

At Campeche a band of about fifty Indians approached as they were filling their casks with fresh water. Invited to follow them, the

Spaniards proceeded warily to the village where they were told in sign language that they must leave forthwith or else be attacked. Convening in a place where there was clear evidence of human sacrifice, they issued an ultimatum to Córdoba in the form of a stack of burning reeds, which, once burned, would signal an attack if they had not yet left. At the same time, more Indians joined them in full war paint, making clear the Spanish were not welcome. The message was clear. Córdoba and his men quickly decided to retreat to the boats and continue their journey, avoiding a battle—this time.

Sailing further for another week along the coast they put in again for water at a place they designated Champotón. Once again, after filling their casks, they found themselves surrounded by Indians, a greater number than at Campeche and more menacing. It was evident from the brandishing of weapons and war whoops that the Indians intended to attack the entire party, making a battle unavoidable. In a fierce engagement where they were greatly outnumbered, they lost fifty men. Indeed, only one member of their party was not wounded in the melee. But fighting with everything they had, they managed to retreat to their boats and cast off. The Spanish called the place "the coast of the disastrous battle."[35]

Following this, Córdoba decided, and all agreed, to return to Cuba. But as they were totally without water and their numbers were fewer they decided to break up one of their ships and sail the remaining two to Florida where one of the captains knew there would be fresh water. Then, they would return to Cuba. In Florida, too, however, there was confrontation and battle with the Indians, who attacked and attempted to seize one of the boats, but the Spaniards beat them back and were able to depart with water casks full, though leaking. Mortally wounded from battle, Córdoba led his men back to Cuba, where he would expire a short time thereafter.

Upon the expedition's return to Cuba, "word spread like wildfire" of their great discovery. They had lost 57 of their 110 and had not captured any slaves, but returned with tales of battles, of gold, of treasure, and of an advanced if warlike civilization. They had encountered only hostile natives bent on opposing them. Nevertheless, they had brought back enough idols, statuary, and artifacts "of many different shapes," to raise

---

[35] Díaz del Castillo, *True History of the Conquest of New Spain*, 1:24-25.

wild speculation of their origins. Some thought that "they belonged to the Gentiles...or the Jews" who had been cast out of Jerusalem. Governor Velázquez in particular was overcome with the discovery of gold. When he questioned the two natives they had brought back with them about the existence of gold mines, they indicated "there was much [gold] in their land."[36]

Discovery of Mexico: The Expedition of Grijalva

Governor Velázquez, greatly excited by the prospect of obtaining gold, reported the discovery to the king's Council of the Indies in Seville, and requested authority to explore further. Although by this time at least two ships per week sailed between Santo Domingo and Cadiz, making communication reasonably quick, Velázquez did not wait for an answer.[37] He proceeded to outfit another expedition to follow the path Córdoba had charted and go beyond it. This expedition would be more powerful than the last to ensure they could overcome all native opposition. Thus, Velázquez assembled four ships with 240 men under the command of his nephew Juan de Grijalva. (Córdoba had sailed with three ships and 110 men.) Whereas Córdoba had sailed with only muskets, swords, and crossbows, Velázquez provided Grijalva with light cannon and war dogs, the large, ferocious and terrifying mastiffs that the Spanish had used in their conquest of the islands, especially of Cuba.[38]

Grijalva's instructions called for him to "obtain by barter all the gold and silver that could be procured, and that if it appeared to be advisable to form a settlement...but if not then...return to Cuba." The expedition left the north coast port of Matanzas, Cuba on April 8, 1518.[39]

---

[36] Ibid., 32.

[37] See Thomas, *Rivers of Gold*, 546, for the list of registered vessels traveling to and from the Indies.

[38] Graham Hancock, "The Spanish Use of Animals as Weapons of War," *Ancient Origins*, October 6, 2013, https://www.ancient-origins.net/opinion-guest-authors/ spanish-use-animals-weapons-war-00898; and John and Jeannette Varner, *Dogs of the Conquest* (Norman: University of Oklahoma Press, 1983).

[39] Díaz del Castillo, *True History of the Conquest of New Spain*, 1:37-39. Other authors mark Santiago as the initial point of departure, either in April or January. See Hubert Howe Bancroft, *History of Mexico,* vol. 1, *1516-1521*, vol. 9 of *The Works of Hubert*

By early May, the sailors sighted present-day Cozumel, where they went ashore. Approaching a village, they saw that all of its inhabitants had fled inland, except for two elderly men and a woman who claimed that she had been shipwrecked on the island. She was from Jamaica and could speak the Mayan tongue, making her very useful as an interpreter.

1.7. Grijjalva' s Expedition, 1518

Re-embarking, Grijalva sailed south along the coast about fifty miles to a cove they named *Bahía de la Ascensión*, before reversing direction and picking up Córdoba's course. Sailing around the peninsula and bypassing Cape Catoche, the ships stopped next at Champotón where Córdoba had suffered a serious defeat. As before the Indians massed at the beach to attack the landing party, but this time the Spaniards were better armed with light cannon and muskets that could penetrate Indian padded cotton armor and war dogs that terrified and panicked the Indians. In the fierce battle that ensued, the 100 men of the landing party suffered eight killed and sixty wounded. The Spaniards, however, savagely crushed the Indians, depleting their ranks, killing over two hundred and driving them out of their village and into the neighboring swamp.

After spending four days ransacking the village, they proceeded along the coast, putting in at two more coves for protection, until they came to the Tabasco River (which they named *Rio Grijalva*). Averting a confrontation, Grijalva managed to engage the Indians in peaceful conversation and barter of goods. The Indians conveyed the idea that while

---

Howe Bancroft (San Francisco: A.L. Bancroft, 1883), 17. Helps, *Spanish Conquest of America,* 2:217, says simply "Grijalva set sail from Cuba on the 5th of April, 1518."

they themselves did not have much gold, the land to the west, which they called Mexica, had "plenty of gold."[40] Proceeding further west, they reached another river where, despite orders to keep the ships together, Pedro de Alvarado sailed his ship up river alone (Alvarado was a conquistador in his own right, who would play a major role later in this history). When Alvarado returned after three days, he was reprimanded severely for putting himself and the others in a vulnerable position. They had been at sea for over two months and after the battle at Champotón, had managed to avoid large-scale battles, but had not obtained or located large amounts of gold.

Around mid-June, they reached a river they named *Rio de las Banderas* because of the welcoming presence of Indians flying white banners on the shore. There they encountered native chiefs who spoke a language their interpreters did not understand. It was clear to them that they had passed into a new territory. Indeed, Grijalva named it New Spain. This was the land of the Aztecs, as we call them today, but which they called Mexica. Their chiefs made it plain that the great ruler of the Mexica, Montezuma, had followed their every move from the time they first spotted Córdoba's ships the year before. They revealed that they knew about the landings and battles at Cape Catoche, Campeche, and Champotón, and that ever since the second battle of Champotón, Montezuma had given orders for them to engage peacefully and not to fight. Staying for a week, the Spaniards bartered goods for gold in the extraordinary amount of 16,000 crowns. But as they explored further, they came upon an island with evidence of recent human sacrifice, which seemed to be an omen and a warning against further encroachment. They named it *Isla de los Sacrificios*.[41]

Assessing their circumstances, Grijalva decided that there was no prospect for establishing a settlement. They were too few and could not guarantee their security against a large-scale attack, or even their food supply. He decided to send Alvarado back to Cuba for reinforcements, which would permit a settlement, but also remove a dissident voice from

---

[40] Díaz del Castillo, *True History of the Conquest of New Spain*, 1:49.
[41] William H. Prescott, *History of the Conquest of Mexico and History of the Conquest of Peru*, (New York: Modern Library, 1843), 125-26.

among them. Alvarado was entrusted with most of the gold and other treasure they had accumulated in the form of idols, and cloth, as well as the wounded. With the departure of Alvarado, their number was now three ships and as they continued to explore the coast, observing many towns along the way, they debated among themselves their future course of action.

As it was now getting into the rainy season, and no reinforcements had come, they decided against further exploration and to return to Cuba. They were forced to stop several times for ship repairs, to obtain water, and await favorable currents. Now that they were on their way out, however, the natives encountered during their return voyage were largely friendly, willing to provide food and to barter gold for beads and other trinkets. On about November 1, the flotilla anchored once again at Matanzas, Cuba, where Grijalva received an order from Governor Velázquez to return immediately to Santiago.[42]

In the meantime, Alvarado's return had both gratified and worried Governor Velázquez. When the governor "beheld the gold," he was "astonished at our having discovered such rich lands."[43] Furthermore, news [of the gold] spread like wildfire throughout the island.[44] The gold booty confirmed the many rumors of vast sources of gold in the Americas, but the hostile reactions of the Indians meant that getting it would not be easy. He had been worried about his nephew from the beginning, sending a small sloop commanded by Cristóbal de Olid to follow him, which unfortunately had been forced to turn back because of a storm. The many wounded men Alvarado brought back, and reports of injuries Grijalva had suffered (several arrow wounds and a couple of broken teeth), concerned

---

[42] Bancroft, *History of Mexico*, 1:30-31. Díaz del Castillo, *True History of the Conquest of New Spain*, trans. Maudslay, 1:61-63, recounts that they stopped at Rio Tonalá for ship repair, and Campeche for provisions, and then reached Santiago in 45 days. In a section preceding the text labeled "Itinerary," lxiv, Maudslay puts Grijalva at Havana on September 30, Jaruco on October 4, and Santiago on November 15. Peck says the fleet left Campeche on September 8 and reached Puerto Carenas (present day Havana) on the 30th, finally arriving at Santiago in early November: Douglas T. Peck, *The Yucatan—From Prehistoric Times to the Great Maya Revolt, A Narrative* (Xlibris, 2005), 242-44.

[43] Díaz del Castillo, *True History of the Conquest of New Spain,* 1:58-59.

[44] Prescott, *History of the Conquest of Mexico and Peru*, 135.

him even more. Perhaps most disconcerting were Alvarado's claims, later shown to have been spurious, that Grijalva had been a weak leader, had feared establishing a settlement, and that he himself had supported establishing one and had taken the lead in exploration and discovery. But most importantly, without a settlement there could be no claim to the land that could not be contested by others.

Accordingly, the governor decided to send a rescue and replenishment mission to Grijalva and include Alvarado in it to help find him. After much deliberation, the governor offered the opportunity to two of his associates, first to Vasco Porcallo and then to Balthazar Bermudez, but neither would agree to the terms the governor proposed, requiring them to finance the expedition.[45] Velázquez then turned to Hernán Cortés, whom he knew had accumulated a small fortune from his gold mining and agricultural endeavors. The motives for the choice of Cortés have varied, from picking him for his financial resources, his leadership skills, or to selecting him in hopes of eliminating him as a competitor, but the fact is the governor obtained a license from the King's Council in Santo Domingo and the two men entered into a contract on October 23, 1518.[46]

With the seemingly modest and limited objective of rescuing a compatriot, the Spanish presence in the Americas entered into a new and unpredictable phase. Governor Velázquez attempted to rescind his contract with Cortés when Grijalva returned safely, but Cortés sailed to the mainland in defiance of his governor's retraction. No one could have foretold that this ignominious beginning would lead to the conquest of the Aztec civilization and establishment of Spanish rule in Mexico.

---

[45] Charles Saint John Fancourt, *The History of Yucatan*, (London: John Murray, 1854), 17-18. Francisco López de Gómara, *The Pleasant Historie of the Conquest of the West India* [...], trans. Thomas Nicholas (London: Thomas Creede, 1596), 17, mentions only Bermudez.

[46] "Instructions Given by Velasquez, Governor of Cuba, to Cortes, on His Taking Command of the Expedition; Dated at Fernandina, October 23, 1518," in William H. Prescott, *Mexico and the Life of the Conqueror Fernando Cortes, in Two Volumes, Illustrated,* vol.2 (New York: Peter Fenelon Collier & Son, 1900), 423-26.

1.8. Diego Velázquez de Cuéllar

Chapter 2

Hernán Cortés
and the Conquest of Mexico

At this moment in history, February 1519, the Spanish enterprise in the Americas was floundering as the king's appointed governors were placing their personal interests above those of the Crown. Governor Pedrarias in Panama had just executed the great explorer Balboa, throwing Castilla del Oro into turmoil (and setting back the discovery of Peru by a decade). Balboa was preparing to set off for the South American continent when Pedrarias arrested him. So, too, with Hernán Cortés: Governor Diego Velázquez of Cuba was doing everything in his power to prevent Cortés from launching his expedition to Mexico. In both cases personal greed overrode the Crown's interest in exploration and discovery of the riches of the Americas. It did not help that King Charles was more interested in the affairs of Europe than America, delegating responsibility for American affairs to his Council of the Indies.

Cortés and Governor Velázquez

In truth, Cortés and Velázquez had a mercurial relationship. When the nineteen-year-old Cortés arrived on Hispaniola in 1504, Governor Nicolás de Ovando, a distant relative, arranged for him to receive a *repartimiento* (distribution) of land and slaves. Cortés worked the land and acted as a notary for the small town of Azua, but after seven years he grew restive, saying "I came to get gold, not to till the soil, like a peasant." In 1511, when Ovando's successor Diego Columbus made the decision to conquer Cuba, assigning Diego Velázquez to command, Cortés signed on. After brutally pacifying the island, Velázquez became governor and rewarded Cortés for his courageous service, naming him as one of his secretaries and allotting him land and slaves.[1]

2.1. Hernán Cortés

Then things soon turned sour. Cortés was a handsome, charismatic man of fine bearing; literate, but not learned; and he was also gregarious and a rake with promiscuous habits. He became romantically involved with Catalina Suarez, one of the daughters of a wealthy Spanish landowner on the island. But his reluctance to marry her caused a rift with Velázquez, who was courting one of Catalina's sisters. Thereafter, Cortés became a magnet for those with a grievance against the governor. They decided to present their complaints to Diego Columbus in Santo Domingo, electing Cortés for the mission. Velázquez discovered their plan and imprisoned Cortés. Although he escaped and found temporary sanctuary in a church, he was caught and imprisoned a second time, and slated for trial. Escaping yet a second time, Cortés saw that his best course would be to marry Catalina and reconcile with the governor. [2]

---

[1] William H. Prescott, *Mexico and the Life of the Conqueror Fernando Cortes, in Two Volumes, Illustrated,* vol. 1 (New York: Peter Fenelon Collier & Son, 1900), 173-74.
[2] Hubert Howe Bancroft, *History of Mexico,* vol. 1, *1516-1521,* vol. 9 of *The Works of Hubert Howe Bancroft* (San Francisco: A.L. Bancroft, 1883), 48-52.

Over the next several years Cortés made a reputation for himself, suppressing his ambition for adventure, growing wealthy from working the land and gold mines, and being elected mayor of Santiago, the new capital of Cuba. He was happy and seemingly content—until opportunity beckoned. Governor Velázquez had sent two expeditions to the mainland in search of gold and slaves. The first under Francisco Hernández de Córdoba in February 1517 had shown promise in regard to both categories. The second, under the command of his nephew Juan de Grijalva a year later, apparently had been lost. The governor decided to send a mission to rescue Grijalva, which prompted Cortés to grasp the opportunity to lead the mission.

Cortés sent word of his interest through mutual friends who were close advisors to the governor. One of these was Velázquez' secretary, Andrés de Duero, who would play a most vital role later in this story. As recompense for interceding with Velázquez, Cortés promised to give Duero a third of whatever he found. When the governor's first choices turned down his call to lead the expedition, Cortés was there, ready and willing to risk his fortune for the chance to discover new land and riches. Accordingly, the governor obtained a license from the king's authorities in Santo Domingo and the two men entered into a contract on October 23, 1518.[3]

Cortés, now thirty-three years old and in the prime of his life, was elated at the prospect of leading an expedition to the mainland. It would be his first adventure since his participation in the pacification of Cuba six years before. It would be his first opportunity to lead a large group of men into battle in a new and unknown land. He reached out to his many friends and any who were thirsting for adventure to contribute to the provision of ships, guns, men, and supplies. They flocked to his banner. Risking much of his fortune, he was well on the way to outfitting his armada, having acquired six ships and recruited three hundred men. Suddenly, Cortés's hopes were placed in doubt with news of Grijalva's safe return.

---

[3] "Instructions Given by Velasquez, Governor of Cuba, to Cortes, on His Taking Command of the Expedition; Dated at Fernandina, October 23, 1518," in Prescott, *Mexico and the Life of the Conqueror,* 2:423-26.

The Grijalva expedition returned to port in Cuba some time in November 1518; by at least one account, arriving in Santiago as late as November 15, three weeks after Velázquez and Cortés had signed their contract.[4] At every stop they were feted royally, as Grijalva regaled all with stories of vast riches in New Spain. Governor Velázquez was "well contented" with the gold brought back, in all the substantial sum of about 20,000 pesos, but angry with Grijalva (in part for not establishing a settlement in so rich a land, even though that was not his primary mission). The venal Velázquez feared that someone else would claim the land and "rob him of his reward."[5]

Indeed, he perceived and was increasingly led to believe by those around him that the usurper would be none other than the man with whom he had so recently signed a contract, Hernán Cortés. The lure of gold had prompted Velázquez to change his mind and he sought to wriggle out of his contract. At first, he tried to dissuade Cortés from proceeding on the grounds that Grijalva had returned, so there was no longer a reason for the expedition. Cortés refused, insisting that a contract was a contract. Then, Velázquez ordered his officials to confiscate Cortés's ships. Upon learning of this decision, Cortés hastily gathered his ships and men and cast off three days later, on November 18, 1518.

For three months, between November 18, 1518 and February 18, 1519, Cortés played the game of catch-me-if-you-can with the governor. Cortés had been in the midst of outfitting his expedition when he cast off on November 18 to elude Velázquez' officials. Attempting to build up sufficient stores for his expedition, he moved from port to port from east to west—Macaca, Trinidad, Havana—even sending an aide to Jamaica for supplies. Cortés eluded, bluffed, or recruited to his cause the governor's men who came with orders to seize him and his ships. By the middle of

---

[4] Arthur Helps, *The Spanish Conquest of America and Its Relation to the History of Slavery and to the Government of Colonies,* vol. 2 (New York: Harper & Bros., 1856), 228. There are various other accounts about the timing of Grijalva's return. See, e.g., Bancroft, *History of Mexico,* 1:30-31, esp. 30n8; and Charles St. John Fancourt, *The History of Yucatan* (London: John Murray, 1854), 21-23.
[5] Bernal Díaz del Castillo, *The True History of the Conquest of New Spain,* trans. Alfred Percival Maudslay, vol. 1 (London: Hakluyt Society, 1908), 63-65; and Bancroft, *History of Mexico,* 1:30-33.

February 1519, he was ready. He now had eleven ships, over five hundred soldiers, one hundred sailors, two hundred native bearers, about two dozen women, fourteen cannon and all the provisions and equipment needed for an extended campaign, including sixteen horses and numerous war dogs.

Departing February 18, 1519 from San Antonio, on the far western tip of Cuba, Cortés sailed first to Cozumel off the northeast coast of Yucatan where, after a stormy voyage, fate smiled. A Spanish ecclesiastic who had been shipwrecked eight years earlier and held captive made his way to Cortés and rescue. Jerónimo de Aguilar would become a valued adviser and interpreter with the Maya whose language he had learned. In discussions with several of the captains who had sailed with Grijalva and had joined his expedition, Cortés planned his initial strategy. Departing Cozumel in early March, Cortés passed by the places where Córdoba and Grijalva had encountered hostile receptions and stopped at the Tabasco River on March 25, where Grijalva had first encountered and had a profitable exchange with Indian chiefs. The Tabascan people were a neighboring tribe to the Aztec Empire, which influenced their policies.

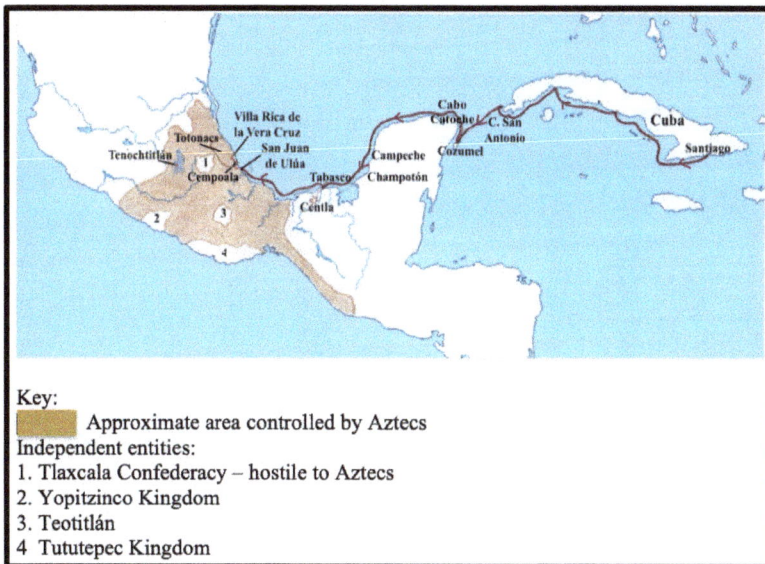

2.2. Expedition of Hernán Cortés to Mexico, 1519

Cortés's reception, however, was "unlike what he had reason to expect" from members of the Grijalva expedition. The Indians attacked his forces as he attempted to land, despite protestations that he had come in peace. The attack was unsuccessful. In retrospect, however, it is clear that Montezuma, ruler of the Aztecs, had decided upon a test of strength. He evidently assumed that he could overwhelm Cortés's relatively small force with numbers. As noted in the previous chapter, Montezuma had a network of intelligence and communication that spanned the empire, so he was able to assess Cortés's strength and movements from the beginning, just as he had earlier followed Córdoba and Grijalva.[6]

After an uneasy night and more skirmishes the next day, Cortés learned that further inland at Centla, a very large force (later reported to be forty thousand natives) was preparing to attack. Cortés responded, as was his wont, by taking the offensive rather than conceding the initiative to the Indians. He decided upon a pincer attack. He sent his foot soldiers, supported by cannon brought from the ships, on a frontal assault against massed Indian forces, while he circled around behind with his armored horses. The result was a major defeat for the Indians, who fled in fright from the booming cannon and the powerful horses, which they had never before seen.[7] While not mentioned by historians cited here, Cortés likely also used his terrifying war dogs as weapons in the battle against the Tabascan warriors. Natives throughout the Americas bred small dogs for food but had never come upon the large, ferocious carnivorous beasts that the Spaniards brought with them.[8]

---

[6] William H. Prescott, *History of the Conquest of Mexico and History of the Conquest of Peru* (New York: Modern Library, 1843), 125n14; Bancroft, *History of Mexico,* 1:100.

[7] Díaz del Castillo, *True History of the Conquest of New Spain,* 1:116-120; Prescott, *History of the Conquest of Mexico and Peru,* 152-57; Bancroft, *History of Mexico,* 1:87-90.

[8]"The Dogs of the Conquistadors," *doglawreporter-Bay-Net,* http://doglawreporter-bay-net.blogspot.com/2011/11/the-dogs-of-conquistadors.html; "Spanish War Dogs, Edible Dogs of the Conquistadors and Aztecs," *El Valle de Anton, Panama...The Volcanic Village...History, Attractions and Information,* https://elvalleinformation. wordpress.com; Graham Hancock, "The Spanish use of Animals as Weapons of War," *Ancient Origins,* October 6, 2013, https://www.ancient-origins.net/opinion-guest-authors/spanish-use-animals-weapons-war-00898.

2.3. Spanish war dogs

The Tabascans had endured enough. Next day, their chiefs approached the Cortés encampment with a peace offering that included many gold ornaments, food, cotton cloth, and twenty slave girls. Cortés, too, offered peace, glass beads, and trinkets, but demanded to know the source of the gold. Their reply was that the source of the gold lay further to the west, in Mexico. Cortés's course was now set; he would head for the capital of the Aztecs. Before departing, he made a display of religious power. He organized a procession to the principal temple of Tabasco, where an altar had been installed and Indian idols had been taken down and replaced with the cross and statues of the Virgin Mary. He insisted that the Tabascans tender their allegiance to the Spanish king and God (whose warriors, the natives had witnessed, possessed the power of thunder and lightning).[9] It was but the first of many instances in which Cortés would systematically tear down the belief system of his adversaries by toppling their idols and replacing them with Catholic symbols. Later, this practice would nearly bring about his destruction.

It is said that success brings its own luck and the victory over the Tabascans seemed to prove it. As his ships sailed west along the coast to Mexico, Cortés discovered that one of the slave girls on board was

---

[9] Prescott, *Mexico and the Life of the Conqueror,* 1:205-06.

educated in both the language of the Maya and Nahuatl, the language of the Aztecs. Thus, within a few weeks of his arrival on the American mainland, Cortés had found two people who would be invaluable, enabling him to communicate with his adversaries.

2.4. La Malinche

The slave girl, whom the Spaniards christened "Marina," but who was called "Malintzen" or "Malinche" by the Aztecs, reportedly was beautiful and intelligent. She became a close adviser, interlocutor, and, eventually, mistress to Cortés, bearing him a son. She would be Cortés's voice when he interacted with Montezuma. Indeed, the Aztec emperor would frequently address Cortés as "Malinche."

Anchoring April 20 off the coast of San Juan de Ulúa, Cortés's first task was to establish a defensible coastal base of operations, as the place where they had landed was a combination of sand dunes and marshes infested with swarms of mosquitoes. Accordingly, he sent out armed reconnaissance teams by land and by sea to find a more accommodating location. The site selected was a bay near Quiahuiztlan, located further up the coast, about 20 miles north of Cempoala, the capital city of the Totonac tribe (the Totonacs were an unhappy people who were tributaries of the Aztecs and were more than amenable to cooperating with the Spaniards). There, Cortés established the settlement of *Villa Rica de la Vera Cruz*.

The establishment of Vera Cruz served a political as well as military purpose. Pursuant to the establishment of the settlement a dispute broke out between Cortés's supporters and a handful of Velázquez's. The latter claimed that Cortés had no mandate to establish a settlement and insisted that they therefore return to Cuba. Refusing to cut short his expedition, the captain put the leaders in irons aboard one of his ships and dispersed the others among his men, winning them over one by one. Nevertheless, Cortés knew that Velázquez remained a formidable threat to his expedition. His lack of a mandate meant that Velázquez could take away everything he might gain in Mexico through legal action in Spanish courts, or by appealing directly to the king.

Therefore, Cortés decided to follow the precedent established by Velázquez himself and set up a legitimate political base, which would enable him to act independently of the governor. A few years earlier, when Velazquez conquered Cuba, he did so under a contract with the governor of Santo Domingo, Diego Columbus. Establishing the city of Santiago, Velázquez abrogated this contract and designated himself as governor of Cuba under the Spanish Crown. The king accepted his fait accompli and legalized his position as governor.[10]

Thus, Cortés sought to do the same. He established the city of Vera Cruz, naming town officials and magistrates, who, in turn, elected him as both captain general and chief magistrate. Being head of a settlement, Cortés argued, superseded his contract with Velázquez and signified that his expedition was no longer under the authority of the governor, but under that of the king. Both Velázquez and Cortés would appeal directly to King Charles for validation of their charges against each other. This, in fact, would be the purpose of the first of five extensive

---

[10]*New World Encyclopedia* (online), "Hernán Cortés," http://www.newworld encyclopedia. org/entry/Hernán_Cortés

letters Cortés would send to the king, which would accompany the shipment of the king's portion of whatever treasure Cortés would find.[11]

Cortés had been warmly welcomed by the local Totonac tribal leaders but was surprised by an equally warm, but unexpected visit by Aztec representatives of emperor Montezuma. Discussions with the Totonac leaders revealed that they were but one of many disaffected tributaries of the Aztecs. Although Montezuma ruled over a vast and populous empire of vassal states, it was rent with dissension and ruthlessly held together by force used to put down frequent outbreaks of revolt. There were some thirty-eight provinces, each paying tribute of various kinds to the capital of Tenochtitlán (the present site of Mexico City).[12]

To enforce the peace and Aztec rule, Montezuma deployed military garrisons in every province to keep order and to protect the tax collectors, who exacted tribute of all kinds, including sons and daughters of vassal states who were sacrificed to the gods. Cortés quickly realized that he could pursue a divide-and-conquer strategy in which he would ally with disaffected tributary states against the powerful Aztec center. His first alliance would be with the Totonacs, whom Cortés promised to protect against the Aztecs, starting with defending their decision to refuse payment of tribute to Montezuma's tax collectors. This audacious defiance of Montezuma served to widen the fissures already undermining his rule, as word spread throughout the empire.

By the time of Cortés's arrival, Montezuma had accumulated a significant amount of intelligence about the invading Spaniards from both direct and indirect contacts with earlier expeditions. He knew they were more powerful than he in every respect but numbers. Each time they had come they came stronger than before, the recent battle at Tabasco revealing new weapons the Aztecs had never before beheld. Thus, soon

---

[11] David Marley, *Wars of the Americas: A Chronology of Armed Conflict in the New World, 1492 to the Present* (Santa Barbara: ABC-CLIO, 1998), 17.

[12] See Matthew Restall, *When Montezuma Met Cortés: The True Story of the Meeting that Changed History* (New York: Harper Collins, 2018) for a more favorable treatment of Montezuma and a negative portrayal of Cortés. See also Álvaro Enrigue, who finds Restall's book to be "less a history than a polemic," in "The Curse of Cortés," *The New York Review of Books* 65, no. 9 (May 24, 2018), https://www.nybooks.com/articles/2018/05/24/mexicocortes/.

after Cortés landed, Montezuma adopted a conciliatory approach, sending emissaries laden with gifts of gold and other Aztec riches.

Montezuma: Uneasy Lies the Crown

It was uncanny that Cortés had arrived at just the time foretold by Aztec prophecy and that he and his men bore a strong resemblance to their chief god, Quetzalcoatl, a bearded white man, who had left in ages past, but who had promised to return to resume his rule over the empire. Indeed, the Aztecs justified their rule in the name of this deity. But it was doubtful that Montezuma believed that Cortés was this god; he had seen enough of the Spanish to know that they were men; powerful men with a technology he could not match, but men, nonetheless. But could he employ Cortés to shore up his own shaky rule? The record is ambiguous, but during the period of late June 1519 through early November when Cortés entered Tenochtitlán, Montezuma appears to have followed a twofold strategy of peaceful talk while setting traps for Cortés, rather than a strategy of direct confrontation proposed by some of his advisers.

2.5. Montezuma II

At first Montezuma sought to dissuade Cortés from visiting his capital. Yet, the tactic he employed to turn Cortés away had the very opposite effect of enticing him in. Montezuma knew the Spanish were after gold, above all. Cortés had told his emissaries that the Spanish were afflicted by a disease that only gold could cure. Thus, it made no sense for Montezuma to send gifts in enormous quantities of the very items that Cortés sought and expect him to turn away. No, the answer must be that Montezuma sought to draw Cortés to him with promises of more gold, attempting to learn about his weaknesses, while setting traps along the way. In short, Montezuma employed a strategy of attrition.[13]

Montezuma's objective was to deplete Cortés's forces by leading him into conflicts with his recalcitrant allies. If that failed (as we know it did), then he would seek to exploit the notion that Cortés was the returning god Quetzalcoatl and claim that the god's purpose was to rule by reinforcing Aztec authority over a fractious realm. It was a risky strategy; it would preclude Montezuma's deployment of his own forces against the presumed deity in whose name he would claim to rule, for such a course could trigger uncontainable revolts throughout the empire. Attrition could work both ways.

At the end of June Montezuma sent another large delegation to Cortés, again laden with gold and treasure. This time, however, it was to inform him that he could travel to Tenochtitlán after all, but with no guarantee that he could actually meet Montezuma. Cortés was excited at this news, but before he could marshal his forces and set off, there occurred an event that forced a delay. On July 1 a single ship arrived from Cuba with a dozen crew professing their interest in joining Cortés's forces. The men were welcomed, but it was the news they brought with them about governor Velázquez that galvanized Cortés into action.

Their news was that the king had issued a decree appointing Velázquez as *adelantado* of Cuba "giving him authority to trade and found settlements." It was Cortés' worst fear because now the governor had the legal right to deprive him of everything he had claimed in Mexico. Cortés decided to inform the king of what he had done and beg his confirmation. Accordingly, he loaded one of his best ships with as much as it could hold

---

[13] Restall, *When Montezuma Met Cortés*, 10.

of the treasure he had so far accumulated, including all he had parceled out
to his men, as his gift to the king. Along with the treasure, he sent his first
letter (which has recently been discovered), as well as a petition signed by
all of his men supporting Cortés in all of his actions.[14]

Departing for Spain on July 26, the ship stopped first in Cuba to
take on food and water, but despite Cortés's admonitions to take
precautions against leaking news of their trip to Velázquez, the governor
discovered it. Although he tried and failed to intercept the ship, which
sailed on to Spain unhindered, the governor now decided to use his new
authority to mount an expedition to Mexico to seize and imprison Cortés
and claim the land for himself. It would be almost a year before the
governor's expeditionary force would arrive in Mexico (June 1520) and
when it did it would trigger a sequence of events that would lead to the
near defeat of Cortés's entire effort in Mexico. But that is a part of the
narrative to be taken up later.

In the meantime, word of the king's decree sparked renewed
unrest in the camp. A handful of men secretly planned to steal a ship and
return to Cuba. Upon learning of the plot, Cortés dealt harshly with the
dissidents, executing the two leaders and severely punishing the others. It
now transpired that Cortés also discovered that his remaining nine ships
were no longer seaworthy, having been weakened by shipworm. One
vessel he was able to salvage, but the others had to be taken apart, sails
and hardware stored, and the rotting planks burned. Cortés offered free
passage aboard the remaining ship to anyone who wished to leave, but
there were no takers. Dismantling his fleet had several positive
consequences. Not only did it strengthen the resolve of his men once they
realized that they had no choice but to march with Cortés, but also, it
strengthened his force by adding roughly a hundred sailors who were now
free to accompany him.

---

[14]Díaz del Castillo, *True History of the Conquest of New Spain*, 1:192-98; and John
Schwaller with Helen Nader, *The First Letter from New Spain: The Lost Petition of
Cortés and his Company, June 20, 1519* (Austin: University of Texas Press, 2014).

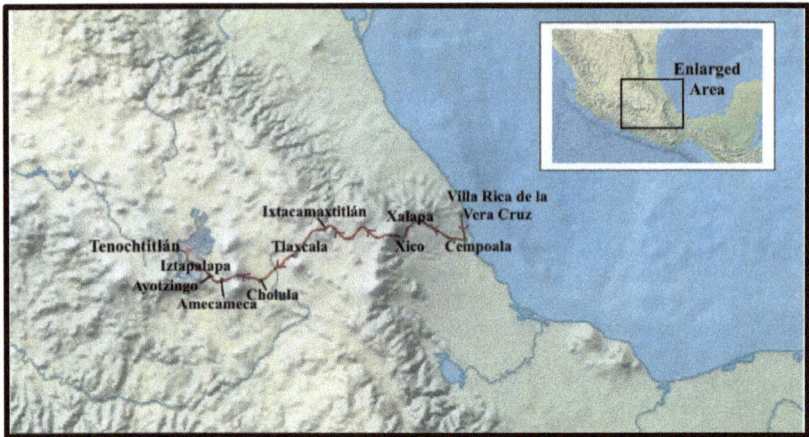

2.6. Cortés's march to Tenochtitlán

On August 16, Cortés set off for Montezuma's island capital of Tenochtitlán with four hundred Spaniards, strengthened by the addition of over a thousand Totonac warriors and porters, plus fifteen horses, a like number of cannon and numerous war dogs. On the advice of his Totonac allies, Cortés headed directly for Tlaxcalan territory in the expectation that he could enlist them as allies, for the Tlaxcalans were determined adversaries whom the Aztecs had never been able to subdue. For the first two weeks, tribes encountered along the march were uniformly friendly and hospitable, welcoming Cortés as a liberator from the Aztec yoke. But, reaching the border of Tlaxcala on August 31, Cortés once again was confounded by what he encountered.

Contrary to what he had been led to expect, the Tlaxcalans immediately began a series of large-scale attacks on Cortés's forces lasting nearly three weeks, including a night attack, which war dog sentries foiled. Although Cortés's forces fought the Tlaxcalans to a standoff, the battles weakened both sides. In the end the Tlaxcala leadership decided to reverse policy; they sued for peace and indicated a willingness to join an alliance with Cortés. It would become one of the most enduring and crucial alliances the Spanish would ever make in Mexico. Having a secure base of operations in the very heart of the Aztec empire would be a critical component of his eventual victory. The question was: what explained the Tlaxcalan decision to attack the enemy of their mortal foe in the first place? The answer lay in the internal politics of the Tlaxcala realm, which was composed of four provinces whose leaders both cooperated and contended with each other for supremacy, even colluding with the Aztecs on occasion.[15]

In the debate over how to deal with the Spaniards, there was considerable disagreement among the leaders. Xicotencatl the Younger, the warrior son of one of the four leaders of the Tlaxcalan confederacy, saw advantage in attacking Cortés, as part of his bid for leadership. Others were opposed, seeing advantage in an alliance for their long struggle against the Aztecs. The decision to attack was therefore not unanimous and dissension spread to the forces in the field. In the end, Xicotencatl the Younger lost not only the battle and his bid for leadership, but later on he would be executed for what was determined to have been a traitorous policy of opposing the decision to ally with Cortés.

Whatever the domestic explanation for the Tlaxcala attack on Cortés's forces, the objective reality was that their battles served the attrition strategy of Montezuma. Montezuma could hardly have been more pleased than to see his two main adversaries facing off against each other in mutually draining engagements. But Montezuma's pleasure soon faded at the grim prospect of having to face both adversaries once they reconciled and entered into alliance against him. Worse, news of Cortés's successes on the battlefield had spread throughout the country, drawing many disgruntled tributaries to his side.

While recuperating in Tlaxcala, where they would spend the better part of a month, Cortés received yet another emissary from Montezuma. The emperor's message was to congratulate Cortés on his military prowess and to offer him tribute in any amount he wished, for as long as he wished, if only he would not come to Tenochtitlán.[16] Accepting the offer of tribute, Cortés courteously insisted that he must meet Montezuma in person to convey the message of his sovereign. A personal meeting would also enable them to "iron out" any misunderstandings. That being the case, the Aztec emissaries were authorized to invite Cortés to proceed by the direct route that passed through the religious center of the empire, Cholula.

---

[15] Ross Hassig, "Xicotencatl: Rethinking An Indigenous Mexican Hero," *Estudios de Cultura Náhuatl*, no. 32 (2001):29-49.

[16] Díaz del Castillo, *True History of the Conquest of New Spain*, 1:264.

Cholula would be the next trap in Montezuma's larger attrition strategy against Cortés. Cholula was the holy city of the Aztecs, the equivalent of Jerusalem for the Christians, or Mecca for the Muslims. Its great pyramid was nearly as large as the grand pyramid of Giza in Egypt. By the middle of October, his troops refreshed and ready, Cortés set out for Cholula accompanied by six thousand Tlaxcalan warriors (most of his Totonac allies had decided to return to their coastal homeland). Upon arrival, the Cholula chiefs warmly welcomed Cortés into the city, but required the Tlaxcalans, who were their enemies, to camp outside the city walls.

After a few days of cordial interaction, the mood changed. Sending several of his Indian aides out on a carefully disguised reconnaissance of the city, what they saw alarmed him. Cortés knew from the outset that Cholula was a strong ally of Montezuma and so he approached the city with caution. His scouts now confirmed his worst fears. Streets were being barricaded, stones (ammunition) placed on rooftops, stake pits to trap horses were being dug and camouflaged, children were being sacrificed to appease their gods, women and elderly were leaving the city en masse, and a large Aztec force was being deployed nearby. Malinche, befriending one of the chieftains' wives, confirmed that their plan was to massacre the Spaniards in the city streets in a close quarter engagement that would neutralize the Spanish advantages of mobility and firepower.[17]

It was a difficult situation, but Cortés reacted in characteristic fashion by taking the initiative rather than waiting passively for his enemies to strike. He set his own trap, informing Cholula's leaders that he would be leaving the next morning and requesting their presence to send him off. When the chiefs and ranking members of the city arrived in the central courtyard the next morning, Cortés confronted them, exposing their plot. His men slammed the gates shut and massacred the people trapped in the courtyard. Cortés signaled his Tlaxcalan allies, who also stormed the city, preventing any assistance from reaching the courtyard.

Cortés had ordered a preemptive attack that thwarted the planned Cholula attack on him. He deliberately eradicated the entire leadership

---

[17] Prescott, *History of the Conquest of Mexico and Peru*, 267-68.

along with several thousand men, removing it as an ally of Montezuma and sending a clear message to the Aztec emperor and his allies that the same fate would attend to them if they resisted. Several neighboring cities quickly sent envoys to Cortés' camp tendering their allegiance. Cortés brought the city back to order, treating its inhabitants with compassion and encouraging a return to normal activity. He also installed pro-Tlaxcala leaders into power, ensuring that his supply line from Vera Cruz to Tlaxcala to Cholula was securely in the hands of allies.

Montezuma hastily sent envoys to Cortés laden with rich presents, disclaiming any connection to the events at Cholula. He explained away the presence of the Aztec force in the vicinity as being there to put down disorders. Renewing his invitation to Cortés to come to Tenochtitlán, Montezuma laid yet another trap. As Cortés's forces advanced, they came upon a fork in the road with one route recently blocked. The other route led through narrow passages and ravines, perfect territory for an ambush. So, taking a page from Hannibal's book, Cortés set off over the mountains to arrive at Tenochtitlán by a more circuitous route that was geographically challenging, but militarily safer.[18]

Cortés in Tenochtitlán

On November 8, the Spaniards appeared on the verge of Montezuma's island capital, having avoided all his snares. The Aztec emperor was forced to implement Plan B, the Machiavellian tactic of keeping one's friends close, but his enemies closer. He did this by literally embracing Cortés as the embodiment of the long-prophesied return of Quetzalcoatl. Welcoming Cortés at the entrance of Tenochtitlán, Montezuma said:

> Our lord, you are weary. The journey has tired you, but now you have arrived on the earth. You have come to your city, Mexico. You have come here to sit on your throne, to sit under its canopy. The kings who have gone before, your representatives, guarded it and preserved it for your coming.... The people were protected by their swords and sheltered by their shields. Do the kings know the destiny of those they left behind, their posterity? If only they are watching! If only they

---

[18] Marley, *Wars of the Americas*, 18.

can see what I see! No, it is not a dream. I am not walking in
my sleep. I am not seeing you in my dreams.... I have seen you
at last! I have met you face to face! I was in agony for five days,
for ten days, with my eyes fixed on the Region of the Mystery.
And now you have come out of the clouds and mists to sit on
your throne again. This was foretold by the kings who governed
your city, and now it has taken place. You have come back to
us, you have come down from the sky. Rest now and take
possession of your royal houses. Welcome to your land, my
lords![19]

Showered with gifts of gold and feted lavishly, Cortés, his men,
and Tlaxcalan allies were housed by Montezuma in the palace of
Axayacatl in the center of the island capital. There can be little doubt that
neither Montezuma nor his chiefs believed Cortés was the god
Quetzalcoatl; but saying that he was reinforced his people's awestruck,
almost reverential reaction to him. It also offered the opportunity to show
that they were allied, thus shoring up his fractious regime against further
defections. Montezuma would rule, but at the behest of the long absent
deity. In co-opting Cortés, Montezuma also bought time to work out a plan
to defeat him.

    After a week of festivities, Cortés began to feel less like a god than
a lamb being fattened for sacrifice. Though its buildings were magnificent,
the layout of the capital lent itself to the feeling of entrapment. The city
was an island fortress that could only be entered or exited by three
causeways across water that could quickly be shut by raising drawbridges.
When the bridges were raised the city was nearly impregnable to attack
from without, but that same feature could isolate those within the city's
walls. Cortés had bearded the lion in his den, but now looked for a way to
escape.

---

[19] Jill Lepore, *Encounters in the New World: A History in Documents* (New York:
Oxford, 2000), 62-65. Compare to the version offered by the Spanish priest
Bernardino de Sahagún, *Florentine Codex*, bk. 12, *The Conquest of Mexico*, trans.
Arthur J.O. Anderson and Charles E. Dibble, 2d. ed., rev. (Salt Lake City: University
of Utah Press, 1975; paperback ed., 2012), chap.16:44. Sahagún rewrites this speech
to omit all reference to Cortés's passage from heaven to earth, coming out of the
clouds, and coming down from the sky. Restall, *When Montezuma Met Cortés*, 17,
offers yet a third rendition.

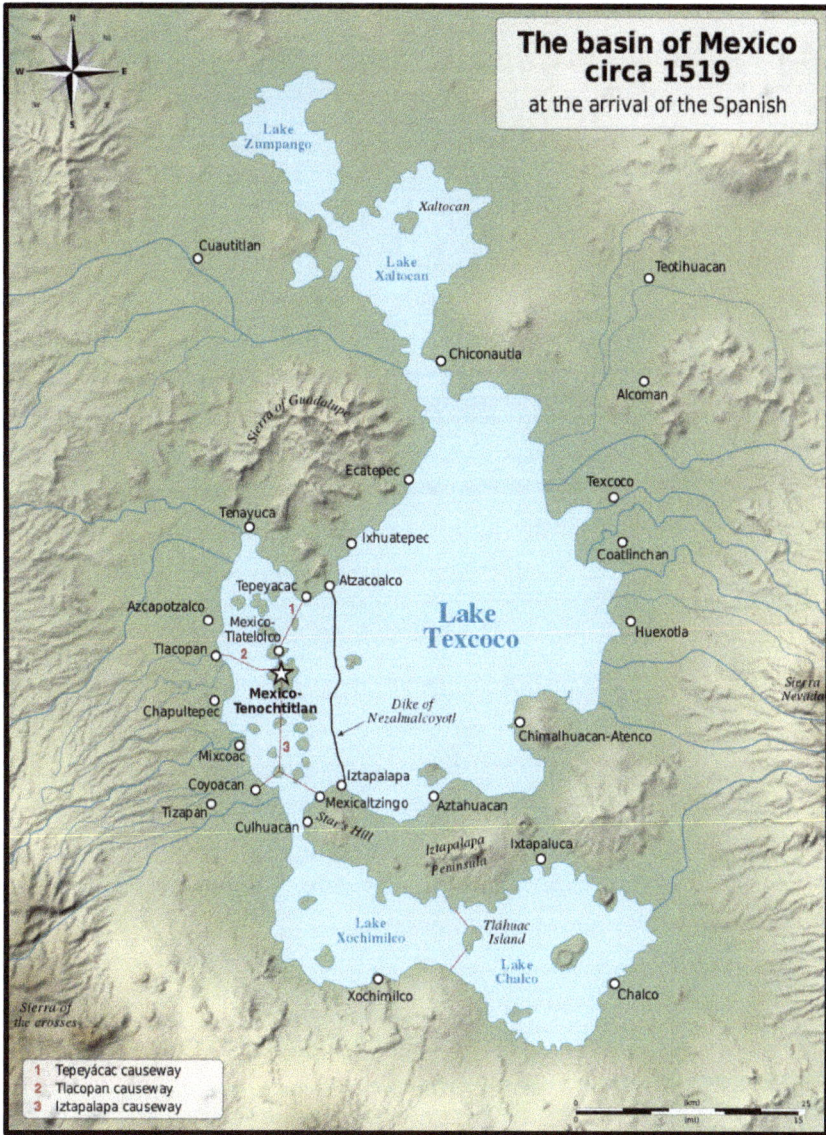

2.7. Tenochtitlán in the Basin of Mexico, 1519.
Map by Yavidaxiu.

Pondering their predicament, Cortés and his officers rejected withdrawal from the city either secretly or openly as leaving themselves vulnerable to attack, especially if caught on the narrow causeways. Even if they should successfully retreat to their coastal base 240 miles away, they would be judged as having failed to achieve their objective. Instead, based upon Montezuma's treatment of him, Cortés hit upon the idea of seizing the emperor and holding him hostage. They would be safe as long as they kept him under control and could rule in his name until they could accumulate sufficient treasure as ransom and arrange for a safe exit. Cortés, too, would keep his friends close and his enemies closer.

Then, an event occurred that offered Cortés the opportunity to put his plan into action. He received news of an attack on their base at Vera Cruz. The Aztec governor of the adjoining province, on the pretext of offering allegiance to Cortés, had drawn the garrison's fifty-man guard into an ambush, with the evident purpose of seizing control of Cortés's coastal base. Although commander Juan de Escalante and his men had beaten off the attack, they had suffered the loss of eight men, including Escalante himself, who died afterward from his wounds. One of their Indian prisoners confessed that the attack was undertaken "at the instigation of Montezuma." Worse, the natives had cut off the head of one of Escalante's men, which they "sent to the Aztec emperor."[20]

Cortés was both outraged and alarmed, for there could be no mistaking the significance of the attack. Capture of their coastal base would have cut them off from any source of reinforcements, communication, or escape. It would be the penultimate turn of the screw isolating them in the Aztec capital from which they would never hope to depart alive. Indeed, there would be no base to which to flee. Requesting an audience with Montezuma, Cortés arrived with an armed guard. Laying out the charge against the attacker and against the emperor as instigator, he demanded an investigation. Montezuma professed his innocence, blaming the incident on one of his enemies, but agreed with Cortés's demand that he summon the accused to stand trial.

Cortés additionally insisted that to insure against any mutinous action, Montezuma should move his residence to Cortés's palace until the investigation had ended. Although vigorously refusing to consent to such a "degradation" of his authority, when confronted with the angry retinue surrounding him, Montezuma complied. Although his nobles were aghast, Montezuma himself made plain that he was "visiting his friends of his own

---

[20] Prescott, *History of the Conquest of Mexico and Peru*, 342-43.

accord," bringing his entire household with him. Ensconced comfortably in the palace of Axayacatl and treated with the utmost deference and homage by the Spaniards attending him, Montezuma nevertheless was now effectively under house arrest and Cortés's hostage.[21]

Upon the accused governor's arrival for trial, Montezuma disavowed him, but the defendant maintained that he served no other sovereign but his emperor. Moreover, he admitted his role in the attack and the killings. Investigation concluded, he and his chief officers were condemned to be burned at the stake in front of Montezuma's palace. Cortés ordered that the funeral pyre be composed of the "arrows, javelins, and other weapons," drawn from the capital's arsenal. To insure against any last-minute eruption, just prior to the execution, Cortés confronted Montezuma, charging him with being the instigator of the entire affair, and fettered his ankles.

When it was over, Cortés released him from his bonds, but declined to permit him to return to his palace, a decision in which Montezuma gloomily acquiesced. As the emperor whiled away his time in captivity over the winter months, Cortés busied himself with devising means of avoiding entrapment in the capital. In a stroke of tactical genius, he decided to begin building two sailing vessels armed with cannon, which could transport fifty or sixty troops. These would enable him to relieve his dependence on the causeways and offer a way to barge out of the city if trapped there. Materials—sails, iron, cordage, nails, even cannon—were sent from the Vera Cruz base in coming days.

Challenges to Empire

Montezuma, meanwhile, faced a two-front challenge from Cortés and internal opposition. His approach was to use one to counter the other. Once his position was strengthened, he would deal with Cortés. A noble of the empire, Cacama, who had once been a rival of Montezuma, concocted a plan to mount an insurrection against the Spaniards ostensibly in order to restore the emperor to power. His scheme contained within it, however, a deeper plan to succeed Montezuma as the vanquisher of the intruders. Cortés discovered the plot, proposing an open confrontation, but

---

[21] Ibid., 344-46.

Montezuma offered a subtler approach, recognizing the threat to himself in any successful rebellion carried out by a rival. Calling for a meeting of the plotters in a town near Tenochtitlán, the emperor had them arrested and imprisoned. He also sent his men to each of their provinces to root out potential rebels.[22]

Having snuffed out an internal threat, Cortés now demanded that Montezuma formally declare his fealty to King Charles. Montezuma agreed, informing his astonished people that the ancient prophecy of the return of Quetzalcoatl to resume his rule over the kingdom had come true. Cortés also suggested that as a sign of good will, Montezuma should send a gratuity to the king. Thereupon the emperor sent his tax collectors to the far ends of the empire to bring back as much gold tribute as they could carry. The emperor himself added to the hoard, turning over several rooms of his palace that were filled to the ceiling with the yellow metal.[23]

When asked about the source of the gold, Montezuma revealed that they obtained most of it from distant rivers and from earlier conquests. Cortés sent men to locate the sources, ascertaining that the Aztecs had obtained gold mainly by panning for it or picking up small nuggets washed down the rivers. Yet this source of gold was insufficient to account for the enormous horde possessed by the natives. Some mines were discovered that showed signs of not having been worked for hundreds of years. It was a puzzle.

The Aztec was a stone-age culture. They had no iron or steel like the Spaniards. Their weapons were of wood and flint. They had no written language, the simple wheel was unknown to them, and they used no currency. Yet, the mines that Cortés's men discovered had been worked with hard metallic tools in the distant past. The same was true of the magnificent temple/pyramids whose stones had been cut by hard-edged instruments. Like the hermit crab or the cuckoo bird, the Aztecs occupied and built upon a habitat that they had not created. Cortés and his men were

---

[22] Ibid., 357-59.
[23] Ibid., 361-63.

too busy collecting loot to ponder this conundrum and simply accepted as fact that the Aztecs were the architects of their domain.[24]

Cortés seemed to have accomplished all he had set out to do. In the name of the king he ruled an empire through Montezuma as large as any in Europe, and perhaps wealthier. But now he took a step too far. He demanded that he and his men be allowed to practice their religion openly in one of the many temples in the city. Although Montezuma was startled by the request, he agreed to turn over a temple. The temple was scrubbed down of sacrificial blood and adorned with the crucifix and a mass was held, attended by Cortés's entire army. It was an extraordinary sight, but a final indignity to the Aztecs who viewed the celebration of a Catholic mass as the profanation of their own religious beliefs. It also directly contradicted Cortés's personification of Quetzalcoatl reborn.

The public desecration of the temple roused the Aztec lords, priests, and people and the emperor was not slow to take advantage of the opportunity. Calling Cortés to his apartments, he insisted that the Spaniards must all leave the country immediately, or "every Aztec in the land will rise in arms against you." Cortés responded that while he would regret leaving the country, he could not yet do so because he had no ships. Were it not for this he would leave at once. Not to be outdone, Montezuma offered to help build new ships. Cortés retorted that if he had to leave under these threatening circumstances, he would have to take the emperor with him.[25]

Over the following weeks, now under an increasingly inhospitable atmosphere in Tenochtitlán, Cortés's and Montezuma's men worked together in Vera Cruz constructing a new fleet. (Cortés, however, passed the word to his men to slow-walk the entire construction process.) The correlation of forces was still adverse. Cortés was surrounded, safe only as long as he held Montezuma hostage, but even that security measure was compromised by the unsubtle inflammatory attempt to flaunt Catholicism in the face of the Aztecs, which only built resentment among the populace, lord and lowly alike.

---

[24] For an incisive exploration of this conundrum, see Zecharia Sitchin, *The Lost Realms* (New York: Harper, 1990), 14-16.
[25] Prescott, *History of the Conquest of Mexico and Peru*, 369-70.

The Spaniards were stuck. Any withdrawal/escape plan required traversing the two-hundred-and-forty-mile distance from Tenochtitlán to Vera Cruz—although there were presumably safe havens along the way at Cholula and Tlaxcala. But would there be ships to sail away on? Moreover, there were possible ambushes along the way, beginning with the problems of departing from the Aztec capital itself. Tenochtitlán, a capital city of 300,000, was the center of a populated area of lakeside towns and villages of close to 400,000 people. Now in early May of 1520, nearly six months after entering Tenochtitlán, "tidings came from the coast, which gave greater alarm to Cortés than even the menaced insurrection of the Aztecs."[26]

Plot and Counterplot—Spanish and Aztec

Earlier, Governor Velázquez, upon learning of the fabulous riches Cortés had discovered in Mexico, had begun to build an expedition to seize them for himself (in the name of the king). Scouring Cuba for ships, men, and weapons, by the spring of 1520 he had assembled the largest expedition that had ever been sent to Mexico. There were eighteen ships, over a thousand men, eighty horses, one hundred and fifty crossbows, eighty riflemen, forty cannon, and one thousand island natives along with ample provisions of food and weapons. The main weakness of the force was not immediately apparent, but it was that many of the men he recruited for the expedition were neither well trained, nor fully dedicated to the governor. They were drawn primarily by the news of Cortés's discovery of Mexico's riches, rather than any allegiance to Velázquez.

Departing Cuba in early March under the command of Pánfilo de Narváez, the armada dropped anchor off San Juan de Ulúa on April 23. Finding this anchorage as unacceptable as Cortés had, he moved his encampment further to the north, near Cempoala and Villa Rica de la Vera Cruz. Montezuma's coastal watchers quickly informed him of the fleet's arrival and the Aztec chieftain sent envoys with gifts and a message of friendship. Narváez reciprocated, condemning Cortés as a rogue profiteer whom he had come to imprison and send back to Spain for trial for insubordination to the king. It quickly became apparent that the two

---

[26] Ibid., 371.

leaders had a common enemy, as their course of action would reflect. Whether fully articulated or not, their strategy was to coordinate their maneuvers. When Narváez began his assault on Cortés, Montezuma was to trigger an uprising from within Tenochtitlán. It was an obvious strategy, but one that would never get beyond its first step.[27]

Whether Cortés learned of their connivance sooner or later was immaterial. He said later that he thought they had secretly "connived" against him.[28] Narváez's very presence on the coast presented the conquistador with the crisis of his life. But Cortés would react the way he had to every other crisis he had faced to date. He would seize the initiative and not passively await the attack being prepared. To throw Narváez off guard and lead him to believe that there was no urgency, Cortés sent several messengers with letters proposing cooperation with him, including an offer to divide Mexico and all of its treasure between them. He also sent agents to sow division among his troops with gifts of gold and promises of much more.

The problem Cortés faced was how to defeat a two-front attack against numerically superior forces? His answer was to hold at Tenochtitlán while striking preemptively at Cempoala before Narváez was ready. Thus, Cortés put one of his top officers, Pedro de Alvarado, in charge of the Tenochtitlán defense. For this purpose, Alvarado would have the majority of their total force—140 men, all of the cannon and most of the muskets. Then, Cortés took his best 70 men and in the second week of May, travelling light, set off for Narváez's encampment outside Cempoala, planning to carry out a surprise attack. Along the way, by prearrangement he stopped at Cholula where he was joined by Velázquez de Leon with 120 men and, further along, met with Gonzalo de Sandoval and 66 more from Vera Cruz. Sandoval had also brought along dozens of

---

[27] "Cortés Struggles with Narváez," in Bernal Díaz del Castillo, *The History of the Conquest of New Spain,* ed. Davíd Carrasco (Albuquerque: University of New Mexico Press, 2009), 209: In his introduction to this section, Carrasco says Montezuma and Narváez formed an "alliance." Marley, *Wars of the Americas,* 20, says "Cortés …is also angry with Montezuma, having learned the emperor secretly contacted his antagonist Narváez during the recent coastal campaign, promising friendship."

[28] Bernal Díaz del Castillo, *The Memoirs of the Conquistador Bernal Díaz del Castillo,* trans. John Ingram Lockhart, vol. 1 (London: J. Hatchard & Son, 1844; Project Gutenberg eBook # 32474, May 21, 2010), 338.

long lances tipped with copper blades for use against Narváez's horsemen. In all, after a series of forced marches over two weeks, he arrived with 266 lightly armed men a few miles from Narváez's encampment on the night of May 28.[29]

There he received another group of envoys from Narváez, one of whom fortuitously was an old friend, Andrés de Duero. Duero was a double agent and secret ally of Cortés who, recall, had been instrumental as secretary to Velázquez in persuading the governor to enter into the original contract with Cortés. He now brought an offer from Narváez. If Cortés would surrender, he and his entire force would be transported safely back to Cuba with no charges to be brought against them. Cortés declined this offer, instead reaffirming the original deal he had made with Duero for one third of all the wealth he obtained in Mexico. Realizing how much more valuable that deal was now, Duero was convinced and promptly disclosed to Cortés invaluable information about Narváez' overconfidence, his lax security measures, and dispositions of troops, cannon, and cavalry.[30]

Cortés decided to strike hard and immediately that very night. The circumstances were perfect. It had begun to rain, a torrential downpour, which would conceal their movements. He assigned the main task of capturing or killing Narváez to Sandoval, giving him sixty men for the job. He gave Francisco Pizarro the task to silence the cannon by pouring wax into the firing holes, also with sixty men. To Leon he gave sixty men to neutralize Narváez's main force under Diego Velázquez. Cortés took twenty men and five horses to use as a mobile reserve and left the remainder of some forty men as a secondary reserve. He also sent a handful of men secretly into Narváez' camp to cut the girths of the horses' saddles.[31]

---

[29] Troop numbers throughout this history are in dispute. These come from Prescott, *History of the Conquest of Mexico*, 383. See also, Sigurdsson, "Battle of Cempoala: Cortés & His Men Defeat Force Sent to Arrest Him," *Burn Pit*, May 24, 2013, who claims that the force was "nearly 400." www.burnpit.us

[30] Prescott, *History of the Conquest of Mexico and Peru*, 387-88

[31] Díaz del Castillo, *Memoirs of the Conquistador,* 1:322-23; and "Conquest of the Aztec Empire, Part II," *Spanish War History*, spanishwars.net.

After midnight, still in a downpour, at the agreed signal Cortés's men mounted the assault. Surprise was nearly complete despite one of the sentries having sounded the alarm. Sandoval's forces climbed up to the temple-top headquarters where Narváez lay asleep and in a brief but fierce battle subdued the commander, literally smoking him out of his quarters by setting fire to the thatched roof of his compartment and by knocking out one of his eyes with a blow from a lance. Claiming that Narváez was killed, Cortés's men quickly persuaded his troops to give in. Cortés had lost but two men in the attack to about a dozen for Narváez, with several more wounded on each side.

It was a complete victory accomplished in a matter of hours. Engaging with Narváez's troops, Cortés won them to his side, again with gold handouts and promises of more to come. He had quintupled his forces to thirteen hundred men augmented by two thousand Tlaxcalan warriors. He also now had ninety-six horses, forty cannon, eighty crossbows, and eighty muskets, all with a full complement of ammunition and stores. Cortés, as he had done before, dismantled most of the ships, reserving their armament, sails, rigging, rudders, compasses, and hardware. Cortés appeared to be in a stronger position with a more powerful force than he had when he originally entered Mexico, but his euphoria was short-lived as news came from Alvarado that Tenochtitlán was in revolt and his forces were under siege.

The uprising at Tenochtitlán was a second major crisis for Cortés, threatening to take away everything he had gained in Mexico. What exactly happened is still shrouded in controversy regarding the origin of the turmoil. Most scholars blame Alvarado for provoking the insurrection by deliberately massacring several hundred Aztec leaders who were peacefully celebrating a feast day in the courtyard adjacent to Alvarado's temple headquarters. The argument professing the peaceful intent of the Aztecs is unconvincing. Evidence suggests that the resulting uprising was consistent with the joint plan Narváez and Montezuma had put together.

The trouble began on May 16 as soon as Cortés had left Tenochtitlán. According to an early Spanish source, "the Mexica intended to have murdered all the Spaniards on this occasion, for which purpose they had concealed their arms in the buildings adjoining the temple. This was told the Spaniards by the women, from whom they always learnt the truth."[32] Another source says that Alvarado tortured several priests who divulged the plan for the insurrection.[33] Still another notes that the uprising was not a spontaneous reaction to the massacre but showed "signs of organization."[34]

It is difficult to believe that Montezuma, who only weeks before had threatened Cortés with a revolution of the entire Aztec nation against him if he did not leave Mexico forthwith, would now meekly request permission from Alvarado to hold a peaceful celebration in the courtyard of the conquistadors' headquarters. More likely, Montezuma saw his opportunity to eliminate the Spaniards' weakened presence in Tenochtitlán as Narváez presumably was destroying Cortés's small force on the coast. Alvarado partially upset this plan by striking preemptively, perhaps triggering prematurely the uprising planned against him anyway.

To Montezuma's surprise, it was Cortés who defeated Narváez. And as soon as Montezuma was informed of this fact, he called off the uprising in Tenochtitlán, although he maintained the cutoff of water and food to Alvarado's embattled troops. The tables had turned once again. Instead of the destruction of Cortés's forces in both places, Montezuma was now confronted with the largest Spanish force he had ever faced, and it was coming to Tenochtitlán. The Aztec leader hastily put another plan into action. He would put the blame on Alvarado for the uprising, denying any responsibility, while laying a trap for Cortés in the capital when he arrived. He would lure Cortés into the capital and then seal it shut, trapping them all inside. The embattled Alvarado would be bait for this trap.

Montezuma's first act was to send a high level four-man delegation to Cortés while he was still on the coast. They tearfully complained that

> Pedro de Alvarado sallied out from his quarters with all the
> soldiers that Cortés had left with him and for no reason at all,

---

[32] Antonio de Herrera, *Historia General de las Indies Occidentales,* 366, as quoted in Díaz del Castillo, *Memoirs of the Conquistador,* 1:397n86.

[33] Buddy Levy, *Conquistador: Hernán Cortés, King Montezuma and the Last Stand of the Aztecs* (New York: Bantam, 2008), 166.

[34] Miguel León-Portilla, *The Broken Spears: The Aztec Account of the Conquest of Mexico* (Boston: Beacon Press, 1992), 77.

fell on their chieftains and Caciques who were dancing and
celebrating a feast in honour of their Idols...[35]

Parsing this complaint, it seems that the story of Alvarado's brutal
massacre of innocent Indians came from Montezuma, and its purpose was
to blame the Spaniards for precipitating the uprising and to exonerate
himself. Montezuma also expected that the news would bring Cortés
quickly back to Tenochtitlán. He was right.

Cortés decided to return to Tenochtitlán immediately, not only to
rescue Alvarado, but also to regain control of the empire. His first
destination was Tlaxcala where he put his forces in order, augmenting
them with two thousand fresh men from his ally. Beyond Tlaxcala the
reception his men received from villages along the way was increasingly
cool, and when he arrived at Texcoco on the east side of the lake,
downright frigid. At Texcoco Cortés received two messages. From
Alvarado came word that hostilities had ceased, but the blockade
continued. From Montezuma came a missive promising to lift the blockade
as soon as Cortés arrived at Tenochtitlán and once again disclaiming any
responsibility for the uprising which he said had occurred against his
orders.[36]

Arriving at the southern causeway entrance to Tenochtitlán on
June 24, the scene was decidedly different from his first entrance the
previous November. Thousands welcomed him along the route the first
time, but now the city seemed deserted, though the gates were open.
Against the advice of his Tlaxcalan allies who smelled a trap, Cortés took
his entire force over the causeway and into the city. Alvarado's contingent
received them with joy, but there was only eerie silence in the rest of the
city. After a testy exchange with Montezuma during which Cortés
demanded that the local markets be reopened, and food and water supplied,
the Aztec emperor suggested that releasing his presumptive heir,
Cuitláhuac, would lead to that result. Instead, when released, Cuitláhuac
became the leader of the revolt.

Within hours, it became clear that the city was up in arms. Hordes
of warriors began to descend upon Tenochtitlán from the surrounding

---

[35] Díaz del Castillo; Carrasco, *History of the Conquest of New Spain*, 210.
[36] Prescott, *History of the Conquest of Mexico and Peru*, 402-03.

countryside and men previously hidden on rooftops in the city emerged armed with stones to sling at the Spaniards. All the entrances to the city were shut and the causeway drawbridges were raised. Cortés realized they had fallen into a trap but believed that his superior firepower would prevail as it had in the past. The entire contingent was lodged in their palace at Axayacatl, a walled enclosure with the usual temple in the center. The walls, however, were not high enough to be a significant barrier to a determined aggressor and higher surrounding temples offered vantage points from which to rain down stones and arrows on Cortés's men.

Thus began the siege of Cortés at Tenochtitlán. Over the next week hordes of Aztec warriors attempted to storm the palace, while the Spaniards responded with their thirteen cannons strategically placed for defense and muskets trained at those who breached the walls. Nevertheless, breaches occurred, resulting in close order hand-to-hand combat. Today, the Aztec strategy would be recognized as a human wave attack designed to reduce the strength of the adversary by relentless charges until eventually overwhelming him. Cortés sought to break through the Aztec lines by repeatedly charging out of the fortress with his cavalry, but the Indians simply withdrew behind hastily constructed barricades only to reemerge when the horsemen retreated. Cortés was winning battles but losing the war to a determined foe possessing seemingly unlimited numbers.

To provide some protection from the slings and arrows, Cortés devised a wheeled wooden canopy called a *manta*, under which two-dozen men could safely advance and fire their muskets. Several were constructed but they proved too heavy and afforded poor visibility. The Aztecs were able to thwart this stratagem by rushing the mantas and pushing them over. Cortés was growing desperate. There was no letup of the siege and food and water were dwindling fast. The only answer was to break out from the blockade and retreat to friendly territory in Tlaxcala where he could regroup and rebuild his forces. However, the causeways leading from the city to the mainland were constructed of stone buttresses spanned by wooden drawbridges. There was constant conflict over the bridges. Cortés's men sought to establish control of the main causeway and its seven bridges, but the Aztecs tore down each connecting wooden bridge as it was rebuilt.

At last, Cortés turned to Montezuma, who initially refused to meet with him, declaring that it was no use: "you will never leave these walls alive." When Cortés promised to leave Mexico and return to Spain if given the opportunity to depart in peace, Montezuma relented and agreed to address his people. Calling to his people from the top of the Axayacatl palace, he declared that any further conflict was unnecessary, as the Spaniards had agreed to depart and leave their land. But the sentiment among the Aztecs was adverse, spurred on by Cuitláhuac, leader of the rebellion and Montezuma's presumptive heir. The throng denounced the emperor, their words followed by a rain of stones and arrows, several of which struck and badly injured Montezuma.[37] He would expire a few days later, at forty-one years of age. Indeed, a council of chiefs had elected Cuitláhuac to be acting sovereign even before Montezuma had addressed the crowd.[38] Cuitláhuac always had been an outspoken advocate for fighting the Spaniards. There would be no armistice. It would be a war of annihilation.

Cortés was truly desperate. They had expended all the ammunition for the muskets and the powder for the cannon was gone. They were down to swords and lances and twenty-three horses. There was no alternative but to attempt a breakout. He had earlier instructed his men to construct a portable wooden span to place over the broken bridges connecting the stone causeway segments. Unfortunately, they had managed to build only one. They would depart well after midnight on June 30/July 1. Although advising his men to travel as light as possible, many were loath to leave behind the treasure in the palace and would attempt to take as much of it with them as they could carry, slowing them down.

They had chosen the shortest of the three causeways for their escape route that led to the lakeside city of Tlacopan two miles distant to the west. To divert attention from their plan, Cortés delivered the dead

---

[37] Prescott, *History of the Conquest of Mexico and Peru*, 420-22; 422n15. Prescott records that Guatemozin (Cuauhtémoc, who acceded to the throne after Cuitláhuac), was reported to have fired the first arrow.

[38] Maurice Collis, *Cortés and Montezuma* (New York: New Directions Publishing, September 15, 1999), 184.

body of Montezuma to the Aztecs, who took him off for ritual burial. In a constant drizzle they set off, with horses' hooves padded to muffle their sound. Using the portable bridge, the advance guard passed over the first damaged segment safely, but before they could move it to the second, they were discovered. The Indians, anticipating the breakout, were arrayed in strength along the banks of the causeway and in hundreds of canoes along its length. It was a massacre, perhaps the worst defeat in Spanish military history. Cortés's men, confined along the narrow causeway and struggling to make it to the mainland, divested themselves of the treasure they carried to lighten their load and speed their pace. The defeat became known as *La Noche Triste*, the night of sorrows.[39]

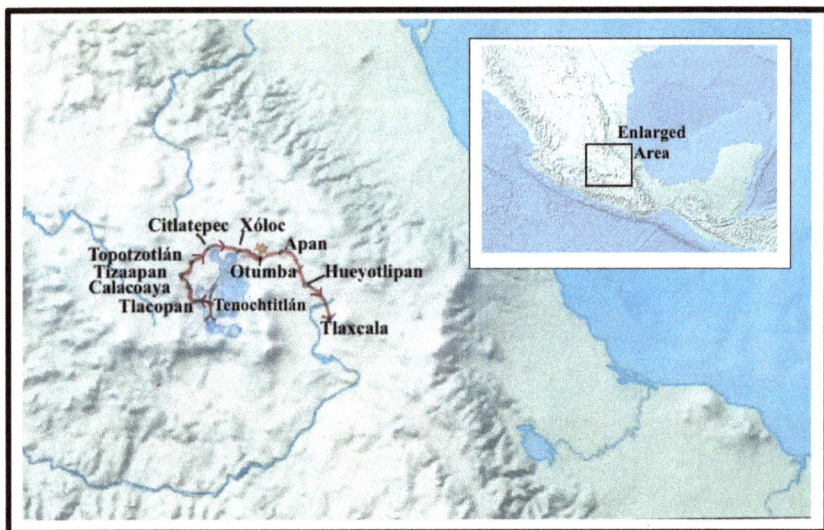

2.8. Escape from Tenochtitlán.

Although their losses were serious, there is no agreement as to the number of deaths sustained in the breakout. Estimates range from 150 to 1,000 Spaniards, and from 2,000-4,000 Tlaxcalan warriors. Most historians credit Cortés with retreating from Tenochtitlán with the same number of troops he had when he first set foot on Mexican soil, about 440, which would set Spanish losses at around 800. But that was small comfort.

---

[39] Stuart B. Schwartz, ed., *Victors and Vanquished: Spanish and Nahua Views of the Conquest of Mexico* (Boston: Bedford/St. Martin's, 2000), 159-60 and 183 ff.

The survivors were badly battered, almost all were wounded, and had only the weapons they carried with them. Traveling northward around the lake, they headed for Tlaxcala. Each village they passed sent out locals to harass the travelers, refusing them either food or water. Oddly, however, the main Aztec army that had driven them from Tenochtitlán had not followed in pursuit.

If Cortés thought fortune had smiled at this welcome breathing space, he was shortly disabused of the notion. For, on the seventh day of the march, at the village of Otumba on the high plain leading to Tlaxcala there appeared thousands of Aztec warriors, many drawn from surrounding principalities, blocking their route and clearly intent on finishing them off. But sometimes fortune smiles in unexpected ways. Unknown to Cortés until later, the reason the Aztecs' main force had not pursued him out of Tenochtitlán was because of a completely fortuitous event.

One of Narváez's black slaves who had traveled with Cortés back to Tenochtitlán had smallpox, which he spread into the Aztec community completely by chance. The Aztecs had no immunity to the disease, which quickly began to ravage the inhabitants, including Montezuma's successor Cuitláhuac, who became incapacitated and would perish in November.[40] The outbreak of the disease disrupted their leadership and debilitated their ranks, causing the Aztecs to delay in the pursuit of Cortés, giving him the needed breathing space. They nevertheless rallied their tributary allies, directing them to intercept Cortés before he reached Tlaxcala. Then, for whatever reason, the Aztecs had decided to wage the final battle against Cortés on open flat ground (the plain of Otumba) that was more favorable to him than to the Aztecs. In fact, even with only twenty horses Cortés directed cavalry charges to disrupt and disorganize the attacking natives.

Still, it appeared that Aztec numbers would be decisive, and as they were about to overwhelm Cortés's forces, the conquistador espied the Aztec commander surveying the course of battle from a small rise. Calling for support from his men, Cortés and a handful of horsemen charged the hill and killed the commander in a brief skirmish. He raised his banner and

---

[40] Noble David Cook, *Born to Die: Disease and New World Conquest, 1492-1650* (Cambridge: Cambridge University Press, 1998), 68-69.

exclaimed triumph, whereupon Aztec forces became disorganized and demoralized, and began to retreat. It was either a brilliant stroke of tactical battlefield ingenuity or luck, but against great odds, Cortés's forces broke through the encirclement to struggle onward to Tlaxcala and safety.

Destruction of the Aztec Empire

While Cortés and his men were tending their wounds and rebuilding their forces at Tlaxcala, the Aztecs were being ravaged by an epidemic of smallpox at Tenochtitlán. By some estimates the population of the capital was decimated from over 300,000 to 200,000 by the fall, including the death of Montezuma's successor Cuitláhuac in late November. By then, the Aztecs too were in recovery mode, rallied by a new emperor, Cuauhtémoc. Smallpox would eventually spread throughout Mexico, devastating the population of five million by ninety percent.

Meanwhile, good fortune continued to smile on Cortés. Governor Velázquez, assuming Narváez had been successful, sent two ships to Vera Cruz loaded with supplies and ammunition, which Cortés's men seized. Around the same time the governor of Jamaica had sent two ships to support an expedition sent to Pánuco, a settlement some 230 miles north of Vera Cruz. In both cases Cortés persuaded the crews to join him. A merchant from the Canary Islands, perceiving a commercial opportunity, sent a galleon loaded with military stores. He was right. Cortés purchased it all with gold, including the ship. These serendipitous arrivals cheered and augmented Cortés's forces by a hundred and fifty men, twenty horses, and copious stores of weapons and ammunition.

Cortés had also sent out his own call for help. During these months, some members of Narváez's expedition had become disenchanted with the life of the conquistadors and wanted to return. Cortés sent them home with messages to his friends in Santo Domingo, Jamaica, and Puerto Rico (but not Cuba), asking for help. His calls were answered during the fall as reinforcements began to trickle in from the islands. By December, Cortés had rebuilt his army to over 1,000 men, including 84 cavalry, 194 musketeers, 680-foot soldiers, several hundred sailors, a handful of cannon, and over 20,000 Tlaxcalan warriors.

Cortés was ready to begin his return to Tenochtitlán. His plan was to turn the tables on the Aztecs. He would lay siege to their capital, destroy the heart of their empire, and restore Spanish rule. He knew the strengths and weaknesses of the island fortress, having occupied it for nearly seven months and having been on the wrong end of a siege there. He would isolate the Aztecs by cutting all sources of food and water. He would persuade or coerce the people of the villages along the lake to turn away from the Aztecs and support him. He would enforce the city's isolation by gaining control of the causeways to it and establish naval supremacy on the lake with his own ships. He commissioned thirteen brigantines, averaging forty feet in length, equipped with sails, and armed with cannon for this purpose.

The Aztec emperor Cuauhtémoc understood Cortés's objectives and sought to counter with a spoiling strategy. Thus, when Cortés sent armed reconnaissance probes to lakeside villages and towns, Aztec forces were there to contest him in the struggle over hearts and minds. When he tried to cut off the water viaduct, they battled to keep it open. When Cortés sought to seize the causeways, Cuauhtémoc's forces contested every foot. When Cortés pushed to gain control of the lake, hundreds of canoe-born Aztecs were there to battle him, including an attempt to drown the Spanish leader at Iztapalapa by opening the canals and raising the water level.[41] However, in each case superior Spanish firepower and determined persistence prevailed.

By the middle of June 1521, with more and more of the Aztec former tributaries flocking to Cortés's side—by some estimates amounting to 75,000 men—his forces reached the gates of Tenochtitlán. The last stand for the Aztecs had commenced. It was savage, long, and decisive. In a two month-long campaign in which no quarter was given by either side, Cortés gradually tightened the blockade while his forces and his Indian allies forced their way across the causeways and advanced through the city in what can fairly be described as house to house and hand to hand combat. To counter the remaining Aztec advantage of attacking Cortés's forces from the temple heights and rooftops of houses, Cortés decided to raze the

---

[41] Díaz del Castillo; Carrasco, *History of the Conquest of New Spain*, 244.

entire city, tearing it down brick by brick and using the breakage to fill in the gaps in the causeways. The capital of the Aztec empire was no more.

2.9. Capture of Tenochtitlan. Jay I. Kislak Collection, Library of Congress.

With Aztec forces weakened to exhaustion by disease and combat, deprived of food and water, and with the end in sight, emperor Cuauhtémoc attempted to flee Tenochtitlán by canoe across the lake with his retinue and wealth but was chased down by one of the brigantines. Brought before Cortés on August 13, 1521, he surrendered. That would not be the end of the killing, however, as the former subjects of Aztec tyrannical rule now exacted their revenge, scouring towns and villages, raping and pillaging everything they considered representative of Aztec rule, despite Cortés's attempts to rein them in. When it was over Cortés brought the leaders of all the former clansmen of the empire to Tenochtitlán to witness firsthand its utter devastation and the superiority of Spanish rule.

Cortés laid the foundation of the Spanish empire in Mexico. He rebuilt Tenochtitlán, which would become the eventual site for Mexico City. He settled new towns across the country, improved the Aztec transportation network and developed gold mining operations, importing thousands of black African slaves for the purpose. As the economy developed, maritime commerce between Spain and New Spain, as it was called, ballooned. The church followed in a plan to convert the natives to Catholicism. Thousands of people poured into Mexico to settle, explore, and marvel at the wonders of the New World.

Years later, Spanish historians would glorify Cortés's exploits, but at the time he was treated shabbily by the Spanish Crown and the Council of the Indies where Governor Velázquez had friends. In the familiar bureaucratic struggle among the Crown, the governors abroad, and the conquistadors, the bureaucrats triumphed. Claiming to fear that he would break with Spain and establish himself as head of an independent country, the Crown moved to ensure control of its great colony by sending administrators to replace Cortés. The king lauded his work, accorded him land and titles, but denied him the authority he wanted in Mexico. Cortés left Mexico for Spain in 1528, returned in 1530 for a decade in which he explored into present-day California searching for the fabled land of *El Dorado*—the rumored repository of gold—before returning to Spain in 1541. He would die six years later attempting to return to Mexico.

Although Cortés had seized a great deal of gold and treasure from the Aztecs, (wealth that they themselves had looted from their enemies), he never discovered the sources he so assiduously sought. The mines he restarted never lived up to their promise, although the slaves he imported proved to be a permanent addition to the land. Gold shipped to Spain in Cortés's time averaged about a ton a year, significant but not the riches that had been expected. Yet Cortés played an important role. He destroyed the Aztec empire and opened the door to the sources of gold and especially of silver that would finance the Spanish empire for the next two hundred years, but he would not live to see it. That glory would accrue to unknown later governors of the colony, and especially in Peru, ironically within but a few years of the return of Cortés to Spain.

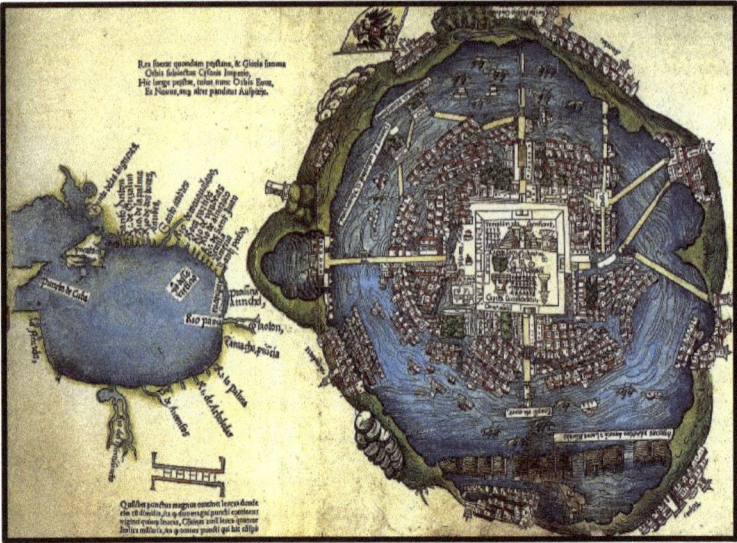

**2.10. Gulf of Mexico and Tenochtitlán at the end of Aztec rule.
Map published by Fridericum Peypus in 1524.**

Chapter 3

Searching for *El Dorado,* Discovering Peru

Of all of the conquistadors, on paper Francisco Pizarro seemed the least likely to be capable of establishing the financial underpinning of a Spanish Empire that would last over a century. He was illiterate, illegitimate, and more than fifty years of age when he discovered Peru, which was old for any soldier of fortune. Yet, a closer look reveals a very intelligent man with great political, business, and military acumen. He learned how to maneuver within the Spanish Crown and colonial bureaucracies to obtain the authorizations necessary to pursue his dream of reaching *El Dorado.* He possessed the intangible qualities that made him well suited for the task, such as military experience and ruthless drive. He also was ambitious, opportunistic, determined to succeed, and willing to take calculated risks. But most of all, Pizarro was a patient man, and like the other conquistadors, he would search for one thing, find something greater, yet not live to see the true fruits of his endeavors.

Little is known of Pizarro's youth; even the date of his birth is uncertain, variously reported between 1471 and 1478. Assuming the earlier date, he was fifteen years older than his distant cousin Hernán Cortés and twenty-two years of age when Columbus returned to Spain after his first voyage. Pizarro was born in poverty, received no formal education, and could neither read nor write. He worked as a swineherd in his youth and joined the Spanish army when he came of age, fighting in the Italian wars alongside his father, an army colonel. It is no surprise, then, in 1502 to find the thirty-one-year-old soldier of fortune on board a ship headed for Santo Domingo, Hispaniola in search of wealth, adventure, and destiny.

In those days the Crown had extended its claims beyond the Caribbean islands to the north coast of the Panamanian isthmus and part of South America, initially naming it *Tierra Firme*. The region was further divided into two sectors: Veragua to the west and Nueva Andalucía to the east, with the meridian at the Gulf of Urabá and the Atrato river. In 1509, King Ferdinand authorized expeditions from Santo Domingo to establish settlements in each sector, naming Alonso de Ojeda governor of Nueva Andalucía and Diego de Nicuesa governor of Veragua. Unable to finance an expedition entirely by himself, Ojeda entered into an agreement with Martín Fernández de Enciso, a wealthy lawyer, navigator and adventurer on the island of Hispaniola. In November 1509, Ojeda sailed first, with a complement of two ships; two smaller, two-masted brigantines; and three hundred settlers and soldiers. As was Spanish practice, Enciso was to follow with additional men and supplies after a few months. Diego de Nicuesa departed for Veragua shortly after Ojeda, his experience to be recounted below.

Pizarro and Balboa

It was on Ojeda's expedition that Francisco Pizarro first received an opportunity to shine, although the circumstances were not ideal. Fighting their way down what is today the Colombian coast, Ojeda's men established the settlement of San Sebastián on the eastern shore of the Gulf of Urabá. Unfortunately, the settlement was poorly sited. Conditions were unfavorable for growing crops and the jungle was impenetrable. Worse, hostile Indians armed with curare-tipped arrows wreaked havoc on the settlers, reducing their numbers by a third. By spring 1510, as Enciso had yet to arrive, Ojeda decided to return to Santo Domingo for supplies and reinforcements, leaving Francisco Pizarro in command. Their agreement was that Pizarro should hold out for fifty days; if Ojeda had not returned within that time, the young lieutenant would be free to take whatever action he deemed appropriate.[1]

Unbeknownst to Pizarro, Ojeda had been blown off course far to the northwest and was shipwrecked. After fifty days had elapsed and Ojeda had not returned, Pizarro decided to return to Santo Domingo, the

---

[1] David Marley, *Wars of the Americas* (Santa Barbara: ABC-CLIO, 1998), 9-10.

expedition a failure. Just after casting off, however, he encountered Martín Fernández de Enciso on the way in with 150 men and full provisions for the beleaguered settlement. In mid-voyage, Enciso had discovered a stowaway on board his ship, one Vasco Núñez de Balboa, later to be renowned as the discoverer of the Pacific Ocean. Balboa, fleeing debt collectors, had decided to seek his fortune on the mainland. Persuaded to allow him to join the expedition instead of depositing him on a deserted island, Enciso made a fateful decision.[2] From their first encounter, Enciso and Balboa were at loggerheads, which ultimately would not end well for Balboa. Initially Pizarro sided with Balboa, a decision Enciso also would not forget.

Incorporating the remnants of Ojeda's men into his own contingent, Enciso determined to head for San Sebastián against the forceful objections of Pizarro and his bedraggled crew. When they arrived, they were met by hostile Indians and found that the settlement had been reduced to ashes. After general discussion, during which Balboa was very persuasive, it was decided to abandon San Sebastián, sail across the Bay of Urabá and establish a settlement where conditions presumably would be better. In September 1510, they established the settlement of Santa Maria de la Antigua del Darién, or simply, Darién.[3]

---

[2] Charles Anderson, *Old Panama and Castilla Del Oro: A Narrative History* [...] (Boston: Page, 1914), 158.
[3] Frederick A. Ober, "In the Land of Poisoned Arrows," *Pizarro and the Conquest of Peru* (New York: Harper & Brothers, 1906), online at Heritage History www.heritage-history.com.

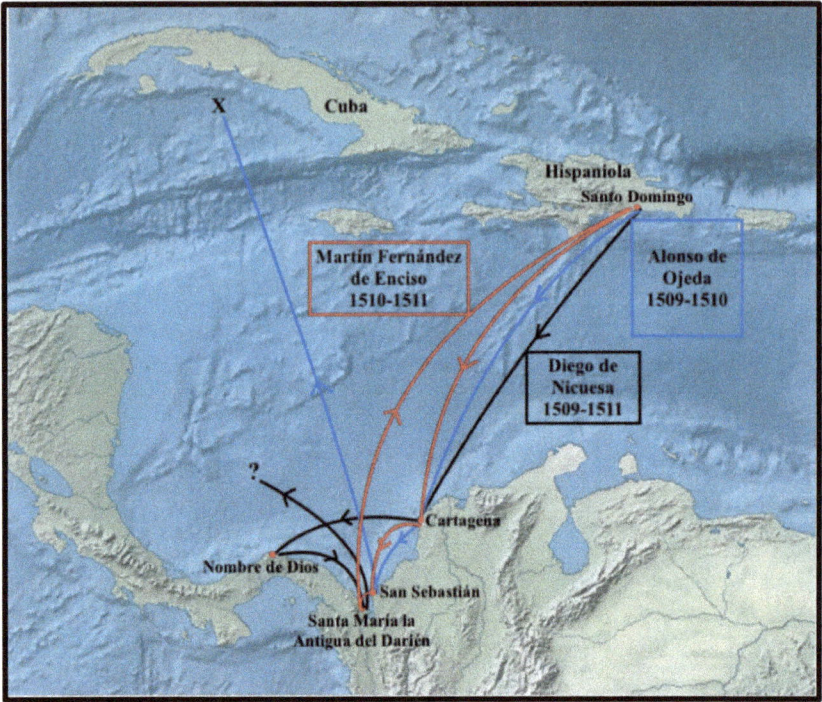

3.1. Expeditions of Ojeda, Nicuesa, and Enciso, 1509-1511

Meanwhile, the expedition led by Diego de Nicuesa had experienced even more troubles than Ojeda. After months of exhaustive missteps and two failed attempts at establishing settlements, Nicuesa founded a settlement at Nombre de Dios on the north coast of the Panamanian isthmus. Although starting out with six hundred men, a group twice the size of Ojeda's, by the spring of 1510 the settlement was on the verge of collapse. Settlers were dying off sharply, mainly due to disease and malnutrition, but also Indian attacks, leaving only a few dozen men. The Indians had pursued a scorched earth policy, leaving no available food for the settlers, and retreated into the jungles hoping to starve the Spaniards out. Were it not for the arrival of Nicuesa's captain Rodrigo de Colmenares in mid-November, the Indians might well have succeeded. He arrived not only with sixty reinforcements and plentiful supplies, but also with news of Ojeda's expedition.

Colmenares had stopped at Darién before sailing on to Nombre de Dios. He found a flourishing settlement under the leadership of Balboa, but also some irregularities. It transpired that upon establishing the settlement at Darién, Enciso had taken charge. He ruled with a firm hand, confiscating the lion's share of all gold accumulated by the settlers. Balboa led a group of disgruntled settlers and overthrew Enciso on a legal technicality based on the fact that Darién was in Nicuesa's sphere of authority: as Enciso was operating under Ojeda's mandate, he had a claim to San Sebastián, but not to Darién. The upshot of the dispute was that the settlers held an election in which Balboa and Martín Samudio were chosen over Enciso to serve jointly as mayors. Balboa then put Enciso on trial, found him guilty of attempting to usurp power, and clapped him in irons.

When Nicuesa learned that a settlement had been established in his designated territory at Darién, and moreover that it was flourishing where his decidedly was not, he determined to take control as governor of Veragua. He sailed to Darién in February 1511, but when he neared the dock, a large crowd led by Balboa refused to let him disembark, demanding that he return to Nombre de Dios. After much futile argument, a desperate Nicuesa pleaded with Balboa to permit him to live in the settlement as one of them, renouncing his title of governor, for the conditions at Nombre de Dios were so deplorable. But the majority of the settlers were opposed. Led by mayor Samudio, they put Nicuesa and seventeen of his followers out to sea on March 1, 1511, in a boat weakened by shipworm. They were never heard from again.

For the next three years the settlement at Darién thrived under Balboa's leadership, ably assisted by now-captain Francisco Pizarro. Fortunately, the natives there did not possess the poisoned arrows used by those at San Sebastián and the settlers were able to defeat various tribes while befriending others, gradually enlarging their territory. They were able to plant food crops, fish, and hunt, while supplementing their efforts with provisions from Hispaniola.

Pizarro learned a great deal from Balboa about governing. He maintained discipline among settlers and Indians alike through coercion and negotiation, earning their respect. He also learned a lesson of loyalty to his men. Balboa had sent Pizarro on a reconnaissance mission with half a dozen men. Ambushed by natives, they had fought a successful retreat, but Pizarro had left a wounded comrade behind. When Balboa learned of it, he reprimanded Pizarro and sent him back to retrieve the man.[4]

Balboa also found success in his search for gold and slaves, learning from friendly Indian chiefs of a great empire beyond the South Sea. Both he and Pizarro were enthralled by the information and determined to seek out this land. The notion of discovering a land to the south that flowed with rivers of gold would stay with Pizarro for the rest of his life. Recognizing that it would require more resources than were at their disposal to realize their dream, Balboa decided to petition King Ferdinand. In letters dated January 20 and March 4, 1513, he described the land of great wealth beyond "the other sea," requested that the king authorize a major expedition to conquer it, and that he send enough men and supplies to build a shipyard for that purpose. He sent the petitions with two of his men aboard the same ship that transported Enciso, whom Balboa had decided to exile to Spain. His men were to plead his case for the expedition and explain his actions against Enciso. One of these men was co-mayor Martín Samudio, whose departure left Balboa in command as informal governor of Darién.

King Ferdinand was elated by Balboa's discovery, but at the same time deeply concerned about the legality of his methods, for Enciso had managed to persuade him that he had been treated unfairly. To resolve his dilemma, in August, the king made three decisions designed to strengthen the Crown's control over the new territories and their presumed holdings of gold. First, based on Balboa's news, he reorganized Tierra Firme, and renamed it *Castilla del Oro*, or Castile of Gold. Then, responding affirmatively to Balboa's entreaties, he authorized the largest expedition to the Indies since Columbus's second voyage and only the second ever financed entirely by the king himself. All other expeditions were financed either privately, or as joint ventures with investors. Third, he named Pedro Arias Dávila, known as Pedrarias, to head the expedition. The king also named him governor of the newly designated lands, as he was familiar with gold mining; and tasked him with resolving the dispute between Balboa and Enciso. Balboa was relieved as governor but was named

---

[4] Anderson, *Old Panama and Castilla del Oro,* 160.

adelantado (explorer and royal representative) of the South Sea, to encourage and facilitate further exploration in that direction.

It would be over a year before Pedrarias's expedition was properly outfitted, departing Spain on April 11, 1514, but news of the king's decisions traveled fast. Learning of the royal resolutions from his emissaries in Spain, Balboa decided to lead an expedition southward. With 190 men accompanied by several ferocious war dogs, the men hacked their way through dense jungle and past hostile tribes, reaching the southern coast of Panama in September 1513. Although Balboa is universally credited with discovering the Pacific Ocean on September 25 of that year, in truth the entire expedition, in which Pizarro played an important role as second in command, deserves credit. All shared in this moment of triumph, for it reinforced their belief that they would find the fabled land of gold and riches once the men and materials had arrived from the king.

Pizarro and Pedrarias

The arrival of Pedrarias on June 30, 1514 with a very large entourage of seventeen ships and two thousand men signaled that the king shared Balboa's conviction, and that he was determined to establish the Crown's control over the colony to secure its financial promise. It also sent the careers of Balboa and Pizarro onto sharply divergent paths. While the king aimed to encourage Balboa's further exploration in search of the wealth he needed, Pedrarias sought to constrain Balboa's activity at every turn because he saw him as a threat. The struggle between the two men was the political context for Pizarro's ascendancy, as he now shifted his support to the new governor.

Among those who had come with the Pedrarias expedition were men who would prove to be consequential in the subsequent Spanish conquest of America. These included: Hernando de Soto, the youthful aide to Pedrarias; Gaspar de Espinosa, mayor and judge; Gonzalo Fernández de Oviedo, royal accountant and future chronicler; Sebastián de Benalcázar, army captain; Pascual de Andagoya, inspector; Diego de Bustamante, army captain; Juan de Quevedo, newly appointed bishop; Louis Carillo, relative of the court; Hernando de Luque, priest; Diego de Almagro, merchant and slave trader; and Martín Fernández de Enciso.

Pedrarias's company dwarfed Balboa's small settlement of five hundred men; it also quickly consumed the meager resources of the settlement. Balboa had no choice but to acquiesce in Pedrarias's takeover, and from the first the new governor sought to draw Balboa's supporters away from him and into his sphere. His first step in this direction was Balboa's *residencia*, the customary review of an outgoing governor's conduct. With the jurist Gaspar de Espinosa presiding, the court found Balboa innocent of any illegal actions against Enciso, but nevertheless levied a large fine against him. Pedrarias sought to return Balboa to Spain, but intercessions by his wife, Doña Isabel, and Bishop Quevedo forestalled any further action against him.

Thus, from the start it was clear that the governor considered Balboa a rival and a threat. Balboa had reported fully to the new governor regarding his plans for a voyage to the south and about the vast amounts of gold to be found there. Pedrarias took note of Balboa's reports but sought to ensure that he and his supporters gained the credit for any discovery, not Balboa. Thus, he ignored the king's orders to support Balboa and denied his request to lead a South Sea expedition. For Pizarro, this meant that if he were to have a future, it was important to distance himself from his former mentor and ingratiate himself with Pedrarias's circle of intimates.

Pedrarias, in turn, cultivated Pizarro's support, relying upon his military experience in the territory and knowledge of the whereabouts of gold and slaves, which he coveted. Thus, Pedrarias sent Pizarro on missions for which he was rewarded with land and slaves.[5] Unfortunately, none of these expeditions succeeded except in the infliction of carnage and pillage upon the native populations, which only inflamed them against the settlers. The king had ordered Pedrarias to establish a "a line of posts from sea to sea, in accordance with the plan of Vasco Nuñez [de Balboa]," as well as to establish a city on the south coast to pave the way for further

---

[5] Frederick A. Ober, "A Compact With the Enemy," in *Vasco Nuñez de Balboa* (New York: Harper and Brothers, 1906), online at Heritage History www.heritage-history.com.

exploration southward, but Pedrarias refused to include Balboa in his plans.[6]

After repeated failures, Pedrarias was persuaded to relent in his antagonism toward Balboa, partly because the king, having heard of their mutual antipathy, sought to strengthen Balboa's position. In an order dated September 23, 1514, the king named Balboa governor of the area to the west of Darién, present-day Panama City. The implication was that Balboa should establish a settlement in this as-yet undeveloped territory. Thus, in addition to his earlier title of *Adelantado* of the South Sea, this new authority to govern territory on the south coast of Panama clearly signaled the king's support of Balboa's intentions.[7] Pedrarias delayed action on the king's order until he had effected a reconciliation of sorts with Balboa by agreeing to the proxy marriage of his daughter, then in Spain, to him.

Against the backdrop of the feud between Pedrarias and Balboa, over the next two years, in addition to seeking the favor of the governor, Pizarro soon found friends among the newcomers. In particular, he developed close relations with Diego de Almagro and Hernando de Luque, cleric, schoolmaster, and confidant of the governor. Pizarro and Almagro bonded "almost immediately," coming from similarly undistinguished parentage and circumstances and being of similar age. Their main difference was that whereas Pizarro had moved along a military path, Almagro had made his way in commerce and service.[8]

The two men pooled their resources to pan for gold and to raise cattle for the settlement. Seeking to expand their business, they petitioned Governor Pedrarias to grant an *encomienda* in the territory where Balboa had authority, which at the time was but a small outpost away from the prying eyes of Pedrarias and his spies. Their commercial endeavors, as well as their service to the governor supporting forays in search of gold and slaves, enabled them to accumulate enough cash to contemplate financing their dream of an expedition to the South Sea. They included Fr.

---

[6] Anderson, *Old Panama and Castilla del Oro*, 189.

[7] Roscoe Hill, "The Office of Adelantado," *Political Science Quarterly* 28, no. 4, (December 1913):653. The king's order was dated September 23, 1514 but did not reach Balboa until the following year.

[8] Paul M. Kochis, *God, Glory and Gold: Journey to the Conquest of the Incas*, vol.2, *The Quest* (Minneapolis: Mill City Press, 2013), 68.

Luque, who had some influence with the governor and funds to contribute; and they named their venture the Company of the Levant. Because their objective seemed so farfetched, Panamanians laughingly called it *"Compañía de Lunáticos,"* and some referred to Luque as "Fernando de Loco" for his involvement. [9]

Meanwhile, news of King Ferdinand's death on January 23, 1516 had reached the Indies and was having a dramatic impact on events. Bishop Quevedo had returned to Spain to report to the new King Charles I on Pedrarias's governorship, (as no doubt other clergy were doing regarding other settlements—all part of the Crown's initial attempts to consolidate control over its burgeoning empire in the Americas).[10] Quevedo denounced Pedrarias's leadership as an unmitigated disaster, persuading King Charles to replace him with the governor of the Canary Islands, Lope de Sosa. (Sosa, however, would die mysteriously on the very day of his arrival in Darién, May 20, 1520. Suspicion fell on Pedrarias, whose adversaries often seemed to die unexpectedly, usually of poison.)

When word of King Charles's decision to install a new governor reached Darién, it had a profound effect on all concerned. Pedrarias decided to eliminate Balboa, fearful of what he would say in the forthcoming *residencia* that would be held when Sosa arrived. His insubordination to the Crown would be fully exposed in his treatment of Balboa. Balboa, on the other hand, decided to move forthwith on his plan to sail to the South Sea before Sosa could stop him. Success would be his guarantee, as discovery of new land and especially the establishment of settlements were the legal bases in those days for royal favor, governorship, and political independence from men such as Pedrarias, or, indeed, from incoming governors.

---

[9] *Enciclopedia Católica* (online), "Francisco Pizarro," https://ec.aciprensa.com/wiki/Francisco_Pizarro; *Encyclopedia.com,* "Luque, Hernando de (?-1534)," https://www.encyclopedia.com/humanities/encyclopedias-almanacs-transcripts-and-maps/luque-hernando-de-1534; and Rafael Olivares, *Ñusta: the Inka Love of Francisco Pizarro* (Bergenfield: Xlibris, 2014), 77.

[10] See J. H. Elliott, *Empires of the Atlantic World: Britain and Spain in America, 1492-1830* (New Haven: Yale University Press, 2006), 117-20, for discussion of the Crown's early efforts.

In April 1517, Balboa established the South Sea Company with two partners, Hernando de Soto and Pascual de Andagoya. It was believed that de Soto served as Pedrarias's eyes and ears in the endeavor, which was located at Acla, a new, small settlement some forty miles to the west of Darién on the north coast. Their plan was to finance and build four ships for an expedition to the South Sea in pursuit of Balboa's dream of finding the land of gold they had all heard so much about.[11] Balboa had asked Pizarro to join him; however, indicative of the latter's allegiance at this time, he declined.

When Pedrarias learned of Balboa's plans, either from his "eyes" de Soto, or from one of Balboa's adversaries, he believed he had grounds for pursuing him on the charge that he was planning to "throw off allegiance to him as soon as he reached the ocean." Anderson thought this information came from one of Balboa's compatriots, Andres Garabito, who longed for Balboa's Indian mistress and saw this false charge as a way of getting him out of the way.[12] Whatever the truth, it would mark the tragic end for one of Spain's truly heroic conquistadors.

Pedrarias proceeded to set a trap for Balboa so he could arrest, try, and execute him on the charge of treason. He sent a letter to him requesting a meeting to confer about his planned expedition. Unsuspecting, the conquistador agreed to meet his "father in law." To disguise his intent, the governor sent Francisco Pizarro, one of his loyal lieutenants, and a friend of Balboa, with a group of men to meet him en route. Taking Balboa by surprise, Pizarro arrested him and brought him before Pedrarias.

A Star Chamber trial was convened in Acla, away from prying eyes in Darién; and Balboa was denied his right to call supporting witnesses. Pedrarias accused him of treason, of planning to usurp power in Castilla del Oro and establish an independent settlement on the South Sea. The governor, supported by Chief Constable Enciso (!) and chief magistrate Gaspar de Espinosa, found Balboa guilty as charged. Denying him any appeal, Espinosa sentenced him and four compatriots to execution

---

[11] Kochis, *God, Glory and Gold*, 2:73; Frederick A. Ober, "Building the Brigantines," *Vasco Nuñez de Balboa* (New York: Harper and Brothers, 1906), online at Heritage History, www.heritage-history.com.

[12] Anderson, *Old Panama and Castilla del Oro*, 204-05.

by beheading. In Pedrarias's view, "since [Balboa] has sinned, let him die for it" (*pues se peco, muera por ello*). The sentence was carried out on January 12, 1519.[13]

With Balboa out of the way, Pedrarias proceeded to carry out his deceased rival's plan for establishing communication between the Atlantic and the Pacific. In the summer the governor decided to relocate his administration to the new town of Panama City on the southern coast of the isthmus, sending Pascual de Andagoya and four hundred settlers to formally found it on August 15, 1519. (Darién thenceforth became a backwater and in 1524 was overrun by the Indians, literally disappearing from the map.) At the same time, he reinvigorated Nicuesa's failing settlement due north of Panama City on the north coast, Nombre de Dios, establishing a road between them. The two ports and the connecting road, known as *Camino Real* (royal road or highway) would thereafter be the main route of passage between the Pacific and Atlantic Oceans. Panama became the center and point of departure for all southward exploration as well as a major entrepôt for the burgeoning slave trade.

In setting up his new capital, Pedrarias rewarded those who had conspired with him against Balboa, parceling out *encomiendas* and slaves on the outskirts of the city. This would seem to support the view of Gonzalo Fernández de Oviedo, Pizarro's "great detractor," who claimed that "not only did Pizarro betray Nuñez de Balboa to Arias Dávila, but that he played a full part in his capture and hanging."[14] In any case, Pedrarias not only acceded to Pizarro's and Almagro's earlier petition for land there, but he also appointed Pizarro as mayor, a highly prestigious post, which moved him into Pedrarias's inner circle. Pizarro's *encomienda* included the island of Taboga just off the coast of Panama and two hundred Indians. He turned the island's plentiful gravel into a thriving business selling ballast for ships.

But all was not sweetness and light between the wily Pedrarias and the now well-ensconced Francisco Pizarro. With increased wealth from the livestock, mining and slave trades, Pizarro and his comrades

---

[13] Ibid., 206-07.
[14] Oviedo, as quoted in Stuart Stirling, *Pizarro: Conqueror of the Inca* (Stroud: Sutton, 2005), 14.

Almagro and Luque were now "among the richest men in Panama."
Indeed, the first appearance of their company in Spanish documents
occurred in 1522 when the three men registered 705 pesos of gold from
their mining profits for shipment to Seville for investment purposes.[15]
Ready and able, they pressed Pedrarias for permission to mount an
expedition to the South Sea.

But Pedrarias had other ideas. News of the expeditions of
Córdoba, Grijalva, and Cortés to Yucatan and Mexico prompted Pedrarias
to send his men exploring northward and westward, reaching as far as
present-day Honduras and Nicaragua, in order to establish a northern
"boundary" against encroachment on his empire.[16] Indeed, multiple
Spanish expeditions clashed there. An expedition under Gil Gonzalez,
with governing authority from the Crown, confronted an expedition under
Hernando de Soto dispatched by Pedrarias's office, and both encountered
a third expedition sent by Cortés from Mexico under Cristóbal de Olid. In
a "wild scramble" for control of territory and gold, Olid was killed.[17] It
was perhaps a portent of what was to come, as Spaniard battled against
Spaniard for wealth and power in the new world.

Pizarro, Almagro, and Luque

Attitudes changed with the discovery of America and its riches,
combined with the realization that the world was a much bigger place than
was thought just a few years earlier. While the Crown still sought the
Malacca Straits as a shortcut to China, the king was increasingly enamored
of the wealth of America as a source of funds for his European wars. Of
course for the men on the ground, plunder and pillage continued to be the
principal objectives.[18] After over two years of exploration to the north and
west with not much gold and silver to show for it, Pedrarias decided to

---

[15] Rafael Varón Gabai, *Francisco Pizarro and His Brothers, The Illusion of Power in Sixteenth-Century Peru,* trans. Javier Flores Espinoza (Norman: University of Oklahoma Press, 1997), 17. Curiously, Manuel José Quintana, *Lives of Vasco Nunez de Balboa and Francisco Pizarro,* trans. Margaret. Hodson (Edinburgh: William Blackwood, 1832; repr., Kessinger, 2010), 91 says that at this time he was "one of the least wealthy inhabitants of Panama."
[16] Kochis, *God, Glory and Gold,* 2:91-92.
[17] Anderson, *Old Panama and Castilla del Oro,* 222.
[18] Kochis, *God, Glory and Gold,* 2:90-91.

turn his gaze southward; and in 1522 when he was ready to authorize an expedition, he gave the task not to Pizarro, but to his close friend Pascual de Andagoya, who had been Balboa's partner and who would use one of the very ships Balboa had constructed for the purpose.

News of Cortés's fabulous success in Mexico as he began to ship treasure back to Spain rekindled old rumors in Panama City and indeed through all of Europe of an undiscovered land of fabulous riches and gold. The dominant legend was of *El Hombre Dorado* or simply *El Dorado* (The Gilded Man). He was said to be a tribal chief who as part of his investiture ceremony would cover himself in gold dust before dipping in a lake to emerge cleansed, reborn and fit to govern. In social gatherings in haciendas and cantinas alike, practically everyone had his own version of this legendary chief and his location. Some believed that it lay to the north, in or beyond Mexico; others thought that it was situated near Lake Guatavita in what is now Colombia; and still others, Pizarro and his friends among them, reckoned that it would be found further to the south, as Balboa had believed, in a land they called Peru.

Pedrarias had bitterly disappointed Pizarro and his friends by appointing Andagoya to lead the expedition south, further alienating them. But their hopes were reborn with Andagoya's unexpectedly early return due to a hypothermia-inducing immersion in which he nearly drowned. He had sailed nearly as far as Balboa and Pizarro had earlier, replenishing at the Pearl Islands (Isla del Rey) and then sailing along the coast to Piñas Bay and the River Jacqué. Though his expedition was cut short, returning in the spring of 1523 he claimed to have seen enough to confirm the stories of a great, rich kingdom still further to the south, as Balboa had held.

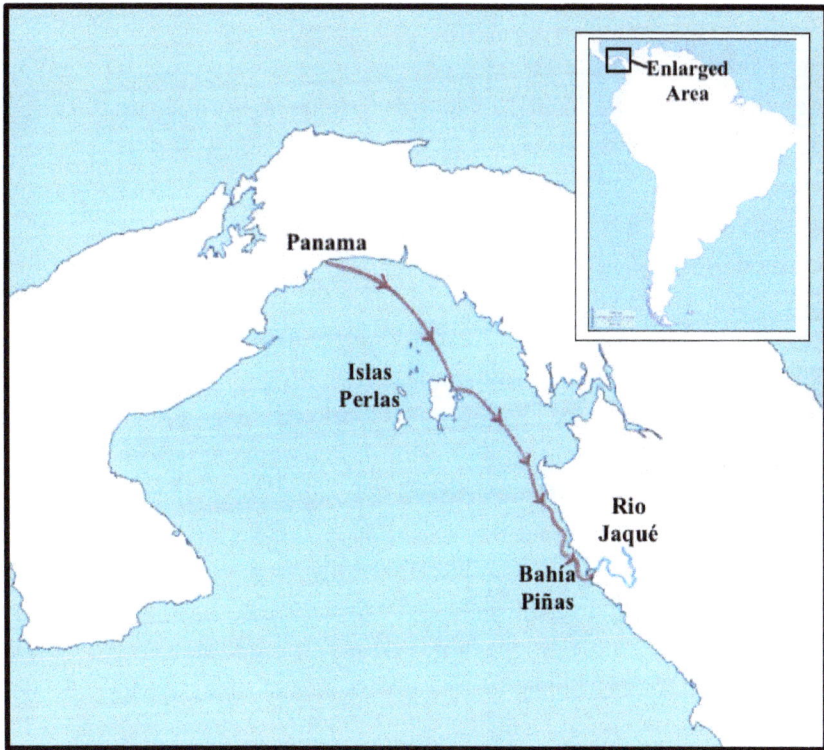

3.2. Andagoya's expedition, 1522-1523

Pedrarias finally agreed to issue a license to Pizarro and his friends Almagro and Luque to carry forward Andagoya's mission; as usual, taking for himself a share of future profits. After months preparing for their expedition, they had acquired two ships and recruited 130 men, including 112 Spaniards, a mix of Indians and blacks, and four horses. Their plan was the standard tag-team approach where Pizarro, captain of the expedition, would sail first in one ship, blazing a trail along the Colombian coast. Almagro would follow in the other ship some months later with reinforcements and supplementary provisions. Departing in mid-November 1524, the rainy season, Pizarro was undaunted, at last underway after years of waiting to pursue his dream of discovering *El Dorado.*

Topping off supplies of gravel, wood, hay, water, and food at Taboga Island off Panama City, Pizarro wended his way along the coast, putting in at promising-looking coves and conducting reconnaissance marches inland. After two and a half months exploring what still is forbidding territory, featuring high rocky bluffs and thick impermeable jungle joining tangled mangrove swamps, the results were disappointing. They came across no habitation and thus no food, let alone gold. Putting into a cove at Humboldt Bay they considered their position. They were dangerously low on food and water, and with no sign of Almagro. In mid-February 1525, Pizarro decided to send his ship under the command of Gil de Montenegro back to the Pearl Islands for supplies.

Camping at a spot they named aptly Puerto de la Hambre (Hunger Port) near the present-day Rio Jurado, Pizarro and his men explored inland along the river, finally coming across some small Indian settlements which they raided for food. But pickings were slim, with only an occasional ear of corn, coconuts, fish, crabs, palm treetops, and some fruits for sustenance. In desperation they boiled the ship's cowhide pump cover to extract whatever nutrients still remained in it. During their wait thirty men died of disease and malnutrition. Undoubtedly, their voyage was not what they expected, and it got worse.

While Montenegro was sailing back to the Pearl Islands, in mid-March Almagro was finally setting out in search of his partner. Sailing from Panama, he, too, replenished at the Pearl Islands and headed for the Colombian coast looking for signs of Pizarro's path in the form of felled or notched trees, and other prearranged markers. Somehow, Almagro and Montenegro missed sighting each other and Almagro never did meet up with Pizarro. At the end of March, Montenegro returned to Puerto de la Hambre with ample provisions amid great acclamations from the nearly famished and emaciated men. After a few days of feasting and recuperation, Pizarro decided to continue on, hoping that they would finally encounter Almagro, who they rightly believed must be on his way to them.

It was now April 1525 and they were observing more open country, finding better rivers, beaches, bays, and coves to explore. Even so, as there were few deep-water anchorages for their ships, exploration had to be by canoe to shore and then on foot inland following river courses.[19] Proceeding southward, now about two hundred and fifty miles along, they reached a place they named Puerto de la Candelaria a few miles north of present-day Solano Bay. Marching inland they discovered a small settlement of Indians who possessed a few gold artifacts, but they also saw evidence of cannibalism. From these natives they received positive reinforcement about the great kingdom to the south. Moving on, they dropped anchor in Solano Bay at a site they would later name *El Pueblo Quemado*, the burned village, for reasons that will become clear in due course.

Close to shore Pizarro found a fortified settlement that seemed to be deserted. Entering, the Spaniards took stores of food and some ornaments of gold. But it was a trap. The Indians, led by a chief whom they called the "cacique of the stones," returned to confront the Spaniards. In serious fighting five members of Pizarro's party were killed and seventeen wounded, including Pizarro himself, who suffered seven flesh wounds. Indeed, he was only saved from death by the heroic action of his men. Afterward, suffering some twenty percent casualties, he decided he had had enough. They re-boarded their ship and headed for home. It seemed to be an ignominious end to a long-held dream. Again, he and his partner, Almagro, moving in opposite directions, failed to connect, like ships passing in the night. The entire expedition had been a fiasco.

Pizarro decided not to return to Panama City to face the wrath of Pedrarias. He decided to stay away because he remembered Balboa's fate; and knew that he would be asked to explain the failure of his expedition, especially the loss of life. Worse, the chance of his being authorized to continue with a second voyage seemed nonexistent. Therefore, instead of returning to Panama City, he sought refuge in what was no more than a secluded camp called Chochama a few miles to the east of the city. After he and his men disembarked, he sent Nicolás de Ribera, his quartermaster, along with those who had decided to quit the expedition and the small

---

[19] See the invaluable account of Robert Cushman Murphy, "The Earliest Spanish Advances Southward from Panama Along the West Coast of South America," *Hispanic American Historical Review* 21, no. 1 (Feb 1941):13.

amount of gold they had accumulated back to Panama to refit the ship and report to Pedrarias.[20]

In the meantime, in June, Almagro proceeded southward along the coast, noting some of the places where Pizarro had anchored, but did not make contact, having overshot his partner. Sailing further, he reached the mouth of the San Juan River. Here was found extensive habitation. Almagro and his crew saw well laid-out settlements, villages, impressive buildings, and well-organized agricultural plantings. Trading with the natives, they accumulated more gold and silver than Pizarro had.

The sheer size of the habitation persuaded Almagro to adopt a friendly approach, realizing that far more men and weapons would be required for conquest. On the way back, he dropped anchor where Pizarro had engaged in the major battle with the "cacique of the stones" near the Bay of Solano—and met with the same reception. The Indians attacked and in a major battle Almagro suffered a serious injury, the loss of sight in one eye. In reprisal, the Spaniards burned the entire Indian settlement to the ground; hence the name "*El Pueblo Quemado*," the burned village.

3.3. First voyages of Pizarro and Almagro, 1524-1525

---

[20] Nicolás de Ribera was one of the very few actual participants to write about Pizarro, as quoted in Stirling, *Pizarro*, 6-7.

Returning to the Pearl Islands, Almagro learned that Pizarro had survived and was holed up at Chochama, and so sailed to join him. In what was at once both a joyous and acrimonious reunion over their missed connection, but safe return, they agreed that a second expedition was more than warranted—if they could obtain the governor's permission. It was agreed that Pizarro should remain out of Pedrarias's clutches and that Almagro should return to Panama City to appeal to the governor for a new license. Almagro would make contact with Luque and hope that with his skillful mediation, together they could persuade Pedrarias to give them another chance.[21]

Upon presenting their petition to Pedrarias, Almagro and Luque were alarmed by his adamant refusal to countenance any further effort in southward exploration. He railed against Pizarro for the extensive loss of life, denouncing his reckless and irresponsible leadership. The emissaries were taken aback and could not fathom the governor's reaction. (They could not have been aware of the pressures on Pedrarias that had caused this outburst. The king and the Council of the Indies were demanding greater treasure; and the governor was putting together an expedition to deal with a rebellious captain in Nicaragua, and undoubtedly wanted no distractions from these tasks.)

Friar Luque assuaged the governor, acknowledging that he was right about Pizarro, but noting that the loss of life was due mainly to disease, not irresponsible action. He also insisted that they now knew for certain what they had only recently thought was conjecture: that there indeed existed a land of great wealth ready for plunder, and it was within reach. Almagro further soothed Pedrarias by offering to buy out his "interest" in the partnership with a one thousand gold peso contribution to help finance the expedition he was preparing for Nicaragua. Though still dubious, the governor approved a new license, but on condition that Almagro agree to be co-captain with Pizarro—and be jointly responsible for all debts incurred.

Armed with their license to prepare a new expedition, they joined Pizarro to tell him the good news. But when Almagro informed him that

---

[21] William H. Prescott, *History of the Conquest of Peru,* partly abridged and revised by Victor W. von Hagen (New York: New American Library, 1961), 148.

the governor had agreed only with the stipulation that he accept the position of co-captain, Pizarro exploded. He felt humiliated by what was in effect a slur against his leadership, and a demotion. Worse, he suspected that Almagro and Pedrarias had conspired against him. However, after hearing Almagro out, Pizarro and his partners agreed to share equally all the expedition's profits—in treasure, land, and slaves. Helps believes, however, that Pedrarias's appointment of Almagro as co-captain was when "ill-feeling between the two friends" began.[22]

There is disagreement over the nature of their profit-sharing arrangement, or whether there was one at all. Prescott argues that the three men entered into a formal contract dated March 10, 1526. Helps claims that there was merely the formalization of an agreement that "had existed practically for some time before."[23] Varón also says the three partners "worked together from at least 1519" and if there was a contract they "perhaps never put [it] in writing."[24] Kochis mentions no contract at all, and relates that Pizarro subsequently pressed Almagro to obtain "a license directly from the Council for the Indies, cutting Pedrarias out of the equation."[25] Anderson takes Prescott's line. According to him, they went to Panama City and ratified the contract before a notary with witnesses who signed for the illiterate conquistadors, on March 10, 1526. But after months of recruiting men and outfitting ships, further financing was required. Friar Luque produced the necessary funding, having entered into a secret side contract with Gaspar de Espinosa, the judge, dated August 6, 1531.[26]

However, there is reason to doubt the existence of anything more than a handshake agreement as opposed to a formal, binding contract. Indeed, over the next several years, in all of the many highly contentious

---

[22] Arthur Helps, *The Spanish Conquest in America, and Its Relation to the History of Slavery and to the Government of Colonies,* ed. Michael Oppenheim, vol. 3 (New York: John Lane, 1902), 301.

[23] Prescott; von Hagen, *Conquest of Peru,* 153-54; and Helps, *Spanish Conquest in America,* 3:293, n.2.

[24] Varón, *Francisco Pizarro and His Brothers,* 18.

[25] Kochis, *God, Glory and Gold,* 2:168.

[26] Anderson, *Old Panama and Castilla del Oro,* 238. The date of this agreement is suspicious coming well after the fact. See especially n8 for further discussion of Espinosa's subsequent involvement in Peru.

arguments that Pizarro and Almagro would have over land, riches and slaves, there was no reference to an actual contract, whose equal shares proviso presumably would have established the basis for settling their disputes.[27] In fact, a copy of the "contract" would not surface until the end of the century, seventy years later, long after the three men had passed away and when third parties would lay claims against their spoils in Spanish courts. [28]

Whatever the form of their arrangement, their differences were resolved for the moment, and La Compañía de Lunáticos was in business. The enterprise had some difficulty recruiting men for the expedition, as Governor Pedrarias was at the same time recruiting for his expedition to Nicaragua. They succeeded, however, in obtaining the services of Bartolomé Ruiz de Estrada, an experienced navigator. By the beginning of summer, they had assembled some two hundred men, including Indians and blacks, two ships, three sturdy canoes, and several horses. Fully provisioned, Pizarro sailed first, with Almagro following a few days later. Their plan was to rendezvous at the furthest point reached by Almagro earlier, the San Juan River. From there they would commence their exploration—or, one should say, conquest.

First Contacts Force Changes of Plan

After meeting at the San Juan River, their early efforts met with some success. They razed several villages, seized some fifteen thousand pesos worth of gold ornaments, and secured provisions from village stores. They established an encampment, and attempted to gather information from several captured natives. Realizing that they needed more men, supplies and equipment and more information about the wealthy people they were told about whose lands lay further to the south, they decided to change plans. Almagro would go back to Panama City with the gold they had collected to "tempt more adventurers to the enterprise," and purchase equipment and supplies.[29] Captain Ruiz would sail on a reconnaissance

---

[27] See James Lockhart, *Men of Cajamarca* (Austin: University of Texas Press, 1972), 70-73.

[28] Varón, *Francisco Pizarro and His Brothers*, 18.

[29] Anderson, *Old Panama and Castilla del Oro,* 239.

mission to the south, while Pizarro stayed put and fortified the camp pending their return.

Almagro and Ruiz departed in February 1527 and were gone for just over two months. At the river base, Pizarro and his men struggled to carve out a meager existence, exploring the land around them, without much success. Ever-watchful natives attacked whenever they found someone alone or inattentive, in one case massacring fourteen men whose canoe had become stuck on a sandbar in the river. Lurking alligators and boa constrictors also took a toll. Constant rainfall, ubiquitous ants, and never-ending swarms of mosquitoes bedeviled them. Disease plagued the settlers and food sources were sparse, approaching famine levels.

Almagro had a better time of it. When he reached Panama City, he was heartened to learn that Pedrarias had been replaced as governor of Castilla del Oro by Pedro de los Ríos. Almagro and Luque pleaded their case to the new governor, who was supportive, giving permission for them to recruit men and purchase supplies. (Later, Pizarro wrote to the king requesting that he direct Governor Ríos to honor their contract with Pedrarias. The king agreed, establishing a direct line of communication with Pizarro.)[30] Within a few weeks Almagro set sail to rejoin Pizarro with forty soldiers, a few horses, and full provisions.

In the meantime, Bartolomé Ruiz had the best luck, making first contact with people who lived on the northernmost fringes of the Inca Empire. Sailing south along the coast, he sighted the Gorgona and Gallo Islands, San Mateo Bay, and Atacames. Further south, off Coaque, in the second week of March, he came upon a great ocean-going balsa raft, sporting twin-masts, a large sail, and two thatch-roofed cabins. Lookouts estimated there were about twenty persons on board, most of whom jumped into the ocean to swim for shore as Ruiz' larger vessel approached.

---

[30] Varón, *Francisco Pizarro and his Brothers*, 15.

3.4. Andean balsa raft

What Ruiz and his men found after securing the balsa astounded them, for it was clearly the product of a civilization more advanced than any they had yet seen. The three men, two women and two children whom they took into custody all wore fine garments unlike the mostly naked Indians they had so far encountered. They told the Spaniards through sign language that they were on a trading trip to barter Inca gold and silver ornaments, wool cloth, mirrors, cups and other items for Indian shells and corals. They also said they were from a place called Tumbes in a kingdom ruled by an emperor named Huayna Cápac. Ruiz assured them that he would release them upon making landfall, but he planned to retain and train a few as future interpreters.[31]

Ruiz continued southward, reaching the equator before turning back. In fact, he and Almagro returned to Pizarro's encampment within a few days of each other. It was just in time, as most of the famished and emaciated men were ready to give up their quest for fortune and return to the relative normality of Panama City. After feasting on the food Almagro had brought and digesting the information and observing the men, women, and children Ruiz had captured, they all resolved to continue their

---

[31] John Hemming, *The Conquest of the Incas* (New York: Harcourt Brace Jovanovich, 1970), 26.

expedition, for they now had tangible proof that the wealthy land they had so long heard and dreamed about was near at hand.

In May, however, from the moment they set out, their troubles mounted. Re-tracing Ruiz' course they immediately had to weather fierce storms, adverse currents, and unfavorable winds. They sought shelter at an island anchorage that Ruiz had discovered, named "Isla de Gallo" by Pizarro because of its prominent cockscomb silhouette; and they spent two weeks there repairing their ships before moving on. As they edged their way southward, they saw increasing evidence of well-ordered villages, large-scale agricultural planting, pastures, roads, and numerous peoples dotting the landscape. The problem was that they were uniformly unfriendly.[32]

Word of the Spaniards' rapacious actions clearly had preceded them, as each time they attempted to land, large Indian forces were there to attack and repulse them. Deaths from disease, malnutrition, and combat continued to reduce their numbers and by the time they had reached Atacames in present-day Ecuador, their numbers had dwindled to fewer than a hundred Spaniards. Raiding coastal villages, their priorities shifted from searching for gold to scavenging for foodstuffs. Finally, they decided to retreat to the relative safety of Gallo Island to rest and take stock of their situation.

The men were on the verge of mutiny. Pizarro and Almagro also quarreled, narrowly averting the drawing of swords. Should they admit defeat and failure and return to Panama City? The majority of the crew appeared ready to quit; some say Pizarro was among them, but this seems unlikely given his long-held passion for El Dorado.[33] The two captains insisted on continuing, if only because returning to Panama City with nothing to show for their outlay meant that they would spend the rest of their days in debtor's prison. Their decision was for Almagro to return once again to Panama City for men, horses, and supplies, while Pizarro waited on the island for them to return.

---

[32] Murphy, "The Earliest Spanish Advances Southward [...]," 25.
[33] Helps, *Spanish Conquest in America*, 3:303, writes that supposedly, "Pizarro was for returning..."

The men demanded they be allowed to send letters home, to which Almagro agreed. But once underway, he seized all of their missives in order to prevent "tales of despair and disaffection" from reaching Panama City. Unfortunately for the captain, one of the letter-writers had secreted his note in a ball of yarn and it escaped confiscation. When Almagro reached Panama City, the letter of woe found its way into the hands of Governor Ríos, who, appalled at the men's dire circumstances, decided to abandon the "mythical" enterprise. Detaining Almagro from sailing, he sent his lawyer, Pedro Alonso de Tafur, to Gallo Island with two ships for the purpose of bringing them all back.[34] Meanwhile, on Gallo Island, disaffection continued to mount. In exasperation, Pizarro directed all who wished to depart to embark with Ruiz aboard their remaining boat and return to Panama City.

Ruiz arrived in Panama City just when Governor Ríos was deciding to send Tafur to Gallo and assigned Ruiz the task of guiding him there. On arrival, sometime in July, Tafur relayed the governor's orders for the remaining crew to return, but he also had a letter for Pizarro from Almagro and Luque containing a quite different message. His two partners encouraged him to stay the course, promising that help was on the way. They exhorted him "to die rather than return to Panama, since he could judge for himself with what shame and ignominy they would be covered if he did not push this discovery to the end."[35]

These were the circumstances under which Pizarro drew his now famous "line in the sand," which only thirteen of the remaining force of eighty-five crossed to stand with their captain. Tafur, upon departing, declined to leave one of the ships, stranding Pizarro and his "thirteen," but did provide them with food and supplies. Ruiz returned to Panama City with Tafur, but only to lend his support for the continuation of the enterprise. It took months of remonstrating with Governor Ríos, but eventually Almagro, Luque, and Ruiz persuaded him not to abandon their marooned comrades. The king's order, mentioned above, no doubt influenced his decision. He agreed to permit them to send a ship with

---

[34] Murphy, "The Earliest Spanish Advances Southward [...]," 25.
[35] Helps, *Spanish Conquest in America*, 3:305n1, quoting Antonio de Herrera, *Historia de las Indias*.

munitions, and provisions, but with only a handful of men and a time limit of six months within which they would have to finish their expedition one way or another.[36]

Meanwhile, Pizarro soon found Gallo Island unsuitable, with little available food and under constant assault by swarms of mosquitoes. Moreover, it was too close to shore and subject to Indian sneak attacks. So, he directed the construction of a large raft that they sailed northward to a larger, uninhabited but wooded island further off the coast, which they called Gorgona. Here, water was abundant, mosquitoes fewer, and fish and game plentiful. They were able to scrabble out a better existence while awaiting the promised help from Almagro, Luque, and Ruiz. It would be three months of waiting and watching before the sails of the promised rescue ship came into view. Aboard were Ruiz and Almagro—with provisions but no more recruits.

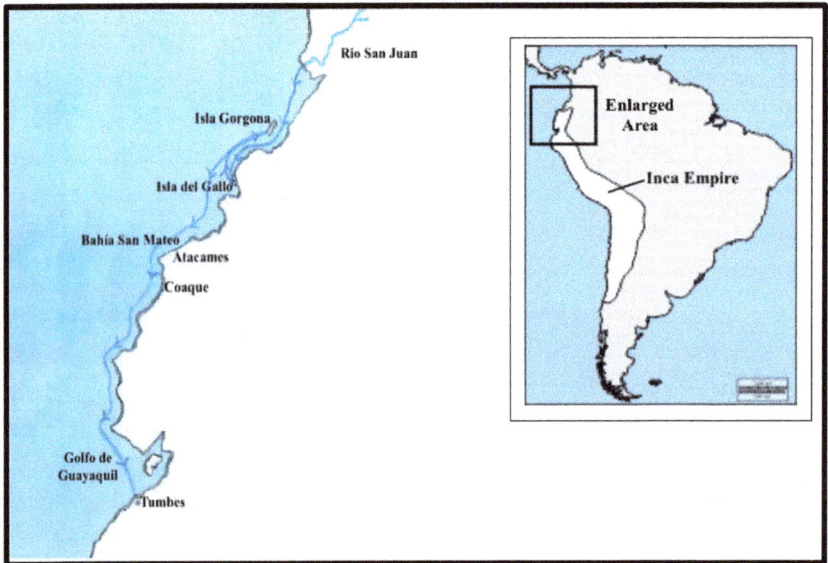

3.5. Pizarro's second voyage, 1527

With no choice and the six-month time clock running, Pizarro resolved to get going. Of course, with only a handful of men, there could

---

[36] Ober, "Success in Sight at Last," in *Pizarro and the Conquest of Peru*, online at Heritage History www.heritage-history.com.

be no thought of conquest. Now, the mission had to be peaceful reconnaissance—the scouting of targets for future exploitation. With a dozen men (two had to be left behind because they were too ill to travel), a few sailors, and the five Peruvian captives that Ruiz had taken from the balsa raft, the little band sailed south, hugging the coastline.

They were headed for Tumbes, the home of their captives, who no doubt helped to guide them. After nearly three weeks, in early November 1527, they reached the large Gulf of Guayaquil, the home of their Peruvian "interpreters." Before them they could observe numerous coastal settlements and the large urban complex of Tumbes. It was clear to them that they had at last reached an outpost of the great civilization they sought. To be safe, they put in at a small island Pizarro named Santa Clara located across the harbor north of Tumbes. In halting Spanish their captives explained that the island was a place where the people made sacrifices to their ancestors, which accounted for the many stone, gold, and silver carved objects they found. As impressive as the precious metal was, their captives expressed that "these riches were nothing compared to those that were to be found" on the mainland. The Spaniards also encountered for the first-time evidence in stone idols of the Incan practice of fashioning the head in an elongated, conical form.[37]

Their plan was to release their balsa captives in hopes that they would communicate their peaceful intent and promote good will among their kinsmen. They could then engage in trade and a chance to gain a closer look at the remarkable city they could see before them. Raising anchor, the next morning they sailed into the harbor of Tumbes. There they saw several large balsa rafts loaded with armed warriors heading toward them, which called immediately for a change in plans. Uncertain of the Indians' intent, the Spaniards prepared for the worst, but their "interpreters" engaged in a lively conversation with the warriors on the balsas as they came near, which resulted in a decision to welcome the leaders of the warriors on board Pizarro's vessel.[38]

---

[37] Helps, *Spanish Conquest in America*, 3:309.
[38] Unbeknownst to Pizarro, the balsas were headed for a raid against the natives of the large island of Puna across the bay, but they changed plans when they sighted his ship.

During a pleasant exchange aboard ship, the Spaniards made plain their peaceful intent and need for provisions. Thus, the warriors on the balsas guided their ships close to shore, where the assembled populace stood entranced at what appeared to be a "floating castle" in the harbor.[39] It was not long before several balsas appeared loaded with provisions of all kinds for the ship. The fleet was headed by a person of obvious rank, who was shown deference by all. He was what was called the *curaca*, a regional governor of the Incan empire. He was distinguished by his stature, taller than the others; and by the gold disks implanted into his elongated ear lobes, which led the Spaniards to call him and others like him *orejónes*, or men of big ears.

The *curaca* came aboard the ship, spending the entire day in "friendly discourse" with Pizarro and his men. The ship was larger than anything the Inca had ever seen, and he had never before seen a horse. But most curious were the tall bearded white men themselves, recalling the legends of their god, Viracocha, to whom the Spaniards bore a superficial resemblance. Incan legend held that in the distant past their gods had come from the heavens, imparted civilization and culture to them, and departed, promising that they would one day return. Were these the ones? It would be an all-consuming question for Incan leaders.

After a dinner of pork roast, vegetables and wine, the captain welcomed the chief's invitation to come ashore. On parting, Pizarro gave the chief several gifts, including two pigs and chickens as well as an iron hatchet, which "greatly excited his admiration."[40] The Inca was a bronze-age culture and had not developed iron implements, which were greatly superior to their stone tools and weapons. Thus, as impressed as Pizarro and his men were at the well-developed civilization they saw before them, they were perhaps not as awestruck as the Inca were of the accoutrements the Spaniards brought.

It was late in 1527, thirty-five years since Columbus first sailed to the new world, that two distinctly different civilizations first began to engage, with the outcome of their interaction unforeseeable. Fortunately for Pizarro and Spain, the outcome would be decisively affected by events

---

[39] Prescott; von Hagen, *Conquest of Peru*, 173-74.
[40] Ibid., 175.

occurring then within the Incan empire that would weaken it, leaving it ripe for conquest. As Pizarro lay anchored off Tumbes, the ruler of the Incan empire lay on his deathbed, stricken by an unknown disease. Huayna Cápac's death would precipitate a succession struggle that would be the dynamic context for Pizarro's conquest. Ironically, European-borne diseases were beginning to ravage the Incan empire from within, as they had the Aztec; just as Pizarro arrived to ravage it from without.[41]

---

[41] The cause of the Incan ruler's illness is uncertain. See Robert McCaa, Aleta Nimlos, and Teodoro Martinez, "Why Blame Smallpox? The Death of the Inca Huayna Cápac and the Demographic Destruction of Tawantinsuyu," paper delivered at the American Historical Association Annual Meeting, January 8-11, 2004, Washington, D.C., online at http://users.pop.umn.edu/~rmccaa/aha2004/. The authors demonstrate not only that smallpox had not yet reached the Quito region at the time of Huayna Cápac's illness, but also that the description of his illness does not fit the symptoms of the disease.

Chapter 4

Pizarro and
the Decision to Conquer Peru

When Francisco Pizarro dropped anchor off the Incan city of Tumbes in November 1527, he believed that he had at last reached the land of *El Hombre Dorado*. Yet he could not have imagined that it would be the beginning of a quest that would enrich him and his followers beyond their wildest dreams, while also leading to his untimely demise and the near-collapse of the entire Spanish enterprise in Peru.

The commonly held but erroneous view that Francisco Pizarro single-handedly conquered the Incan Empire with one hundred and sixty-eight men and sixty-two horses still prevails. This view, generated by early Spanish historians, was essentially a form of cultural chauvinism, a myth designed to glorify the power of Spanish men at arms while at the same time exculpating the Crown from any blame for its excesses. The core of this myth has endured even though modern historians have acknowledged its internal contradictions and the contributions made by others, including Andean peoples subjugated by the Inca.[1]

It is my view that the history of Pizarro's conquest must be considered anew because extant works are still very thin in explaining the why and how of events. Plainly, as Kamen notes, Spanish historians deluded themselves with the thesis that the empire was built by Spaniards alone. This may have been a reaction to the almost universal resentment toward Spain as it grew wealthy from the conquest; or a function of the

---

[1] John Hemming, *The Conquest of the Incas* (New York: Harcourt Brace Jovanovich, 1970).

nation's insularity in thought and culture; or sense of inferiority to surrounding cultures, including the Andean.[2]

Whatever the reason, the narrative that persists is a brutal caricature of the conquest, an oversimplification compounded by the paucity of contemporaneous records. Unlike Cortés, Pizarro left no personal account explaining his actions. The Inca possessed no writing system and therefore also left no concurrent written record of events.[3] The result is a one-sided narrative largely composed well after the events. It is replete with contradictions and includes more supposition than fact, more partisan recrimination than analysis of strategy and politics, designed to serve the interests and reputation of the Spanish Crown.

Pizarro would not have succeeded without significant contributions by Incan leaders and subjugated peoples, along with the key variables of intelligence, chance, and superior military technology. Disease, often cited as a factor, does not appear to have played a large role in the initial stage of the conquest. What stands out across the centuries is Pizarro's character: his singular courage and political vision combined with avarice, which were the critical elements propelling him to decapitate and topple an Incan empire already in the throes of collapse from its internal conflicts and contradictions.

The later Spanish portrayal of the conquest as a civilizing mission to bring Christianity to the heathen was also a way to justify and deflect attention from the Crown's true objective of subjugating the Incan empire and extracting its vast wealth to support Charles V's ambition for Spanish domination of Europe. There is a clear sense that the king, his court, and the clergy were conflicted over the conquest and enslavement of native

---

[2] Henry Kamen, *Empire: How Spain Became A World Power, 1492-1763* (New York: Harper Collins, 2003), 510.

[3] Francisco de Xeres, Pizarro's secretary, wrote a report on Pizarro's "itinerary" during the crucial years of 1532-33, to establish the conquistador's full compliance with the terms of the *Capitulación de Toledo*. His account is essentially the conquistador's log replete with statements such as "In order to comply with the commands of his Majesty, and that the natives might come to be converted..." See Clements Markham, ed. and trans., *Reports on the Discovery of Peru* (London: Hakluyt Society, 1872; repr. New York: Burt Franklin, 1970), 21.

peoples, but in the end were willing to subordinate their humanitarian concerns to the siren calls of wealth and power.[4]

The conquest of Peru was an event of epic proportions whose impact stretched well beyond Spain. Indeed, the extraction and transfer of wealth that commenced with the conquest would transform global political and economic relations, fueling extreme inflation (the so-called "price revolution") and the rise of competing empires. Such transformative effects require that its origins be reassessed in more strategic terms in order to provide a clearer view of its significance.

At the same time, the history of the Incan Empire is shrouded in myth. The nature of the regime and its achievements, strengths, and weaknesses need further scrutiny. Although the thesis of the Incan "collapse" has recently come under criticism, more study is required to explain the period in a way that goes beyond notions of the Spanish subjugation of a grand, benevolent (though despotic) and peaceful Incan empire.[5]

Problems with the Historical Narrative

While the conquest narrative of Peru is reasonably coherent *after* Pizarro captured the Inca Atahualpa on November 16, 1532, that is not the case for the preceding five-year period, which is the subject of this chapter. In particular, Pizarro's first visit to Tumbes, and what he learned about the state of the Incan empire during his stay there; his return to Panama and subsequent trip to Spain; the Crown's decision to authorize the conquest and the effort to assemble the resources for the expedition; and its initial phase, all suffer serious chronological compression and analytical inconsistencies. Recent literature and scholarship, however, permit a tentative reconstruction of this formative period.

---

[4] Geoffrey Parker, *Emperor: A New Life of Charles V* (New Haven: Yale University Press, 2019), 372-73, portrays Charles as conflicted between his desire for American wealth and his need to assuage his "delicate conscience."
[5] David Cahill, "Advanced Andeans and Backward Europeans: Structure and Agency in the Collapse of the Inca Empire," in Patricia McAnany and Norman Yoffee, *Questioning Collapse: Human Resilience, Ecological Vulnerability, and the Aftermath of Empire* (Cambridge: Cambridge University Press, 2010), 207-38.

When Pizarro first sailed into the Bay of Guayaquil off Tumbes in November 1527, he unknowingly had reached the northern part of the vast Incan Empire. What he saw amazed and gratified him, for it seemed to fulfill even his loftiest hopes and dreams. He believed he had found the fabled realm of *El Dorado*. At Tumbes he looked out over a city as grand as any he had ever seen, and certainly as populous. Yet, Pizarro's time in Tumbes typically is described as a brief, two- or three- day stopover during which he himself did not even set foot in the city; although he sent three of his crew ashore at the invitation of the local chief. After promising to return, Pizarro is said to have continued his voyage another several hundred miles, reaching the mouth of the Santa River at the 9th latitude, before turning back to Panama.[6]

On the face of it, this is a dubious narrative. An alternative rendition is facilitated by reconsidering the importance of Quispe Sisa, an Incan princess (*Ñusta*) who became Pizarro's mistress/wife—and perhaps was an interpreter and confidante, as the Aztec Malinche had been for Hernán Cortés in Mexico. Such a characterization is presented in a novel by Rafael Olivares, in the form of a diary of Quispe Sisa's granddaughter, who preserved her grandmother's recollections of life with Pizarro.[7] Although avowedly a work of historical fiction, it inspires a re-imagination of events that fills in key points left unclear by the original chroniclers.

4.1. Quispe Sisa

---

[6] Pedro de Cieza de León, *The Discovery and Conquest of Peru*, ed. and trans. Alexandra Parma Cook and Noble David Cook (Durham: Duke University Press, 1998), 116-118.

[7] Rafael Olivares, *Ñusta: The Inka Love of Francisco Pizarro* (Bergenfield: Xlibris, 2014).

Relatively little is known of Quispe Sisa's life, and much of that is in question—including maternal genealogy and lifespan. Her father was Sapa Inca Huayna Cápac.[8] Thus she was the sister or half-sister of Atahualpa, Huayna Cápac's successor, and his brother/rival Huáscar, among many other children who were sired by Huayna Cápac with his principal or secondary wives and concubines. Quispe Sisa's mother probably was Contarhuacho, a highborn woman from the Huaylas valley in Peru, and one of the Sapa Inca's secondary wives.[9] The girl was born sometime in the early 1500s; a basic Internet search for "Quispe Sisa" mostly turns up a lifespan of 1518-1559, but without much evidence. More likely, she lived well into the latter half of the 16th century.[10]

In the conventional historical record, Quispe Sisa, also known as Doña Inés Huaylas Yupanqui following her Christian baptism, first appears only in 1532-1533, during the imprisonment of Atahualpa by Pizarro's forces in Cajamarca. Supposedly, Atahualpa gave his sister to Pizarro in a gesture of amity or payment of ransom. Stirling says that she may have been no more than 12 years of age at the time, which seems implausibly young. Similarly, Karen Vieira Powers describes Quispe Sisa as "a beautiful fifteen-year-old, in the full blossom of her youth," in contrast to the fifty-six-year-old Pizarro. Peruvian historian Raúl Porras

---

[8] "Sapa Inca" means the supreme Incan ruler or emperor, though the word "Inca" also frequently is used to denote the ruler as well as the people.
[9] Maria Rostworowski, *Doña Francisca Pizarro, Una Ilustre Mestiza 1534-1598,* cuarta edición; primera edición digital (Lima: Instituto de Estudios Peruanos, 2017), 24; Stuart Stirling, *Pizarro, Conqueror of the Inca* (Stroud: Sutton, 2005), 216; Rafael Varón Gabai, *Francisco Pizarro and His Brothers, The Illusion of Power in Sixteenth-Century Peru*, trans. Javier Flores Espinoza (Norman: University of Oklahoma Press, 1997), 177. Some sources say that Quispe Sisa's mother was an Ecuadorian princess, Paccha Duchicela, daughter of the last indigenous ruler of Quito before the region was subsumed into the Incan empire, and that Quispe Sisa was born around 1510. See Piedad Peñaherrera de Costales and Alfredo Costales Samaniego, *Huayna Cápac* (Cuenca: CCE-Núcleo del Azuay, 1964), cited in Wikipedia, "Paccha Duchicela," https://es.m.wikipedia.org/wiki/Paccha_Duchicela. This article says that Paccha Duchicela also may have given birth to Atahualpa ten years earlier, but others believe his mother was related to Huayna Cápac, though a secondary wife.
[10] Rostworowski, *Francisca Pizarro*, 45; 90, cites legal proceedings involving Doña Inés Yupanqui, Quispe Sisa's Christian name, in the 1560s; and a church record indicating a possible burial date of 1575.

Barrenechea contends that she was probably 18 years old when Atahualpa gave her to Pizarro.[11]

It is generally agreed that she bore two children with Pizarro: a daughter, Francisca (1534) and a son, Gonzalo (1535).[12] Her union with Pizarro lasted until 1537; she was then married off to one of his aides, Francisco de Ampuero. She had three more children with Ampuero, though the marriage probably wasn't a happy one. Indeed, Doña Inés was said to have collaborated with witches in an attempt to poison her husband.[13]

In Olivares's historical novel, Quispe Sisa claims to have met Pizarro almost six years earlier than the conventional timeline, during the conquistador's initial sojourn at Tumbes, when she herself was 25 years of age. According to this account, she had learned the Castilian language from four Spaniards who were part of an expedition up the Amazon that got lost in the jungle and wandered into Incan territory several months before Pizarro arrived.[14] When Pizarro reached Tumbes, she was called upon to act as official interpreter. She became Pizarro's mistress, traveled with him to Spain, was recognized as his wife and was instrumental in his procurement of the royal *Capitulación* authorizing the conquest of Peru.[15]

---

[11] Stuart Stirling, *The Inca Princesses,* ebook ed. (History Press, 2013); Karen Vieira Powers, *Women in the Crucible of Conquest, The Gendered Genesis of Spanish American Society, 1500-1600* (Albuquerque: University of New Mexico Press, 2005), 75; Porras, cited in Varón, *Francisco Pizarro and His Brothers,* 182.

[12] Rostworowski, *Francisca Pizarro,* 24-25; and Powers, *Women in the Crucible of Conquest,* 75.

[13] Rostworowski, *Francisca Pizarro,* 42-53. As part of the marriage arrangement, Pizarro established an *encomienda* for the couple. Meanwhile, Pizarro had taken Atahualpa's royal wife, Cuxirimay (Doña Angelina) as his new mistress, later fathering two sons with her. After Pizarro's assassination, Cuxirimay married Juan de Betanzos, whose history, *Narrative of the Incas*, relies heavily on the recollections of his wife. Perhaps as an indication of ill feeling between her and Quispe Sisa—the two women cohabitated with Pizarro for several years—Betanzos omitted all mention of Quispe Sisa in his narrative.

[14] Olivares, *Ñusta,* 17; 51-54; 59. These men could have been part of the failed expedition of Alejo Garcia, the first European to encounter the northern outposts of the Incan Empire in 1524-25. See Kim MacQuarrie, *The Last Days of the Incas* (New York: Simon & Shuster, 2007), 31n.

[15] Olivares, *Ñusta,* 16-17; 83-106. Jennifer Brooks, *Marriage, Legitimacy, and Intersectional Identities in the Sixteenth Century Spanish Empire* (Macalester College: History Honors Project, Paper 21, 2016), 62, while subscribing to the conventional

She was therefore with him from the first moment he encountered the Incan civilization and stayed with him throughout the conquest, contributing her wisdom and knowledge of the Inca until 1537 when they separated. She claims she bore three children with him, not two: a male who died just after birth in Spain in 1529, in addition to their daughter Francisca and son Gonzolo, both born in Peru.[16]

Her account as represented in the "diary" provides an intriguing perspective on the period in question; and there is some consistency with other descriptions of Pizarro's entourage. Several authors note that Pizarro took with him from Tumbes a few natives whom he intended to train as interpreters. MacQuarrie, like most, identifies two: a native they named Felipillo and another called Martinello.[17] Murphy recounts that Pizarro took "three Indian youths to serve as subsequent interpreters."[18] Kochis says there were three from Tumbes and a fourth from the second voyage, a "translator who had become close to Francisco," without further identifying them.[19]

When Pizarro went to Spain to meet with the king, it is known that he brought his comrade Pedro de Candia with him as well as several native Peruvians. Quintana notes that Pizarro took with him "some Indians dressed in the habit of their county," without identifying them.[20] In Olivares's "diary," Quispe Sisa claims that she was one of those.[21]

---

timeline of Quispe Sisa's relationship with Pizarro, notes that under both the Incan tradition and Spanish law of that period, they would have been considered married.

[16] Olivares, Ñusta, 76, 80.

[17] Macquarrie, Last Days of the Incas, 33.

[18] Robert Murphy, "The Earliest Spanish Advances Southward from Panama Along the West Coast of South America," Hispanic American Historical Review 21, no. 1 (Feb. 1941):27.

[19] Paul M. Kochis, God, Glory and Gold: Journey to the Conquest of the Incas, vol. 2, The Quest (Minneapolis: Mill City Press, 2013), 229.

[20] Manuel José Quintana, Lives of Vasco Nunez de Balboa and Francisco Pizarro, trans. Margaret Hodson (Edinburgh: William Blackwood, 1832; repr., Kessinger, 2010), 132.

[21] A painting of Pizarro's meeting with Charles V by Ángel Lizcano Monedero contains suggestive evidence. In the far-left corner of the painting is a barely visible figure. When that segment of the painting is enlarged, however, one sees the head of a figure wearing what could be Inca ceremonial hairstyle or headdress. The painting, "Entrevista del Emperador Carlos V con Francisco Pizarro antes de partir para la conquista del Perú," was first exhibited at the Exposición Nacional de Belles Artes in

When did Pizarro reach Tumbes and how long did he stay? Accounts marking his arrival range from "the end of 1527" to "late April 1528." [22] According to Olivares, Quispe Sisa recounts having met Pizarro as "official interpreter" for the *curaca*; she seduced him and became his mistress during his stay, which she claims to have been several months, not days. [23] Indeed it seems highly unlikely that Pizarro would have left the fabled city of Tumbes after a mere two days; and impossible for him to have learned of its many advanced features—the viaducts, extensive road system, postal service, large stone buildings, palaces filled with walls lined with gold and silver, fine clothes, abundance of food, large population—in that brief time. In addition, to argue that Pizarro failed to set foot on land at Tumbes is completely at variance with his practice of going ashore wherever he anchored to claim territory for Spain.

One would have thought that having confirmed the existence of a large, fabulously wealthy civilization he would have headed swiftly for home. Yet all accounts further state that upon leaving Tumbes, Pizarro sailed blithely south for another several hundred miles, making several stops until reaching the River Santa, near the 9th latitude below the equator. At that point, supposedly he decided to return to Panama, again stopping at several places, including one they named Santa Clara where a female *curaca* entertained him royally. Returning, he stopped at Tumbes once again, taking two or three natives with him and leaving two of his crew behind. [24] So goes the conventional narrative.

The problem with this part of the narrative is that if, in fact, Pizarro reached the 9th latitude, a point specifically identified by virtually all

---

Madrid in 1881. Six years later it appeared in *La Ilustración Española y Americana* 31, no. 1 (15 de Enero 1887), entitled "Entrevista del Emperador Carlos V con Francisco Pizarro, en el Alcázar de Toledo." I am most indebted to Abigail Thornton for locating the painting and its promise. See Appendix I.

[22] Arthur Helps, *The Spanish Conquest in America and Its Relation to the History of Slavery and to the Government of Colonies*, ed. Michael Oppenheim, vol. 3 (London: John Lane, 1902), 312, puts it late in the year, while Michael Wood, *Conquistadors* (London: BBC Books, 2010) 114, places it in April.

[23] Olivares, *Ñusta*, 51, 60, 79.

[24] In addition to Cieza de León, *Discovery and Conquest of Peru*, 116-118, William H. Prescott, *History of the Conquest of Peru,* partly abridged and revised by Victor W. von Hagen (New York: New American Library, 1961), 178-85; and Quintana, *Lives of Balboa and Pizarro*, 123-30, are typical.

historians, he would most certainly have seen and landed at a number of cities that dotted the coast. Indeed, the most impressive city on the coast at that time, Chan Chan, was located at about 8.1° S, slightly northwest of the present-day city of Trujillo. Chan Chan, the capital of the Chimú civilization before the Inca conquest, was an enclosed coastal city of twelve square miles and over fifty thousand people, with many large pyramids, plazas, and a vast irrigation canal network. Yet, there is no mention in the record of Pizarro having landed at Chan Chan, or even having seen it. Victor W. von Hagen, the distinguished archeological historian who published the revised and abridged version of Prescott's *Conquest* cited above made the same point, although somewhat obliquely, observing: "Chan Chan with its high walls and enormous Sun temples could have been seen from the sea." [25]

When did Pizarro decide to go to Spain for assistance? Most accounts state that it was only after he had arrived in Panama and failed to convince Governor Ríos to support a new expedition. Also, there is said to have been indecision about who among the partners would travel to Spain. In Olivares's "diary," Quispe Sisa recalls that Pizarro made the decision to go to Spain while still in Tumbes, once he realized that only the Crown's resources would be sufficient to undertake a major conquest. Moreover, he asked her to accompany him and she agreed, bringing a sizable amount of gold, silver, fabric, and even two llamas, as well as a substantial retinue. The artifacts would be proof that the wealth of Peru existed, and Quispe Sisa, Pizarro's consort, would be living proof that some Peruvians supported him in his quest for it. [26]

There were other reasons to suggest that Pizarro made the decision in Tumbes and not Panama; the most important of which was to secure the exclusive right of conquest for himself and deny it to all others. Varón says obtaining exclusive rights directly from the Crown not only eliminated competition and middlemen, but it also facilitated raising money. "These were the reasons Pizarro halted his advance and went instead to Spain." [27] MacQuarrie arrives at much the same conclusion:

---

[25] Prescott; von Hagen 397n30.
[26] Olivares, *Ñusta,* 72-73.
[27] Varón, *Francisco Pizarro and His Brothers,* 36.

> Pizarro was worried [that]…other Spaniards might soon get the
> idea of heading south themselves and of stealing from him a
> potentially lucrative conquest. There was only one thing for
> Pizarro to do—he had to return to Spain. Only by petitioning
> the King and Queen in person could he hope to obtain the
> exclusive rights to conquer and sack what appeared to be an
> untouched native kingdom.[28]

Pizarro, from the beginning, was not out to steal a little gold and seize a few slaves, which was the scope of what the governor of Panama could authorize. He was planning on capturing an entire nation and subjecting it to the will of the king of Spain. For that, he needed the backing of the king himself. This is why the decision to go to Spain would have been made in Tumbes, as soon as Pizarro realized the magnitude of the prize and the task. The case would be even stronger if he learned then that the empire was in the early stages of convulsion, which would offer an unparalleled opportunity for action.

Upon returning to Panama, far from pleading with the governor to support a new expedition, Pizarro surely must have been at pains to avoid him because he had grossly violated his direct orders to return within the six-month time period the governor had set for him; and he would have wanted to avoid any risk that the governor would prevent him from undertaking an additional voyage. Furthermore, the notion that the governor would refuse to support a new expedition led by someone else flies in the face of everything known about the tenor of the time, when dreams of *El Dorado* were everywhere. The argument that the three penurious partners could barely scrape up the 1,500 pesos for Pizarro's trip to Spain also is subject to question. In Olivares, Quispe Sisa claims she brought substantial wealth with her, enough to pay for their voyage and sustain them in Spain for the year and a half they would reside there before they returned to Panama and the year they would spend in Panama prior to embarking on their expedition.[29]

Most accounts agree that Pizarro departed for Spain sometime in early 1528, which means that he could not have spent much time in Panama. They disagree, however, on when he met King Charles. The

---

[28] MacQuarrie, *Last Days of the Incas*, 34.
[29] Olivares, *Ñusta*, 69, 82.

reported time ranges from mid-1528 to the first week of March 1529.[30] A meeting in mid-1528 raises questions about the lengthy delay in finalizing the authorization for conquest, the *Capitulación*, which was dated July 26, 1529, while a meeting in March 1529 raises questions about the reasons for the lengthy delay in arranging the appointment in the first place. Such discrepancies in the narrative of the pre-Conquest period compel its re-examination.

Pizarro's Tumbesian Bargain

In addition to being impressed by what he saw at Tumbes, Pizarro would have been dumbfounded to find that by sheer chance there was among its inhabitants an Inca princess who could speak Castilian. Communication being all important, the presence of an interpreter would enable a higher level of interaction, information flow, and mutual understanding than would have been possible through sign language; or by means of the youths from Tumbes whom Bartolomé Ruiz had picked up from the balsa a few months earlier, whose Spanish was rudimentary at best.

It is plausible that Pizarro learned from his conversations with the local chiefs and Incan governor that the empire was in a state of upheaval. The Sapa Inca Huayna Cápac died suddenly of a virulent disease before he could name a definitive successor, setting off a struggle for leadership between two of his sons, Atahualpa and Huáscar.[31] MacQuarrie says that Pizarro had arrived in Tumbes at the moment Huayna Cápac was expiring, but sources differ over the date of the Inca's death, placing it sometime between 1524 and 1529. [32]

---

[30] Hemming, *Conquest of the Incas*, 26-27, says Pizarro was received by Charles in mid-1528; while Kochis, *God, Glory, and Gold*, 2:259, says the meeting took place in the first week of March, 1529.

[31] The debate over what killed Huayna Cápac is long and convoluted. The latest scholarship is Robert McCaa, Aleta Nimlos, and Teodoro Hampe Martinez, "Why Blame Smallpox? The Death of the Inca Huayna Cápac and the Demographic Destruction of Tawantinsuyu (Ancient Peru)," paper delivered at the American Historical Association Annual Meeting, January 8-11, 2004, Washington, D.C., online at http://users.pop.umn.edu/~rmccaa/aha2004/. The authors discount smallpox and lean toward placing the blame on the Inca themselves and their destructive policies.

[32] MacQuarrie, *Last Days of the Incas*, 47-48.

Placing his death *after* Pizarro's first visit to Tumbes, as Prescott does, permits the argument that the empire "was not yet torn asunder by the dissensions of rival candidates for the throne."[33] On the other hand, Stirling and MacQuarrie place his death "probably" and "around" 1527.[34] Markham says 1525.[35] Garcilaso de la Vega dates the Inca's death even earlier, in 1524.[36] So does Sarmiento de Gamboa.[37] The point is, the earlier the Inca's death, the stronger the case for the argument that civil strife had been under way when Pizarro first arrived in Tumbes and that he learned about it then.

A related question is: when did the succession struggle begin? Hemming says there were "a few years of quiet" after Huayna Cápac's death before the civil war broke out.[38] While under captivity, Atahualpa reportedly implied that the conflict had begun in 1531 after several years of "peace."[39] However, most accounts note that tension arose between the half-brothers almost immediately over Atahualpa's objection to the appointment of Huáscar as successor. Markham says that if there was a period of quiet between them it was of "a very short continuance." [40]

Incan burial rites dictated that the dead Inca's mummified body should be transported the over eighteen hundred miles from Quito to Cusco for formal interment with appropriate ceremony. As part of this ritual, all members of the royal family were to accompany the cortege and pay homage to Huáscar, the newly appointed Inca. Atahualpa, however, although sending representatives with gifts, declined to join personally in this ceremonial procession to Cusco, declaring that he must remain in Quito to look after affairs there. Outraged by his disrespect, Huáscar had

---

[33] Prescott; von Hagen, *Conquest of Peru*, 178
[34] Stirling, *Pizarro*, 23 and MacQuarrie, *Last Days of the Incas*, 48-49.
[35] Clements R. Markham, *The Incas of Peru* (New York: Dutton, 1912), 242.
[36] Garcilaso de la Vega, *The Royal Commentaries of the Inca and the General History of Peru*, abridged (Indianapolis: Hackett, 2006), 89.
[37] Pedro Sarmiento de Gamboa, *History of the Incas,* trans. Clements R. Markham, Peruvian Series (Cambridge, Ontario: In Parentheses, 2000), 145.
[38] Hemming, *Conquest of the Incas*, 29.
[39] Francisco de Xeres in Markham, *Reports on the Discovery of Peru*, 64.
[40] Markham, *Incas of Peru*, 243.

the messengers executed.[41] In consequence, Atahualpa consolidated his position in Quito, while Huáscar strengthened his in Cusco, essentially defining a geographical/factional conflict between Quiteños and Cuscoans. It is clear that there was tension from the outset between the two half-brothers, although Huáscar commanded the allegiance of the vast majority of the people of the empire.

Atahualpa's refusal to pay homage to Huáscar offers a reason for Huáscar's decision to take up arms against him, even if not immediately; and establishes an earlier as opposed to later timeframe for the actual outbreak of the conflict. If this sequence of events occurred any time between 1524 and 1527, then Pizarro would have been well informed of the growing crisis in the empire, which would have been building for some time. It follows from the Olivares account that his principal informant could have been Quispe Sisa.

Assuming that the civil war already had begun, what was the balance of forces in late 1527? As Prescott notes, "in Atahualpa's first encounter with the troops of Cuzco he was defeated and made prisoner near Tomebamba, a favorite residence of his father, in the ancient territory of Quito and in the district of Cañaris."[42] He managed to escape and return to his capital of Quito where he was joined by the top generals of Huayna Cápac's army, Chalcuchima, Quiz Quiz, and Ruminavi and their forces. Atahualpa was on the defensive.

If, during the initial phase of the civil war the advantage lay with Huáscar, as Atahualpa's early defeat implies, the essential content of the discussions between Pizarro and his hosts at Tumbes, who included the regional Incan governor, can be inferred. Although not discussed in the "diary," Quispe Sisa may not have been merely an interpreter, but an intermediary, who sought Pizarro's entry into the Incan civil war on the side of her brother Atahualpa, in return for which Pizarro would be rewarded with bountiful wealth. It is logical that she would have felt less loyalty toward Huáscar than to Atahualpa, whose mother, like her own,

---

[41] Juan de Betanzos, *Narrative of the Incas,* trans. Roland Hamilton and Dana Buchanan (Austin: University of Texas Press, 1996), 193-94.

[42] Prescott; von Hagen, *Conquest of Peru,* 209-10. See also Bernabé Cobo, *History of the Inca Empire*, trans. Roland Hamilton (Austin: University of Texas Press, 1979), 165; and Quintana, *Lives of Balboa and Pizarro,* 162-63, who tell the same story.

was not Huayna Cápac's sister-queen.[43] Pizarro, of course, had his own objective, disguised for the moment, which was to mount a conquest of the Inca. This objective would be enormously facilitated if it occurred under the guise of coming to the assistance of Atahualpa in a civil war against his half-brother.

Of course, neither could have known that by the time Pizarro would return to Peru two and a half years later with the necessary forces, the tide of battle would have swung to Atahualpa. But if indeed a bargain was struck in early 1528, Pizarro's assistance would have been welcome, because Atahualpa's forces were outnumbered by as many as four to one. Besides, as Sarmiento notes, Atahualpa assumed the Spaniards to embody the return of Viracocha, the long-absent god who had promised one day to return.[44] An alliance between Viracocha and Atahualpa would be decisive militarily as well as religiously compelling, giving legitimacy to Atahualpa's claim to rule.

La Capitulación de Toledo

In my view, the essential proposition that Pizarro took to Spain was for King Charles to authorize a Spanish expeditionary force to intervene in a civil war on the side of Atahualpa. Whether Pizarro met with the king shortly after his arrival in Spain in mid-1528, or later in March of 1529, it is apparent that the Crown wrestled with his request for several months. The issue was not merely an authorization to conquer the heathen *Indios*. All understood the Inca to be a quite advanced civilization. As the queen put it, "Peru was a rich and fertile land, inhabited by a people more reasonable than any other than has so far been discovered."[45] In Olivares's story, Quispe Sisa reinforced that favorable view. She claims that during their stay she "connected" with Queen Isabella and met secretly and privately with her on several occasions, and that her friendship with

---

[43] Brooks, *Marriage, Legitimacy, and Intersectional Identities*, 61, states that Quispe Sisa "probably grew up under the control and supervision of both her mother and her half-brother, Atahualpa" as the latter was contesting with Huáscar to become Inca.
[44] Sarmiento, *History of the Incas,* 160.
[45]Varón, *Francisco Pizarro and His Brothers,* 16.

Isabella was instrumental in gaining the queen's approval for the Capitulation.[46]

It seems obvious that the Crown's decision would not have been merely the product of private meetings between the queen and Quispe Sisa. Larger issues had to be taken into consideration, especially the idea of interfering in the internal affairs of a sovereign nation as populous as if not more so than Spain itself; and the enslaving of native people, especially those of advanced cultures.[47] The subjugation of native communities to the will of Spanish conquistadors already was inflaming court politics, as clerics such as Bartolomé de las Casas and Domingo de Soto were objecting to the notion that Spain could exercise jurisdiction over any foreign peoples.[48]

The king faced a dilemma. To accede to the protests of his priests would mean to step away from empire, declining further conquest and the riches that would accrue from it; as well as cripple his drive for dominion in Europe. On the other hand, to authorize conquest would maintain the flow of wealth from America, and support his European dreams, but at the cost of undermining his religious beliefs and being labeled a moral hypocrite.

The king's decision was to compromise. He would distance himself from open intervention in a civil war on the side of the rebels and authorize a straightforward policy of "conquest and settlement of the province of Peru," but insist on a humanitarian approach to the treatment of conquered peoples.[49] Even so, when Pizarro returned to Peru his express

---

[46] Olivares, Ñusta, 69, 96-97, 103-104

[47] Spain's population may have been nearly 7 million in 1500 and a little over 8 million in 1600, according to Angus Maddison, *The World Economy: A Millennial Perspective* (Paris: OECD, 2001), 232, Table B-2. As for the Incan Empire, historian Gordon Francis McEwan gives 6-14 million as a generally accepted range. Gordon McEwan, *The Incas: New Perspectives* (ABC-CLIO, 2006), cited in "Inca Population: How Many Incas Were There?" online at worldhistory.us.

[48] See Martti Koskenniemi, "Empire and International Law: The Real Spanish Contribution," *University of Toronto Law Journal* 61, no. 1 (2011):5. Koskenniemi cites "the efforts of the Crown of Castile to regulate the process of colonization, including by prohibiting the use of slave labor and officially allowing the Indians to live in their communities under their native caciques," and the influence of prominent clerics on official policy.

[49] Ibid.

plan was to support Atahualpa against his enemies in the civil conflict and establish him as the Inca.

The king's need for wealth crowded out moral concerns. Moreover, Charles was careful to ensure that whatever wealth would result from the expedition would accrue solely to Spain. The issue was his imminent coronation as Holy Roman Emperor. To insure against any third-party claims, it would be expedient for the king to distance himself from the authorization. In the event, he departed Toledo and had Queen Isabella sign the Capitulation in her capacity as Regent of Castile.[50] The Capitulation was endorsed by Juan Vázquez de Molina, secretary to the Council of Regency; and the Council of the Indies, represented by its president, the Count of Osorno, and one of its members, Dr. Diego Beltrán.[51]

Recent scholarship has confirmed that Pizarro had been in contact with the king at least since his second expedition. When Pedro de los Ríos replaced Pedrarias as governor of Castilla del Oro, Pizarro sent a letter to the king requesting that the new governor respect the arrangements he had made with Pedrarias, a request the king honored with a royal *cédula* (letter or order) to Ríos dated May 17, 1527. Then, during Pizarro's second voyage south, the king, realizing Pizarro's value, sent a *cédula* dated June 5, 1528 to Licenciado Juan de Salmeron, *alcade mayor* (chief administrator) of Tierra Firme, instructing him to "show favor to Captains Pizarro and Almagro."[52] Pizarro's friends in Panama, Father Luque and Gaspar de Espinosa, also sent letters to their friends in the licentiate and the Council of the Indies promoting his cause. Whether these efforts had any effect in a court "teeming with intrigue," it is clear that the king was

---

[50] There is disagreement among historians as to which Queen/Regent gave the authorization: Isabella, Charles' wife, or Juana "The Mad," his mother. For example, Markham, in *Reports on the Discovery of Peru*, 12n8, names Juana. But according to Varón, in *Francisco Pizarro and His Brothers*, 38, and 62n14, it was Isabella.

[51] Text (in Spanish) of *La Capitulación de Toledo*: "1529, 26 de julio. Toledo. Real Cédula aprobando la capitulación concedida por Carlos V a Francisco Pizarro para la conquista y población del Perú," archived at La Biblioteca Virtual Miguel de Cervantes, www.cervantesvirtual.com. See Appendix II herein for a full translation.

[52] Varón, *Francisco Pizarro and His Brothers*, 15.

well acquainted with Pizarro's explorations and aspirations long before he met him.[53]

Thus, Pizarro was no ordinary petitioner waiting in line to plead his case to the king, or, as Stirling put it a "virtually unknown colonist," who "each day…joined the long line of petitioners to the chambers of the Council of the Indies."[54] During his year and a half in Spain he spent time, money and effort ingratiating himself with the powerful figures around the king, the queen, and the high officials of the Council of the Indies. Also, as noted earlier, in Olivares, Quispe Sisa says she was meeting secretly with the queen at the same time. Stirling notes Pizarro's discussions with García Fernández Manrique, the third Count of Osorno, who was president of the Council of the Indies.[55] Varón notes his interaction with Juan de Samano, who was secretary to Francisco de los Cobos, the king's secretary, and with Juan Vázquez de Molina, the queen's secretary. [56] These entities and Pizarro combined their efforts to produce the *Capitulación de Toledo*, the authorization for the conquest of Peru.

The Capitulation is described by some historians as offering nothing more than "trifling assistance" to Pizarro, with the Crown staking "nothing itself on the…enterprise," or at most making "cautious" and conditional pledges.[57] In my view, the Crown made a significant commitment to Pizarro and staked substantial resources on his success. The document gave him exclusive rights to the discovery, conquest and settlement of "the province of Peru," an area defined as spanning two hundred leagues (over six hundred miles), "more or less," along the Andean Pacific coast from "a village that in the language of the Indians is called Tempula, later named Santiago by you, until the village of Chincha is reached."[58] Chincha is located at roughly the 13th latitude below the

---

[53] Ibid., 36.

[54] Stirling, *Pizarro*, 2.

[55] Ibid., 2-3.

[56] Varón, *Francisco Pizarro and His Brothers*, 37.

[57] Prescott; von Hagen, *Conquest of Peru*, 190 and Varón, *Francisco Pizarro and His Brothers*, 38.

[58] Cieza de León, *Discovery and Conquest of Peru*, 137, quoting from the Capitulation. "Teninpulla" in the text is sometimes written as Tenumpuela, or Tempula, as in Cieza. There is some disagreement over the northern boundary of Pizarro's governorate. For example, Markham, in *Reports on the Discovery of Peru*, 12n8, says the two hundred

equator. With no Spaniard having yet sailed beyond the 9th latitude, it is a mystery how anyone could have known to set the boundary at this particular place, hundreds of miles further south. Was it Quispe Sisa?[59]

There was a seeming irony in the manner in which King Charles treated Cortés and Pizarro, who both appeared before him, that highlights the significance of the Crown's concessions to Pizarro. The king denied Cortés's petition to be reinstated as governor of New Spain (Mexico), even though he had already delivered on his conquest; but the Capitulation named Pizarro governor of Peru even though he had not yet set out on his. The difference in treatment was striking; but the king likely sought to avoid giving Cortés a stronger position from which to pursue any move toward Mexican independence, while aiming to encourage Pizarro's conquest of new territory in Peru with the promise that he could rule it.

The Capitulation, dated July 26, 1529, and affirmed the following month by Pizarro, was comprised of twenty-eight parts.[60] While the Crown did not provide men, ships, or money, what it did provide was a sustained legal, logistical, and infrastructural commitment to Pizarro to the exclusion of all others. Pizarro was promised the titles of governor and

---

leagues began at "the island of Santiago or Puna," which is in the Gulf of Guayaquil. Similarly, Helps, in *The Spanish Conquest in America,* vol. 3, 313, "thinks" that Tenempuela means the island of Puna. Others say the upper boundary was further north at the mouth of the Santiago River, near the Ecuador-Colombia border. See Rebecca Seaman, ed., *Conflict in the Early Americas: An Encyclopedia of the Spanish Empire's Aztec, Incan, and Mayan Conquests* (Santa Barbara: ABC-CLIO, 2013), 69; and Warren R. DeBoer, *Traces Behind the Esmeraldas Shore: Prehistory of the Santiago-Cayapas Region, Ecuador* (Tuscaloosa: The University of Alabama Press, 1996), 171, who says that "Another major coastal center, perhaps located near the mouth of the Santiago River, was Tenumpuela, a settlement that Pizarro named Santiago in his 1529 *Capitulación* to the queen of Spain."

[59] Cieza de León, *The Discovery and Conquest of Peru,* 118, says that when Pizarro arrived at Santa, he had "great desire to discover the city of Chincha, about which the Indians had related great things." But it is unlikely that much beyond generalities would have been conveyed by natives in sign language or by his interpreters-in-training, who were from northern Peru and probably had never seen Chincha themselves. The city is not very far from Cusco, the Inca capital, so it is plausible that Quispe Sisa had been there.

[60] Text (in Spanish) of *La Capitulación de Toledo:* "1529, 26 de julio. Toledo. Real Cédula aprobando la capitulación concedida por Carlos V a Francisco Pizarro para la conquista y población del Perú," archived at La Biblioteca Virtual Miguel de Cervantes, www.cervantesvirtual.com.

captain-general of Peru, as well as *adelantado*, chief justice, and *alguacil mayor* (chief constable*)*, although from the outset his men referred to him as "the governor." He was given a lifetime income to be derived from his conquests; and the power to grant *encomiendas* to his followers. In one of the many royal decrees issued to effectuate the Capitulation, Pizarro also was granted a knighthood. [61]

In the nearly four decades since Columbus, Spain had established an extensive if not yet robust logistical infrastructure spanning the Atlantic. The Canaries, and Cape Verde Islands constituted the outbound stepping-stones and replenishing depots. The offshore islands of Hispaniola, Jamaica, Puerto Rico, and Cuba were the first points of contact when reaching America. Panama, Nicaragua, Guatemala, the North coast of Colombia, the Pearl Islands and others, like Taboga, were all within the ambit of Tierra Firme, the Spanish Main. The Crown put much of the resources of this infrastructure at the disposal of Pizarro.

While it was up to Pizarro to acquire the ships, men, and supplies he would need, the Capitulation was very nearly a blank check to help finance it. Two hundred and fifty men were deemed sufficient for the initial phase of the expedition, of which one hundred and fifty were to be recruited in Spain and one hundred in Tierra Firma. The Crown authorized him to purchase on credit the weapons and ammunition he needed. For example, he was authorized to spend up to 300,000 maravedis (Spain's basic monetary unit at the time) on the purchase of artillery, which the Tierra Firme treasury would reimburse. Officials in the Casa de la Contratacíon in Seville were directed to provide him with a storehouse for his supplies. He was also authorized to take fifty slaves from Spain without cost.[62]

Officials in Jamaica were ordered to provide him with a hundred horses, half of them mares, and the mayor of Nombre de Dios in Panama was ordered to "give" him three artillery pieces (cannon) and all the lead, sulphur, and saltpeter he needed for ammunition. All of the Isla de las Flores near Panama would be his to govern and use in return for an annual payment of 200,000 maravedis for as long as Pizarro should so desire.

---

[61] Varón, *Francisco Pizarro and His Brothers,* 38-39; 299-300.
[62] Ibid.

Furthermore, none "of the Indians or properties belonging to Pizarro, Luque, and Almagro in Tierra Firme shall be taken away." [63]

As important as the Crown's provisions of equipment were, the indefinite tax breaks, exemptions and waivers Pizarro received were even more valuable. He was allowed to purchase on credit and proceed without paying duties or taxes on items he purchased. Indeed, he would only be required pay for the items he purchased out of future earnings, a significant subsidy. He was also granted a waiver from all lawsuits originating from debts accrued in Peru.

Curiously, the Capitulation built in conflict between Pizarro and his partner Almagro. Pizarro's men, most of the original "thirteen," were granted respected status as Hidalgos. However, Pizarro garnered the greatest benefits for himself, including the knighthood, which would elevate him to the top ranks of Spanish society. Almagro, on the other hand, was named a *hidalgo* like the original "thirteen," and given command of the fortress to be built at Tumbes, honors he felt were demeaning and hardly worth having. Luque was named to the future bishopric of Tumbes, an appropriate position.

Pizarro would claim that it was the Crown that insisted on a single command, but the great disparity in the honors bestowed upon Pizarro and Almagro can only be explained by Pizarro's insistence on being given sole power to command. Recall Pizarro's humiliation when Pedrarias forced him to accept Almagro in a joint command during the second expedition. Was this a case of "turnabout is fair play?" In any event, the subordination of Almagro in the Capitulation nearly doomed the expedition from the start and would lead to no end of troubles later for the "partnership."

To inject a sense of urgency, the Crown decreed that Pizarro must leave Spain for Panama within six months of the agreement and then depart Panama for Peru within six months after arriving there. Once the agreement was completed, therefore, Pizarro went directly to Trujillo, his hometown, in the province of Extremadura, to reaffirm his family ties. (The Crown had sent an inspector there to conduct a background check to ensure that he was eligible for the knighthood.) While there, Pizarro began

---

[63] Ibid.

the process of recruiting men for the expedition and the first he sought were members of his family.

Although his parents had both died, he connected with his kinsmen whom he had never met. Four half-brothers would join him and become his loyal cohort. These were: Hernando, age 33, who would become effective second-in-command; Juan, 19 and Gonzalo, 17, and Francisco Martín de Alcántara, also 19. Hernando was the only legitimate offspring of the Pizarro marriage. Alcántara was descended from the mother's side; and Juan and Gonzalo from the father's side, all "illegitimate," like Francisco. It should be noted that in 16th-century Spain fully half of all those born were "illegitimate" under Spanish law; thus it was not a sign of disgrace and not an insuperable impediment to advancement, as Pizarro had just demonstrated.

Recruiting would not be easy. Pizarro was only able to gain seventeen villagers from Trujillo to join his cause and thirty-six from all of Extremadura. It was not a matter of disinterest, but money. All who joined had to provide for their own equipment; a horse, armor, sword, or other weapon and most of those he encountered were dirt-poor peasants. It was only in Seville, where he was able to draw from a larger pool of wealthier, more adventuresome souls, that he could fill out more of his force. Still, in all, he would only be able to round up one hundred and twenty men, some thirty short of his allotment.

The six-month deadline for departing from Spain was January 26, 1530, but Pizarro made a hasty departure nearly a month early. According to Prescott he had received intelligence that the Council of the Indies would be sending inspectors to "ascertain how far the [Capitulation's] requisitions had been complied with."[64] Quintana adds that the Council may have been "instigated by some enemy of Pizarro.... An order was despatched [sic] for examining the vessels, and for their detention in case of failure."[65]

To avoid any possibility of a last-minute fiasco and to obscure the facts that he had neither the 150 men, nor the prescribed number of priests or accountants stipulated by the Capitulation on board, Pizarro devised a

---

[64] Prescott; von Hagen, *Conquest of Peru*, 192.
[65] Quintana, *Lives of Balboa and Pizarro,* 138.

clever stratagem to avoid discovery. He cast off with one of his three vessels, leaving the other two with Hernando, telling him that if the inspectors raised questions about the number of men to say that they had sailed ahead with him. Their plan was to meet at Gomera in the Canaries, and thence to sail together across the Atlantic. The inspectors were satisfied and Hernando set off with the remaining two ships loaded with their "volunteers, horses, mules, mastiffs, goats and pigs."[66]

Partnership in Discord

Crossing the Atlantic uneventfully, Pizarro put in at Santa Marta, a small port on the north coast of Colombia where several of his men disembarked having decided to quit, fearful of what lay ahead. The trip to Nombre de Dios was also uneventful, but the meeting with Almagro and Luque, who had traveled there to meet him, was not. Pizarro explained that the best he could obtain for his partners was that Luque was to be given the future bishopric of Tumbes and Almagro control of its government. Upon hearing this and that Pizarro had been awarded sole command of the expedition (not a joint command as they had agreed), and that he would be governor, *adelantado*, chief justice, and chief constable— in effect, viceroy of all Peru—Almagro was infuriated.[67]

Not only was Almagro denied equal status, but also Pizarro had another unpleasant surprise. He introduced his four half-brothers in a way that implied family came before their partnership. Even worse, Hernando and Almagro despised each other from the moment of their introduction. Nothing Pizarro said soothed his disadvantaged partner, who at length declared that the money, men, and supplies that he had collected while Pizarro was in Spain were his alone, to do with as he chose. He further announced that he would organize his own separate expedition. It seemed as if, once again, the dream of conquest would be nipped in the bud before it began.

For months over countless meetings they haggled. Pizarro argued, pleaded, and promised that they would cooperate as of old, but Almagro

---

[66] Stirling, *Pizarro*, 13. War dogs rarely are mentioned by the chroniclers, but the conquistadors routinely took ferocious mastiffs along with them.
[67] Quintana, *Lives of Balboa and Pizarro,* 139-40.

was unmoved, as the bonds of their partnership and friendship were frayed to the utmost. Each suspicious of the other, they moved to build loyal, separate followings. Hernando Ponce de León had arrived from Nicaragua with two ships and slaves to sell. Pizarro, seeking to counter the "defection" of Almagro, struck a bargain with him and his partner Hernando de Soto.[68] In return for the two ships and slaves, Pizarro promised to reward them with the "finest land in the territory we would conquer."[69] By this time the six-month deadline established by the Crown for commencing the expedition had come and gone.

At last, Luque and Gaspar de Espinosa, who had come over from Santo Domingo and who, recall, had his own financial interest in the success of the expedition, mediated a settlement. To Almagro, they noted that a separate expedition was out of the question because the Capitulation prohibited it.[70] They asked Pizarro to compromise and he assured Almagro that he would relinquish the post of *adelantado* to him, and promised to petition the king to confirm it. He also promised not to seek any post for any of his brothers before Almagro had been provided for. Finally, the three men reaffirmed their original agreement to share equally in any "gold, silver, jewels, [and] slaves...acquired by the conquest." [71]

The compromise healed their breach, if only temporarily. From this time there emerged two groups: the Pizarrists and the Almagrists, as their differences seemed more and more to reflect those between the men from Extremadura and Castile. Their reconciliation served the purpose of enabling them to gather the necessary men, ships, and supplies to commence the expedition, but, as Prescott notes, "it was only a thin scar that had healed over the wound, which, deep and rankling within, waited only fresh cause for irritation to break out with a virulence more fatal than ever."[72]

Although months behind schedule, at last they were ready. It was late December 1530. As was their previous practice, Pizarro would set out first, with Almagro following in a few months. Pizarro had in fact

---

[68] Ibid., 142.
[69] Stirling, *Pizarro,* 17, citing Pedro Pizarro, Francisco's kinsman and page.
[70] Prescott; von Hagen, *Conquest of Peru,* 195.
[71] Quintana, *Lives of Balboa and Pizarro,* 143.
[72] Prescott; von Hagen, *Conquest of Peru,* 195.

assembled the prescribed complement of 250 men, but only 180 were soldiers. The rest were slaves, sailors and porters. Thirty-six horses were also aboard.

It was customary for conquistadors to keep the Crown informed of their movements, and before setting out, Pizarro may have sent a letter to the king explaining his plans. One student of the period envisions it thus:

> *Dear Royal Highness,*
>
> *I am writing to you from Panama. The time is right to strike the Inca Empire.*
>
> *The Inca are powerful, their territory stretches more than 2,500 miles north to south, and 500 miles east to west. But they are weakened by the bitter struggle between the half-brothers, Huascar and Atahualpa, who both want to rule. You'll remember the death of Huayna Capac five years ago divided the empire.*
>
> *Also, the Inca have the most power of any Native American nation in the Western Hemisphere. They have made a network of stone roads connecting all the kingdom together, which makes communication swift, and these roads will make traveling for my army easier.*
>
> *My plan is to take about 180 men with firearms from here in Panama to Peru. Once there, I plan to take Atahualpa prisoner and make him head of the empire. That would make me the real ruler of the Inca Empire.*
>
> *So, King Charles I, that is my plan. I will let you know how it goes.*
>
> *Your humble servant,*
>
> *Francisco Pizarro*[73]

The letter depicted here is consistent with the thesis of this chapter. It is undated, but its content suggests that it was written in December 1530 just prior to Pizarro's departure. It contains information he could only have acquired from someone familiar with Incan politics and geography, and that someone could have been Quispe Sisa, who, in

---

[73]Study Resource (online), *Age of Exploration*, chap. 15, "Maritime Revolution," 30. https://studyres.com / doc / 4338157 / chapter-15-maritime-revolution.

Olivares's "diary," claims that she wrote all his letters for him.[74] Furthermore, the only time he could have acquired the knowledge contained in such a letter was when he was first at Tumbes. The missive indicates a sophisticated understanding of the dimensions of the Inca Empire and its principal features, like the extensive road and communication system that Pizarro planned to utilize in his conquest. Indeed, knowledge of Incan geography and the road system could explain the nature of Pizarro's movements from the moment he landed.

Pizarro's understanding of the political situation of the empire "weakened" by civil war, as portrayed in the letter, also could only have derived from someone who was conversant with it. Thus, reminding the king of Huayna Cápac's death "five years ago" indicates that Pizarro knew of the Inca's death while at Tumbes and had discussed its significance with the king when they met. Similarly, he could only have learned about the struggle between "the half-brothers, Huáscar and Atahualpa," while in Tumbes. Proposing "to take Atahualpa prisoner and make him head of the empire" and then to rule through him is an implicit reference to taking the side of Quispe Sisa's favored brother in the civil war.

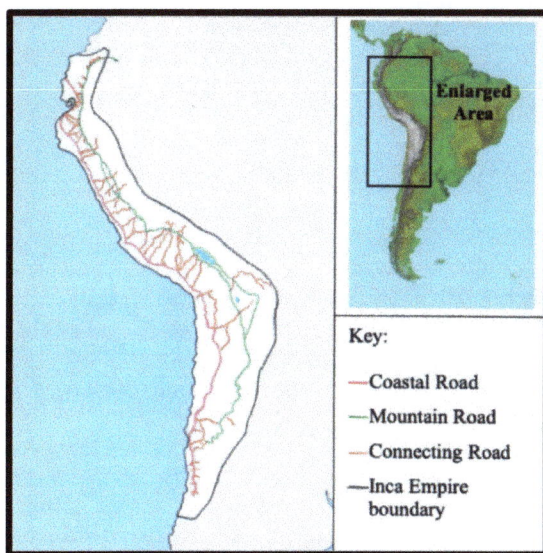

4.2 Inca road system

---

[74] Olivares, *Ñusta*, 84.

A Change of Circumstances

Pizarro's plan was obviously highly secret, and it is doubtful that he shared it with anyone, even his closest confidants. Although he discussed tactics with his top aides, strategy he kept to himself. Departing Panama in early January 1531 with three ships piloted by the redoubtable Bartolomé Ruiz, Pizarro sailed along the Ecuadoran coastline for thirteen days until he heaved to at a point on the northwest coast. There is, however, confusion in the record as to the initial landing site, and more importantly, why he chose it.

Prescott says it was Pizarro's intention to steer directly for Tumbes, but that after thirteen days, "his little squadron came to anchor at the Bay of St. Matthew (in Spanish, San Mateo), about one degree north..." That latitude is in the Esmeraldas area of Ecuador, near the border with Colombia. Cieza, Xeres, Quintana, Stirling, and Kochis, all say that he disembarked his forces at San Mateo Bay and marched southward to Coaque, and then to Puna. Thomas agrees that the place was in Esmeraldas, but calls it San Marco. For Hemming, the decision to land so far north of Tumbes was "inexplicable."[75]

Prescott points to "headwinds and currents" that "baffled" his approach.[76] Yet the ocean circulations along the Ecuadoran coast—particularly the Humboldt Current—are strongest well to the south of Esmeraldas. As Neil and Jorgensen note:

> The warm equatorial current that bathes the northwest coast of Ecuador brings with its moist air and rainfall. During most years, the warm equatorial current pushes farther to the south of the equator for a few months, December to April generally, bringing rainfall and warm, moist air to the areas of the central and southern Ecuadorian coast that are under the influence of the dry, cool Humboldt Current the remainder of the year. This phenomenon is known locally as El Niño (the Christ Child)

---

[75] Prescott; von Hagen, *Conquest of Peru,* 196; Xeres in Markham, *Reports on the Discovery of Peru,* 12-13; Cieza de León, *Discovery and Conquest of Peru,* 149; Quintana, *Lives of Balboa and Pizarro,* 144; Stirling, *Pizarro,* 26-28; Kochis, *God, Glory and Gold,* 2:306; Hugh Thomas, *The Golden Empire* (New York: Random House, 2010), 223.

[76] Prescott; von Hagen, *Conquest of Peru,* 196.

because the annual rains usually begin in mid- to late December, around Christmas.[77]

Strategy is a more satisfying explanation for why Pizarro stopped where he did. He was not headed for Tumbes, but for the closest coastal landfall to Quito to be in position to come to Atahualpa's aid, if Huáscar's forces were still besieging him. Thus, landing at the mouth of the Esmeraldas River put him at the closest point he could be to reach Quito. As Enock notes, "the distance from the town of Esmeraldas to Quito is forty-six leagues, of which twenty-two can be performed in boats up the river."[78] (Forty-six leagues are roughly one hundred and sixty miles, of which nearly half was navigable by boat.) No other landing spot along the coast was as close. Pizarro was, in short, exactly where he intended to be.

According to Diego de Trujillo, a member of Pizarro's expedition, "many Indians came down [the] river in canoes to observe us, though unwilling to land."[79] Despite their reticence, Pizarro could have made contact with some, learning the news that the tide of battle had changed dramatically. At this point, Atahualpa and his armies were no longer besieged at Quito but had turned the tide against Huáscar. Early in 1531, just as Pizarro was landing at San Mateo Bay, Atahualpa's forces had won a major battle at Mochacaxa, south of Quito. Although the overall outcome was still in some doubt, with battles then raging, Atahualpa now had the initiative as his forces were surging southward.[80] For Pizarro it meant that not only was proximity to Quito now irrelevant, but also that his plan had been overtaken by events.

After pondering his options for ten days, Pizarro decided to disembark his force and march southward along the coast, in rough parallel with the course of the battles taking place in the mountains. Passing through Atacamez and Quiximies, both deserted, he reached Coaque in early March. Coaque was a large, prosperous village of over four hundred huts surrounding several large temples inhabited by over a thousand

---

[77] David Neill and Peter Jorgensen, "Climates," in The *Catalogue of the Vascular Plants of Ecuador*, Missouri Botanical Garden (online), www.mobot.org.

[78] C. Reginald Enock, *Ecuador: Its Ancient and Modern History, Topography and Natural Resources* (London: T.F. Unwin, 1914), 120.

[79] Diego de Trujillo, quoted in Stirling, *Pizarro*, 26.

[80] Betanzos, *Narrative of the Incas*, 198.

people. Pizarro's men, having trudged over a hundred miles and perhaps frustrated at their inability to find anything of value thus far, fell upon the unsuspecting villagers, plundering "whatever could be found."[81]

The Indians at first fled in terror, but, Pizarro, remonstrating with their *cacique*, persuaded him to call his people back and to arrange for them to provide the Spaniards with provisions. This outcome pleased Pizarro so much that he decided to stay on for a time. In fact, he would remain at Coaque for seven months; in my view, monitoring the course of battle in the mountains. Unfortunately, the Spanish occupation of the village and their poor treatment of their hosts led to a gradual deterioration of relations with the natives, who, becoming disillusioned "took to the forest and left them their houses."[82]

Although no longer willing to assist the Spaniards, the natives nevertheless continued to watch them from a distance and, using the well-organized messaging system employing runners called *chaskis*, "kept sending notices about everything to the representatives of the Incas, who passed the information to Cusco and Quito and everywhere."[83] In other words, it is safe to conclude that both Atahualpa and Huáscar were kept as well informed of Pizarro's activities, as he was of theirs.

Unfortunately, while at Coaque, a hot, humid, unhealthy, rainy tropical area, the Spanish were afflicted by what were later diagnosed as two debilitating contagious diseases, Oroya fever and Verruga peruana. The former killed more quickly through high fever and anemia, while the latter inflicted crippling muscle, joint, and bone pain followed by the appearance of large nodules and boils.[84] Most were affected, several died, and all cursed the scourge, for which the Spaniards had no cure.

If Pizarro's strategy indeed was to "take Atahualpa prisoner and make him head of the empire," as described earlier, it would need to be redrawn. It now appeared that Atahualpa would become emperor by his own efforts. Pizarro would need to devise another strategy to "take Atahualpa prisoner," which meant getting close enough to him to seize

---

[81] Quintana, *Lives of Balboa and Pizarro*, 144.
[82] Cieza de León, *Discovery and Conquest of Peru*, 150.
[83] Ibid., 153.
[84] Linda Newson, *Life and Death in Early Colonial Ecuador* (Norman: University of Oklahoma Press, 2005), 144-47.

him. I believe Pizarro's new plan was built upon the old. He would still offer to help Atahualpa in vanquishing his enemies, as the means of getting close to him. There was still much fighting to do. The civil war had crippled the Incan Empire as nearly every former tributary sought independence; either by defying both sides, or siding with one over the other. In the future, Pizarro would use these divisions to his own advantage, but for the moment they provided him negotiating leverage with Atahualpa.

For this plan to have any chance of success, Pizarro realized that he needed to augment his forces. He sent all three of his ships back, two to Panama and one to Nicaragua; altogether loaded with some twenty thousand pesos of gold, silver, and jewels expropriated from the natives at Coaque. His hope was that the booty would entice more men to join him and enable him to acquire more horses and provisions. He sent letters to all of his friends, Almagro and Luque foremost among them. Just after his ships departed a vessel arrived, undoubtedly by prearrangement, loaded with some reinforcements and provisions. Aside from this, Pizarro and his men were left to fend for themselves at Coaque. Almagro was conspicuously absent. It is likely that Pizarro tracked the course of the civil war; Quispe Sisa's knowledge would have been a key resource.

Convergence at Cajamarca

To recapitulate, after escaping from his imprisonment at Tomebomba and returning to Quito, Atahualpa began to assemble his armies under the leadership of three of Huayna Cápac's top generals, Chalcuchima; Quiz Quiz, whom he placed in charge of his assault forces; and Ruminavi, who was given the task of maintaining the Quito base. The victory at Mochacaxa also offered Atahualpa an opportunity to solidify his claim to be Inca. He discovered that among the captured soldiers was his cousin Cuxi Yupanqui, whom he welcomed into his camp. He would make Cuxi second in command of his armies.

Accompanying Cuxi was his sister, Cuxirimay, then ten years old. She was not only the niece of Huayna Cápac and a descendant of Manco Cápac, founder of the empire, Cuxirimay was also related to Atahualpa, as their mothers were sisters. Marriage between them would ensure the purity of the Cápac line and strengthen Atahualpa's claim. Thus, Atahualpa took Cuxirimay as his principal wife in connection with his acceptance of the *borla*, or symbolic appointment as Inca. It was a marriage in name only, but one that would have profound consequences later.[85]

Atahualpa's first order of business after the victory at Mochacaxa was to consolidate his base in the north. Discovering that the neighboring Cañari tribe had sided with Huáscar and had sent troops to support him, Atahualpa first moved mercilessly to crush the Cañaris, forcing survivors to eat the roasted flesh of their defeated leaders. His approach was to deal harshly with enemy leaders but welcome the fighting men into his armies. He also applied this approach to another neighboring province, that of the Pasto people. The news spread, resulting in many other tribal leaders switching sides to join Atahualpa, greatly augmenting his forces. But such alliances were fleeting; and reprisals were constant and harsh to punish defections, as would be the case with the Pastos.[86]

Meanwhile, after months at Coaque, in mid-October, 1531, Pizarro decided to leave the pestilential base and move south, for that is where Atahualpa was heading. Just before setting out, however, at the end of the month, the ships sent to Panama finally arrived with the hoped-for men, provisions, and horses. Almagro was not among them, but he and Luque sent missives promising to arrive soon with additional support. Aboard the ship were the three officials that the court had assigned to the expedition, but who had missed connections earlier. These were: treasurer Alonso Riquelme; inspector García de Salcedo; and accountant Antonio Navarro, there to ensure that the king would receive his "fifth" of any treasure found.[87]

Reinforced, Pizarro now set out to the south. His plan was to proceed along the coast establishing friendly relations where possible, dominating where necessary but above all remaining in position where he could be reinforced by sea. He would continue this process of establishing coastal enclaves until the time was right to move inland—when the

---

[85] Josh Provan, "Atahualpa's Rook: Chess and Murder During the Conquest of Peru," *Adventures in Historyland*, March 10, 2019, adventuresinhistoryland.com; and Betanzos, *Narrative of the Incas*, 181.

[86] Betanzos, *Narrative of the Incas*, 197-98, 200-01, 203-04, and 232-33.

[87] Cieza de León, *Discovery and Conquest of Peru*, 153.

combatants in the civil war were weakened from their internecine fighting and he was stronger. Pizarro's route generally paralleled but lagged behind what he estimated to be the movement of Atahualpa's armies in the mountains, as they won major battles at Bombón and Jauja. Along the coast, Atahualpa's forces were carrying out a reign of terror against Huáscar's allied tributaries, apparently keeping one or two steps ahead of Pizarro, who came upon village after village that showed signs of recent fighting.

Kubler notes that on the march southward Pizarro was in contact with "representatives of both factions," referring to Atahualpa and Huáscar, who "came to Pizarro during 1531 and 1532."[88] Indeed, he cites Pedro Pizarro, who says that "Francisco Pizarro actually negotiated with Huáscar's party before the ascent to Cajamarca" to meet with Atahualpa. Kubler observes that several early Spanish historians, including Garcilaso de la Vega, Zarate, Montesinos, and Valasco made the same claim.[89] (Atahualpa's armies crushed Huáscar's forces and took him prisoner in March 1532, although there is some evidence that Huáscar was in contact with Pizarro after he was imprisoned.)[90]

A few days after leaving Coaque, Pizarro reached the village of Pasado some fifty miles down the coast. Here, the local *cacique* had decided to adopt a friendly approach, offering provisions in return for protection. His next stop was a large settlement in the Bay of Caraquez where his reception was quite different. The natives welcomed the Spaniards, but plotted behind their backs, killing a number of them. Pizarro's response was to make an example of their perfidy by killing several natives in retaliation. Still, Pizarro was able to appeal to the chief to maintain friendly relations with the Spaniards, which he agreed to do.

Marching further, they arrived at another impressive settlement at Puerto Viejo a few miles inland. Here, the impact of the civil war was evidenced by the scarcity of able-bodied men. With few men and no help forthcoming from the Inca, the *cacique* decided to "show them good will

---

[88] George Kubler, "The Behavior of Atahualpa, 1531-1533," *Hispanic American Historical Review* 25, no. 4 (November 1945):416.

[89] Ibid.

[90] Prescott; von Hagen, *Conquest of Peru*, 260.

and provide them with what was available in their region because [the Christians] were just passing through." As the rainy season had begun Pizarro demurred, deciding to spend several weeks in Puerto Viejo assessing his circumstances. While there he welcomed the arrival of the ship originally sent to Nicaragua. Aboard was Sebastián de Benalcázar, a highly regarded conquistador, who arrived with thirty men and a dozen horses.[91]

It was now early December 1531. Almost a year had passed, and Pizarro had yet to make contact with Atahualpa. Leaving Puerto Viejo, Pizarro's men reached Santa Elena where signs of war and devastation were recent and everywhere. Here, there was a good news/bad news story. The good news was that while at Santa Elena, on December 1, another ship arrived from Nicaragua bringing Hernando de Soto with one hundred men and two dozen horses. The bad news was that de Soto came with an understanding he had reached with Almagro that he would be named second in command of Pizarro's expedition.

Had Almagro attempted to undermine Pizarro? It was a delicate situation, which the governor handled about as well as could be expected. He told de Soto that Almagro could speak for their partnership in Panama but had no authority to determine his command arrangements in Peru authorized by the king. He also said how much he valued de Soto's presence and expertise, but that Hernando was his second in command and he declined to change that. However, he named de Soto Captain of the cavalry unit, welcomed him into his War Council and promised him a prominent role in reconnaissance missions.[92] Hernando de Soto would be an invaluable aide throughout the conquest, although inclined to act impetuously at times.

In early January 1532, Pizarro's forces made their way to Puna Island in the northern portion of the Bay of Guayaquil, prior to going to Tumbes on the southern shore of the bay. The natives of Puna and Tumbes, recall, were mortal enemies whose conflict had reached a climactic point in a Puna victory. Pizarro decided to make camp on the island until the end

---

[91] Cieza de León, *Discovery and Conquest of Peru,* 157.
[92] Stirling, *Pizarro,* 30, claims that the governor's refusal to name de Soto second in command was a "betrayal," but if it was such, it was Almagro's.

of the rainy season. Although welcomed by the head *cacique*, other chiefs plotted to destroy the Spaniards. The upshot was that in preempting one plot by Puna chiefs, Pizarro precipitated a major conflict; and although the Spaniards beat back a large Puna attack, conditions on the island were no longer bearable and Pizarro decided to move on to Tumbes.[93]

In moving from Puna to Tumbes, Pizarro went from the frying pan into the fire. The flourishing Incan outpost he had first visited four years before was now a devastated wasteland permeated by the stench of death. Almost all of the people had fled and those who remained were hostile; indeed, they ambushed and killed three Spaniards. The only buildings still standing were the large, polygonal stone temples and a few mud brick huts. All the rest had been reduced to rubble. The scene bore the distinct mark of Atahualpa's extermination campaign against Huáscar. After a time, several chiefs approached Pizarro providing information, offering assistance, and seeking the protection of the powerful strangers.[94]

Pizarro now learned that the civil war had reached a decisive stage. In March, Atahualpa's armies had defeated Huáscar's forces in a major battle at Quipaipan near the Apurimac River outside of Cusco and had captured Huáscar. The war of succession was, therefore, over; but major fighting continued, as Quiteños sought to exterminate their Cuscoan factional enemies. Indeed, Atahualpa's generals, Chalcuchima and Quiz Quiz, were then carrying out an extensive ethnic cleansing campaign killing as many of the Cuscoan elite, including women and children, as they could round up. Their objective, on Atahualpa's explicit orders, was to preclude any possible future challenge to the new Inca based on purity of bloodline.[95]

Atahualpa, meanwhile, had not accompanied his armies to Cusco, but, rather, positioned himself with a force of some eighty thousand troops outside of Cajamarca, the mid-point along the mountain highway between Quito and Cusco. From there he could reinforce in either direction, as needed, and prevent any link-up of northern and southern forces against him. Reestablishing control over the empire would be a lengthy and

---

[93] Cieza de León, *Discovery and Conquest of Peru,* 166.
[94] Stirling, *Pizarro,* 31.
[95] Betanzos, *Narrative of the Incas,* 242-46.

gargantuan task; therefore, according to Sarmiento de Gamboa, Atahualpa "rejoiced greatly" at news of the arrival of Pizarro's forces.[96]

Pizarro, on the other hand, realized that the moment had come for him to take action, as Atahualpa's forces were dispersed as widely as they ever would be, engaged in suppression campaigns in the south and pacification operations in the north. Therefore, in May, he moved along the coastal road that began at Tumbes to position his forces closer to Atahualpa. After a misstep at Tangarara, he established a settlement at San Miguel de Piura, about 40 miles further to the south.[97] From this base he could continue to receive provision ships from Panama and be within relatively close range to Atahualpa, some ten to twelve days and three hundred miles distant in the mountains.

Pizarro received news from one of the provision ships that his partner, Almagro, was "preparing an armament and enlisting men, for the purpose of setting forth, on his own account, as a discoverer." In fact, he had written to the king requesting permission to captain an expedition beyond Pizarro's jurisdiction, which the king denied.[98] But Pizarro did not know that. For him, it was the worst possible news, portending failure of the expedition, as competing conquistadors vied for the favor of contending Incas. Thus, Pizarro, employing the Machiavellian principle of keeping one's friends close, but his enemies closer, wrote to Almagro entreating him "by all of the confidence that had formerly existed between them, to forget misunderstandings, cast aside his doubts, and come immediately to him."[99]

One wonders if he had also revealed to him the arrangement he had made to meet with Atahualpa. According to Mavor, it was during his stay at his settlement in San Miguel, that

> his alliance and assistance were sought by Atahualpa, which he readily promised and by these means was allowed to march his troops in safety across the sandy desert between St. Michael

---

[96] Gamboa, *History of the Incas,* 161,

[97] Prescott; von Hagen, *Conquest of Peru,* 220.

[98] Hemming, *Conquest of the Incas,* 556n72.

[99] Quintana, *Lives of Balboa and Pizarro,* 158; Xeres in Markham, *Reports on the Discovery of Peru,* 22-24.

[Miguel] and Motupe, where their career might easily have been stopped.[100]

Thus, at the end of September 1532, Pizarro could afford to wait no longer. After a year and a half, Almagro and his promised reinforcements had yet to appear. Even worse, it was unclear what Almagro's position would be when he did arrive. With no more time to lose, therefore, Pizarro and his band of one hundred sixty-eight men and sixty-two horses began to move inland; southward and then eastward, up into the mountains to rendezvous with Atahualpa.

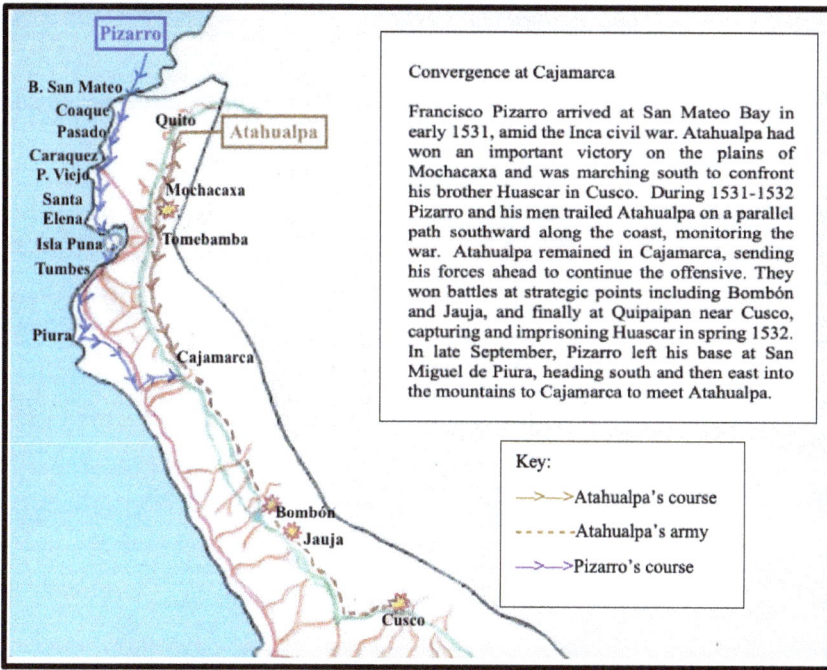

4.3 Parallel courses of Pizarro and Atahualpa toward Cajamarca

Along the way, Pizarro's men were well received by native leaders and his advance scouts made repeated contact with Atahualpa's envoys, who sometimes stayed for a few days, bringing gifts and provisions to ease

---

[100] William Mavor, *History of the Discovery and Settlement to the Present Time of North and South America and of the West Indies* (London: Richard Phillips, 1806), 154. Stirling, *Pizarro,* 33-34, describes the first meeting as being between de Soto and Atahualpa's representatives at the town of Cajas, east of San Miguel.

the Spaniards' journey.[101] They informed Pizarro that they would meet at Cajamarca.[102] Still, it would take nearly two months of marching across bitter cold high mountain passes, treacherous steaming valleys, and turbulent rivers before he reached the mountain town of Cajamarca, guided there during the last part of their journey by yet another envoy.[103] It was November 15, 1532, and Pizarro had a date with destiny.

---

[101] Olivares, *Ñusta*, 22. Quispe Sisa, who accompanied Pizarro on the march, claims that one of these envoys was none other than Atahualpa's top general, Chalcuchima, whom she recognized: "I knew him well." He had come personally to observe and evaluate Pizarro's forces.

[102]Helps, *Spanish Conquest in America*, 3:353-57.

[103] Quintana, *Lives of Balboa and Pizarro*, 174.

Chapter 5

Conquest and Consequences

In the course of a single year, from November 1532 to November 1533, Francisco Pizarro traversed virtually the entire span of Peru, to conquer the Incan empire. He accomplished this astounding historical feat with a relatively small handful of men against a nation of over ten million people. How that occurred is the story of this chapter. As always with such sweeping claims, they need explication; in this case, of Inca culture, Pizarro's romantic liaisons, the internal Spanish political struggle, the difficult geography of Peru, and Spanish military/technological prowess. The historical moment, too, was critical, and not accidental. Pizarro arrived at the very time that the Incan regime was convulsing into self-destruction in a war for succession, a war in which much of the ruling class was being exterminated. And Pizarro entered the fray determined to place his hand on the scale of history in order to influence the outcome to his advantage.

It is said that victory erases all mistakes, but not always and not all of them. Pizarro became increasingly aware that his strategic conception was incorrect and strove to change it. His strategic plan was to take Atahualpa's side in the civil war, make him Inca, and then rule Peru through him. But it was not long before he realized that he had taken the wrong side in the war, and shifted his allegiance to the Cusco southern faction against the Quito northern faction. Then, he discovered that his new partners were themselves opposed by the majority of the Andean people. Unwilling or unable to switch a second time, Pizarro decided to prop up Inca rule, rather than ally with the conquered peoples the way Cortés had done. There would be a terrible price to pay for his misconceptions.

Double Deception at Cajamarca

Why Atahualpa fell into Pizarro's trap at Cajamarca is one of the most puzzling issues that has bedeviled historians of the conquest. This befuddlement stems from a faulty premise: that Atahualpa underestimated Spanish strength and overestimated his own. The issue, however, was not the balance of military forces, but political expectations and tactical execution. Both leaders were proceeding to a prearranged meeting whose ostensible purpose was to strike an alliance against Huáscar. Yet, in approaching this meeting each was deceiving the other as to his ultimate objective. Pizarro sought a meeting in order to capture Atahualpa and rule Peru through him, while Atahualpa, having already defeated Huáscar, sought the meeting as his means of acquiring Spanish military technology to reinforce his rule. Atahualpa simply fell victim to a preemptive strike by Pizarro.

If we accept Olivares's premise, introduced in the previous chapter, that Quispe Sisa had become Pizarro's mistress and interpreter (even intermediary) in 1528 during his first sojourn at Tumbes,[1] then Pizarro's plan for the encounter at Cajamarca was the more complicated. It would involve deceiving not only Atahualpa, but his sister, too. After convincing them of his willingness to serve Atahualpa as a mercenary, he would present them with a *fait accompli*.

For Atahualpa, on the other hand, the long-term issue was paramount. The civil war had torn the empire asunder as Atahualpa decimated Huáscar's Cusco elite, and vassals and tributaries sought to break free of Incan rule. Indeed, Atahualpa's forces were not well received in the south and were, in effect, an occupation force. The acquisition of Spanish military technology would offer him the means of reimposing Incan rule, which required a much longer perspective. Horses, guns, and steel swords could only be a short-term expedient unless he also acquired the means to produce them himself and, most importantly, develop the skills to use them. Thus, I believe Atahualpa went to Cajamarca with the objective of acquiring Spanish military technology one way or the other. He would either enlist Pizarro as an ally or coerce him to train his soldiers

---

[1] Rafael Olivares, *Ñusta: the Inka Love of Francisco Pizarro* (Bergenfield: Xlibris, 2014).

in the use of these new weapons. His goal was to incorporate Spanish military technology as a permanent feature of Incan power.[2]

Descending that afternoon of November 15, 1532 into the high valley of Cajamarca, an oval-shaped plateau roughly ten miles wide by fifteen miles long, Pizarro and his band saw below them a town of several hundred dwellings. There was a central square surrounded by well-ordered cultivated fields separated by a system of irrigation viaducts and hedgerows. Off in the distance they also saw the steam rising from the hot baths of Huamachuco, where Atahualpa already was encamped. They could make out thousands of white tents dotting the hillside, indicating a large force estimated to be at least fifty thousand men.[3]

Contrary to Hemming, it was not by "extraordinary coincidence [that] Atahualpa happened to be camped in the mountains at Cajamarca" when Pizarro arrived.[4] As recounted in the previous chapter, Atahualpa had chosen the town for their meeting place and his envoys had led Pizarro to it. In addition, as he would quickly learn, the Incan leader had ordered the town to be evacuated so Pizarro and his men could use it for their lodgings. The only inhabitants left were a few hundred women in a temple—the local finishing school where young women learned essential skills like textile weaving, wine brewing, and how to serve their masters.

The town center was dominated by a large trapezoidal expanse, enclosed by an eight-foot high wall and divided into three sections. At one end, commanding a view of the entire area was a three-story cylindrical fortress. Below the fortress in the middle section were extensive gardens surrounding a temple where the women resided. The main feature of the enclosure was the third section: a large plaza of six hundred square feet. There were long, one-story barracks-like buildings situated on three sides,

---

[2] Bancroft says that after Huáscar was captured, some of Atahualpa's counselors urged him to immediately kill the Spanish invaders, while others advised taking them alive and "by making slaves of them, ingraft their superiority into their own incipient civilization." Hubert Howe Bancroft, *History of Central America,* vol. 2, *1530-1800,* vol. 7 of *The Works of Hubert Howe Bancroft* (San Francisco: A.L. Bancroft, 1883), 19n5.

[3] William H. Prescott, *History of the Conquest of Peru,* partly abridged and revised by Victor W. von Hagen (New York: New American Library, 1961), 235-38.

[4] John Hemming, *The Conquest of the Incas* (New York: Harcourt Brace Jovanovich, 1970), 30.

each with multiple doorways opening onto the plaza. In one corner was a two-story fort with several smaller buildings clustered around it. The only access to the plaza was through two gates on either side of the enclosure.

Whatever Atahualpa thought about his selection of Cajamarca for their meeting, Pizarro saw the layout of the plaza (see drawing) as fitting his plans perfectly. Its walls allowed him to limit the number of Incan troops that could enter, which meant that he could separate Atahualpa from the bulk of his army while the two gates controlled entry. He could also command the high ground from the fortress and concentrate force in a confined space. Presumably, Atahualpa, too, thought that the confined space of the plaza would suit his purposes—either as a convenient place for the high-level negotiation that had been agreed, or as a way to contain and overcome Pizarro—if it went bad.

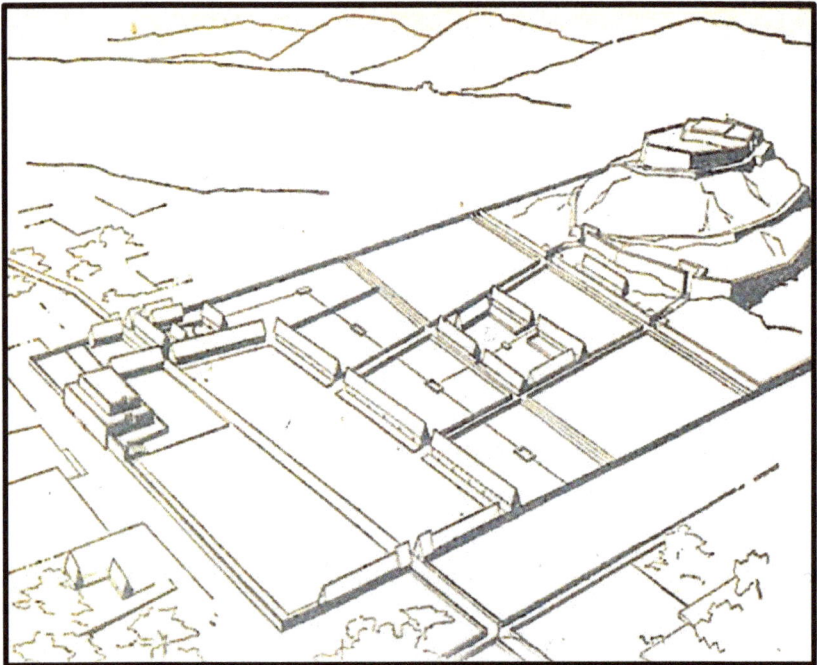

5.1. Layout of Cajamarca. Drawing by Ing. Emilio Harth-Terré in Prescott; von Hagen, *Conquest of Peru,* **236.**

It was evening as Pizarro's force entered the town and a cold rain had begun to fall. He sent his men into the barracks for cover while he walked around the entire enclosure inspecting it. At the same time, he sent Hernando de Soto and Felipillo the interpreter with fifteen men on horseback to inform Atahualpa that he had arrived and to ask for further instructions. As soon as de Soto left, however, Pizarro had second thoughts and sent his brother, Hernando, after him with twenty more horsemen. The two captains met with Atahualpa, who was ensconced at the baths surrounded by his chieftains and many serving women. Over drinks of *chicha*, a corn-based, Incan alcoholic beer-like beverage, they engaged in some testy conversation, reiterating willingness to fight Atahualpa's enemies. Following this and a demonstration of horsemanship by de Soto, the two Spaniards extended Pizarro's invitation to visit, and left.

The Incan leader indicated that he would come the next morning to meet, directing that Pizarro and his men should "lodge in the three great chambers in the courtyard, and that the centre one should be set apart for himself."[5] When Pizarro was told that Atahualpa would come the next morning, the governor sat down with his captains to decide what to do. Their plan depended on what Atahualpa did. If they could entice him to enter the walled plaza, they could separate him from the bulk of his troops, making it a relatively simple matter to seize him. It is easy to see Cortés's seizure of Montezuma as the inspiration of this plan. On the other hand, if they could not draw him into their trap and Atahualpa insisted on holding their meeting at his camp outside the plaza, they would be forced to maintain a friendly attitude and await another opportunity to seize him.[6]

They would plan for both contingencies, but, as Hemming notes, it was agreed that "Governor Pizarro should decide on the spur of the moment the course of action to be adopted."[7] With no time to lose, Pizarro decided to conceal Hernando, de Soto, and Benalcázar in two of the three barracks structures, with twenty horsemen and a dozen foot soldiers for each man. He took two-dozen shield-bearing soldiers with him into the

---

[5] "Letter of Hernando Pizarro to the Royal Audience of Santo Domingo," in Clements Markham, ed. and trans., *Reports on the Discovery of Peru* (London: Hakluyt Society, 1872; repr., New York: Burt Franklin, 1970), 115-16.
[6] Prescott; von Hagen, *Conquest of Peru,* 243, maintains that a trap was his plan all along.
[7] Hemming, *Conquest of the Incas,* 37-38. Cf. Hugh Thomas, *The Golden Empire* (New York: Random House, 2010), 236.

third barracks. He deployed Pedro de Candia with his four cannon, a dozen muskets, a few crossbowmen and a squad of trumpeters on top of the three-story fortress overlooking the plaza and placed several soldiers at the two gates. No one was to move or make a sound until Pizarro gave the signal. They spent a tense night with horses saddled, armor on, and sentries alert.

In Olivares, the planned encounter with Atahualpa alarmed Quispe Sisa, who says that she had only learned after their arrival that the two leaders were to meet the next day, and hurriedly decided to warn her brother. Acting on a "premonition that something terrible would happen," she "sent one of [her] *yanaconas* [servants] to get a message to Atahualpa....to be extra careful." It was important, she said, "not to trust the Spaniards."[8]

Indeed, he would not. According to MacQuarrie, unbeknownst to Hernando and de Soto when they left Atahualpa after their meeting with him at the baths, the Inca already had made the decision to

> capture the foreigners, kill most of them, and castrate the rest to use as eunuchs to guard his harem. Atahualpa would then seize the magnificent animals the foreigners rode in order to breed them in great numbers; the giant animals would surely make his empire even more powerful and would instill fear in his enemies.[9]

Having decided how to deal with Pizarro, Atahualpa spent the night preparing for his visit to him. It would be a carefully orchestrated deception. He would approach their meeting on the pretense of negotiating but capture them before they realized what had happened to them. Unfortunately, according to Betanzos, Atahualpa had done a great deal of *chicha* drinking during their preparation and by the next morning "he was very drunk."[10]

It was nearly noon before Atahualpa arose the next morning, still in a stupor, and he was not ready. So, he sent a couple of messengers, including the one "who had already met the Governor on the road" to tell

---

[8] Olivares, *Ñusta,* 16-17,19, 21.
[9] Kim MacQuarrie, *The Last Days of the Incas* (New York: Simon & Shuster, 2007), 67-68.
[10] Juan de Betanzos, *Narrative of the Incas,* trans. Roland Hamilton and Dana Buchanan (Austin: University of Texas Press, 1996), 261-63.

Pizarro that Atahualpa would put off his visit to the afternoon.[11] According to Betanzos, this messenger was Ciquinchara, who, having observed the Spaniards on several occasions, reported to Atahualpa that they were few and weak and that "it would not be any trouble to tear them to pieces and capture them."[12]

Ciquinchara also had a second task. As Hernando Pizarro recounted, this messenger "Conversing with some Indian girls in the service of the Christians, who were their relations, told them to run away because Atahualpa was coming that afternoon to attack the Christians and kill them." [13] If Quispe Sisa already was at Cajamarca, as Olivares relates, she and her *yanaconas* could have been among the women who were being warned to flee to safety. In that context, the import of the message would have been that any notion of her brother's collaboration with Pizarro should be dismissed.

It was well after midday on November 16 when Atahualpa's men struck camp and began to make their way in a well-ordered procession toward Cajamarca. But in the late afternoon about a half-mile from the town the procession halted, and his men began to pitch camp, a development that alarmed Pizarro. If this meant that Atahualpa intended to call for their meeting *outside* Cajamarca, they would have to cancel their entrapment plan. There could be no question of contending with Atahualpa's entire army on the open plain. Thinking quickly, Pizarro sent a messenger who had learned some Quechua to urge Atahualpa to come to his quarters in Cajamarca before nightfall for he had prepared a feast for their meeting.[14]

In what was a most fateful decision, Atahualpa agreed. Sending a messenger to Pizarro, he apologized, according to the chronicler Pedro de Cieza de León, saying:

---

[11] "Letter of Hernando Pizarro To the Royal Audience of Santo Domingo," in Markham, *Reports on the Discovery of Peru*, 116-117.

[12] Betanzos, *Narrative of the Incas*, 262. Helps identifies the *curaca* Maycabilica as the one who reported to Atahualpa that the Spaniards were "no great warriors." Arthur Helps, *The Spanish Conquest in America and Its Relation to the History of Slavery and to the Government of Colonies*, ed. Michael Oppenheim, vol. 3 (New York: John Lane, 1902), 360.

[13] "Letter of Hernando [...]" in Markham, *Reports on the Discovery of Peru*, 116.

[14] Ibid., 117.

> He would have already come to see him, but he could not
> convince his people because they had such great fear of the
> horses and dogs, and this fear became deeper seeing them at
> closer range. Therefore, he begged him—if he wished to meet
> him—to order that the horses and dogs be firmly tied and that
> the Christians should all hide, some in one place and others in
> another, so that none would appear while they conversed
> together, and thus his people would lose the great fear they
> felt. [15]

The historian Antonio de Herrera offered a close paraphrase of Cieza de
León's account:

> He would have arrived much earlier but had been retarded by
> the great dread his people entertained of the horses and dogs,
> and there he entreated him, as a mark of his complaisance, to
> order that these animals should be tied up, and the people
> confined within their lodgings, that when he should reach
> Cajamarca his Peruvians might not be alarmed, since the nearer
> he approached the city, the more fear they exhibited. [16]

Thus, Atahualpa's plan was as deceptive as Pizarro's. He asked
Pizarro to tie up his horses and dogs and sequester his men, while he
entered Cajamarca with an entourage disguised in full ceremonial regalia
accompanied by high-ranking chiefs, musicians and servants. Included
among them was a security detachment of several thousand men equipped
with concealed arms. [17] Hemming softens it, saying that Atahualpa "left
most of the armed men outside on the plain, 'but brought with him five or
six thousand men, unarmed except that they carried small battle-axes,
slings and pouches of stones underneath their tunics.'" [18]

---

[15] Pedro de Cieza de León, *The Discovery and Conquest of Peru,* ed. and trans.
Alexandra Parma Cook and Noble David Cook (Durham: Duke University Press,
1998), 206-07.

[16] As quoted in Manuel José Quintana, *Lives of Vasco Nunez de Balboa and Francisco
Pizarro,* trans. Margaret Hodson (Edinburgh: William Blackwood, 1832; repr.,
Kessinger, 2010), 182n. As a general rule, Spanish historians have omitted mention
of war dogs from their accounts, although they are included in many paintings of battle
scenes. It was common practice for conquistadors to include them in their forces.
Atahualpa's specific mention of them confirms their presence with Pizarro at
Cajamarca and indicates the Indians' great concern.

[17] Olivares, *Ñusta,* 21. Quispe Sisa says that "in any situation where the Inca himself
was to be involved, the army should be 5,000 to 7,000 strong."

[18] Hemming, *Conquest of the Incas*, 39.

While the majority of his army remained outside the plaza, his security detachment that entered into it was armed. The Incan inventory of bronze-age weapons consisted entirely of axes, slings, knives, spears, clubs, and *ayllos*, which were Incan bolas. In other words, Atahualpa's security guard entered Cajamarca armed with nearly the standard Incan weapons complement concealed under their tunics.[19] In delaying his entry until close to sunset Atahualpa was acting on faulty intelligence from Ciquinchara, who claimed that the horses were "powerless at night without their saddles."[20]

Atahualpa's security detail was clad in a distinctive uniform—a tunic with a black and white checkered vest over a red undergarment. High-ranking chiefs were decked out in bright blue livery, with gold and silver headdresses, while Atahualpa himself was bedecked with the dark crimson headband called a *borla* denoting him as the supreme leader. All of the nobles were festooned with gold and silver ornamentation. Brightly colored bird feathers and jewels, mainly emeralds, completed their outfits. Atahualpa was carried by numerous men on a litter elaborately decorated with silver and gold leaf on which he sat, as on a throne.

Atahualpa's extravagant entourage, accompanied by sweepers clearing the path ahead, drummers establishing a cadence for the marchers, and singers chanting Incan songs, preceded him into the plaza opening a path for his uncovered litter to occupy center stage. The entire proceeding gave every indication that he had come for a negotiation involving a celebration, not a battle, but that impression quickly changed. Atahualpa stood up on his litter and, looking out over the square filled with his men, but no Spaniards, called out: "Where are they?"[21]

At this, Pizarro sent Friar Vincente de Valverde out to greet Atahualpa. He approached the Inca holding a cross and a breviary accompanied by the interpreter Felipillo. He first invited Atahualpa to enter into the barracks where he said Pizarro was awaiting him, but the Inca declined. Then he recited a somewhat bowdlerized presentation of the

---

[19] Later, enemies of Pizarro, like Oviedo and las Casas, would charge that he carried out a massacre of innocent and completely unarmed natives.

[20] George Kubler, "The Behavior of Atahualpa, 1531-1533," *Hispanic American Historical Review* 25, no. 4 (November 1945):420.

[21] Hemming, *Conquest of the Incas,* 39-40.

Requerimiento, the ultimatum required by the Crown to be read prior to a resort to bloodshed.[22] With Felipillo attempting to translate, he laid out the Christian cosmology: belief in God as creator, with Jesus Christ as part of a trilogy; the pope as intermediary between god and man; the king as the pope's representative; and Pizarro as the king's emissary. He, Atahualpa, must agree to this hierarchy and become a tributary, or face the wrath of God as delivered by Pizarro.

Atahualpa responded to Valverde with the argument that his god, the sun, was better, alive and with him every day. He asked on what authority he spoke, and Valverde pointed to the breviary he was holding. He handed it to Atahualpa, who fumbled with it before managing to open it. He looked at the words on the page, which meant nothing to him, and then held the book up to his ear and said: "this is silent, it tells me nothing" and threw the book to the ground.[23] As the interpreter scrambled to recover the breviary, Atahualpa stood up on his litter and told his men to "prepare themselves for battle."[24] Then he addressed Valverde: "Tell your comrades that they shall give me an accounting of their doings in my land. I will not go from here till they have made me full satisfaction for all the wrongs they have committed."[25]

The Capture and Cooptation of Atahualpa

The moment had arrived. With Valverde stumbling back to Pizarro demanding that he act, the governor took out his white scarf and waived it to Candia, the signal to commence fire from the fortress heights and to slam shut the two gates to the plaza, trapping all inside. Within seconds, the trumpeters sounded the call and Candia fired off several volleys from his cannon, muskets, and crossbows. The boom and smoke from his guns shocked the Incan troops as they saw men mysteriously

---

[22] Hemming, *Conquest of the Incas*, 40 says Martinello accompanied Valverde. Prescott; von Hagen, *Conquest of Peru*, 250, and Helps, *Spanish Conquest in America*, 3:369, say it was Felipillo.

[23] William Mavor, *The History of the Discovery and Settlement to the Present Time of North and South America and of the West Indies* (London: Richard Phillips, 1806), 155.

[24] MacQuarrie, *Last Days of the Incas*, 81.

[25] Prescott; von Hagen, *Conquest of Peru*, 251.

falling to the ground injured or killed by what to them were invisible weapons.

Immediately following the initial barrage of gunfire, Pizarro unleashed his cavalry. Horses fitted with silver rattles to give them a more menacing aspect, their riders armed with spears and swords, they charged into the crowded mass of Atahualpa's men shouting "Santiago, Santiago," the traditional Spanish battle cry, stunning them into inaction. They were too cramped to use their slings and bolas because the Spaniards, nearly invulnerable in their chain mail and helmets, were into them very quickly, slashing and cutting through their padded cotton protection, while their steeds kicked and pawed them front and back, trampling all who fell in a stunning display of skill and savagery.

Pizarro, with a few of his men, headed quickly for the litter where Atahualpa's bearers were attempting to keep him aloft, even as they were being slashed and mutilated by the horse riders. Atahualpa seemed mesmerized by the display of Spanish power, perhaps still feeling the effects of the previous night's *chicha* binge. Shouting "take him alive" Pizarro grabbed Atahualpa's arm before he realized what was happening. He pulled him from his litter, receiving a small cut from one of his own men in the process, and dragged him to the safety of one of the barracks.

As the cavalry charged into Atahualpa's men, those who could attempted to flee, heading for a part of the walled enclosure that was slightly lower than the rest. As they surged against it, the upper portion gave way, allowing many to scramble over it into the plain. But there was no escape from the carnage as Pizarro's horsemen accompanied by war dogs pursued them onto the plain, chasing them down, gnashing, slashing, spearing, trampling. At the same time, after the first volley of cannon, muskets, and crossbows, Candia trained subsequent fire on the area outside the gates to prevent Atahualpa's army from coming to his rescue.

In less than two hours, as darkness fell, the Spaniards had slain some two thousand of the men who had entered into the compound and captured Atahualpa himself.[26] Amazingly, when Pizarro's horsemen rode out onto the plain where the main army was encamped they fled in panic

---

[26] Prescott; von Hagen, *Conquest of Peru*, 253, says "it did not much exceed half an hour." Hemming, *Conquest of the Incas*, 43, says "two hours."

or were captured. This may have been because, as Kubler noted, "Atahualpa…was attended at Cajamarca only by raw recruits," not his main forces, which were away on the march.[27] When Pizarro signaled for the trumpets to call for their return, his men brought back into the compound some three thousand prisoners, many of whom he immediately put to work clearing and cleaning up the plaza. The Spaniards had suffered not a single casualty.

While the cleanup was going on in the plaza, Pizarro sat down with his prisoner. After providing him with a change of clothes, the governor invited his captive to join him for dinner. Over their meal, the governor attempted to portray himself as a great, but just conqueror. He explained that "in every country to which we Christians had come there had been great rulers and we had made them our friends and vassals of the Emperor by peaceful means or by war." His aim was not to kill him but to befriend him. Relieved, Atahualpa asked to speak with some of his officers, who confirmed the worst. He then sent them to those who were still encamped outside Cajamarca to tell them that he was still alive but a prisoner and that all should cooperate with the Christians.[28]

Pizarro asked Atahualpa why he had "walked into such an obvious trap?" He replied that "he had intended to capture the Governor…take and breed the horses and mares, which were the thing he admired most." He would have sacrificed some of the men and castrated others for service in his household. But he had miscalculated. He "could not conceive that with the odds so completely in his favor the Spaniards would be the first to attack…before he had even held his meeting with Governor Pizarro."[29] After dinner, they retired. Both men spent the night sleeping in the same room, but obviously dreaming very different dreams.

When the smoke cleared the next morning, November 17, Pizarro realized that he had done what he had set out to do in capturing Atahualpa, but he was himself surrounded by his captive's armies. The first perplexing question was: how would Atahualpa's generals react? Now that they knew he was alive, would they marshal forces in an attempt to rescue

[27] Kubler, "The Behavior of Atahualpa, 1531-1533," 417.
[28] Hemming, *Conquest of the Incas,* 44-45.
[29] Ibid., 45.

their leader? Would they fall into disarray? Would they subordinate themselves to the Spaniards? To get an answer Pizarro sent de Soto with thirty horsemen to the encampment where the army was still bivouacked. Upon arriving, it was evident to de Soto that the troops were tense, but completely passive, many giving the prearranged signal of the sign of the cross to indicate their submission. Still, the concern that Atahualpa's forces would attack would be a constant worry.

De Soto ransacked the encampment, accumulating a horde of gold and silverware, mostly Atahualpa's table service; along with over a dozen precious jewels. In all, the estimated worth, according to Xeres, was "eighty thousand pesos, seven thousand marcs of silver, and fourteen emeralds."[30] He returned to Cajamarca "with a troop of men, women, sheep [llamas], gold, silver, and cloth," presenting Pizarro with an enormous logistical problem, notwithstanding the joyous welcome of great wealth. The llamas were so numerous that they "encumbered the camp," making movement difficult if defense against attack were required. The additional men and women had to be housed and fed.

Pizarro's solution was to release the llamas into the countryside, on the assumption that the Christians could kill as many as needed for sustenance. As for the Indians, he parceled out some for service with his men, and released the vast majority to return to their home provinces unharmed. This last was a stroke of genius because these people spread the word throughout the empire that the Christians had come to liberate them from the Inca. As the governor put it: "they should not desire to be like those Indians, in their cruelties and sacrifices, which they perpetrate on those they capture in war. Those who died in battle were more than enough."[31]

Over the next several days Atahualpa slipped into what might be called depression over the fact of his confinement, refusing to eat and overindulging in *chicha*. Quispe Sisa and Pizarro visited him several times, attempting to restore his sense of well-being. Determined to treat him with all due respect, Pizarro transferred him to separate quarters where he was free to move about in a form of house arrest. He was also allowed

---

[30] Xeres in Markham, *Reports on the Discovery of Peru*, 59.
[31] Ibid., 59-60.

to have some of his serving women and wives to attend him, and to meet daily with visitors, even his officers. Stirling avers that it was during one of Quispe Sisa's visits that "he gave her as a gift to Pizarro," but if Quispe Sisa was already Pizarro's "woman" (as in Olivares), this would only have been a formality sanctioning an existing situation.[32]

Pizarro knew from the beginning that the civil war had split the regime into two broad factions centered around Atahualpa and Huáscar who represented Quito in the north and Cusco in the south, respectively. Atahualpa had won the war, but his victory had been short-lived. When Pizarro seized Atahualpa, he had delivered a crippling blow to a regime already staggering to its knees, as the Quitan leader was in the process of physically exterminating the entire Cuscoan elite class. Even as a prisoner Atahualpa continued his efforts to eliminate as many members of the Cusco royal family as he could.[33]

The evisceration of the ruling class encouraged the regime's many vassals and tributaries to free themselves from Incan rule. Many simply ceased to obey the commands of what remained of the Incan infrastructure in the provinces, as their enforcement power withered. Others, like the Cañari and Huanca peoples, sought to ally with the Spanish conquerors. From tribal leaders who had come to pay homage to him, Pizarro had learned that Huáscar was alive, nearby, and Atahualpa's prisoner. He commanded that Huáscar be brought to him, something whose

---

[32] Stirling, *Pizarro*, 45, says that Quispe Sisa was only twelve years old, yet acknowledges that "Pizarro installed her in the chamber that served for his lodging, facing the central square of the town. Several witnesses attest to the affection he showed the young girl, whom he openly called his 'woman', giving her the nickname 'Pizpita', the name of an Extremaduran songbird because of her liveliness." It is highly unlikely that Pizarro would have called a twelve-year-old his woman, with all of its sexual implications. Peruvian historian Raúl Porras Barrenechea, cited in Rafael Varón Gabai, *Francisco Pizarro and His Brothers, The Illusion of Power in Sixteenth-Century Peru*, trans. Javier Flores Espinoza (Norman: University of Oklahoma Press, 1997), 182, says that she probably was eighteen years old. In Olivares, *Ñusta, 59,* Quispe Sisa says she was twenty-five years old when she met Pizarro in Tumbes in 1528; she would have been about thirty years of age, and Pizarro's mistress for five years, at the end of 1532.
[33] Hemming, *Conquest of the Incas,* 54, describes how Atahualpa sent men to assassinate two half-brothers, Huaman Titu and Mayta Yupanqui on their way to Cusco.

implications alarmed Atahualpa. At first, Atahualpa said that Huáscar was dead, but then admitted that he was still alive and that he would send word to bring him to Cajamarca. [34]

The danger to Atahualpa lay in the fact that Huáscar's power base was in the south, the capital of the empire. Even though Atahualpa's armies had conquered Huáscar's, his generals Chalcuchima and Quiz Quiz were commanding occupation forces in the key cities of Jauja and Cusco and garrison forces in Vilcashuamán and Bombón. They were not welcome by the southerners and could maintain stability only by means of a harsh military presence. Atahualpa realized that Pizarro would see Huáscar as a better choice to undertake the liberation of Cusco than himself, a hated Quitan.

Atahualpa decided on a bold, clever, and risky scheme to make Pizarro the instrument of his own deliverance while also weakening the Cuscoan faction in the south: he offered to ransom himself. In Olivares, Quispe Sisa claims the idea was hers, and that she suggested it to both men.[35] The plan was based on the Spaniards' overwhelming desire to acquire gold and silver, metals which held only religious and symbolic significance for the Inca, but which were prized as a source of wealth by the Spaniards. Atahualpa proposed that in return for his freedom he would provide Pizarro with enormous wealth, enough to fill three large rooms, one with gold and two with silver. As a result of this bargain, Pizarro would free Atahualpa to return to Quito to rule in peace, while he went on to conquer Cusco and the rest of Peru. Pizarro agreed, having a notary write up the contract, which both leaders initialed.[36]

Atahualpa declared that he could fulfill his ransom promise within two months, but it shortly became evident that the distances and the problem of transport meant that it would take much longer. Cusco alone was nearly twelve hundred miles from Cajamarca and lay at the center of the empire, high in the mountains. Thus, he suggested that Pizarro send men to Cusco, the capital and location of the great treasure house of

---

[34] Stirling, *Pizarro*, 46.
[35] Olivares, *Ñusta*, 30.
[36] Hemming, *Conquest of the Incas,* 48 and MacQuarrie, *Last Days of the Incas*, 97-99.

Coricancha, to oversee the project. He would provide safe conduct for them. Pizarro promptly sent three of his men to Cusco; but he was perhaps unaware that in directing him to strip Cusco of its treasure, Atahualpa was enlisting the Spaniard in weakening his adversary's southern base. Atahualpa specifically enjoined Quiz Quiz, his general in Cusco, to prevent the Spaniards from desecrating the tomb and properties of Huayna Cápac.

Meanwhile, Huáscar had heard of the ransom deal and sent word to Pizarro that he would double any amount that Atahualpa promised. Huáscar's message offered to make Pizarro the beneficiary of a bidding war from which he would benefit greatly, but it was anathema to Atahualpa, who learned of it. To avoid any possibility of losing out, Atahualpa sent word to Chalcuchima to kill Huáscar, and leave no trace. The order was carried out by drowning Huáscar in a river near Andamarca, en route to Cajamarca.[37]

When word reached Pizarro that Huáscar had been killed, he confronted Atahualpa, the obvious culprit, who, however, denied any involvement and lamented his brother's death. The governor was dubious. Nevertheless, with Huáscar's death Atahualpa had preserved his position as Inca—but perhaps unwittingly signed his own death warrant. With Atahualpa still alive and presumably free once he paid the ransom, Pizarro would be faced with a potential threat from Atahualpa yet be linked to him. He could only march south as a conqueror, not a liberator, but it would be some months until he came to that realization.

The Arrival of Diego de Almagro

Meanwhile, in late December 1532, the long-awaited Diego de Almagro had reached the port settlement of San Miguel de Piura with three ships, one hundred and fifty-three men, fifty horses and ample provisions. Along with him, however, came rumors that his aim was to mount his own conquest of Quito, not to reinforce Pizarro. This news prompted the governor to send back an appeal to avert a breach. As Prescott put it: Pizarro said that "whatever might have been Almagro's original purpose…the richness of the vein he had now opened in the land would be

---

[37] Cieza de León, *Discovery and Conquest of Peru*, 225-26.

certain to secure his cooperation in working it."[38] According to Cieza de
León, Pizarro also informed Almagro "about how they had imprisoned
Atahualpa, from whom they expected great treasures, and that he should
come quickly because *they would all get portions of it.*"[39] Hoping to
convince Almagro, Pizarro misled him into believing that he and his men
would share in the treasure.

Pizarro was under no illusions about Almagro's aspirations, nor
that he now had the power to pursue them. To set the stage for what he
hoped would be an amicable resolution of their differences, he decided to
get his half-brothers out of the way so he could deal with Almagro one-
on-one. The governor told Hernando, Gonzalo, and Juan that he wanted to
investigate the constantly swirling rumors that Incan armies were
mobilizing for attack; and in early January 1533, he sent them with a small
contingent of horsemen to reconnoiter Huamachuco, Atahualpa's earlier
encampment and staging ground. When he arrived, Hernando was
received warmly by the natives there and found no signs of hostility.

Before he left, however, Pizarro sent him additional instructions
to proceed to the temple complex of Pachacamac, some five hundred miles
south from Huamachuco, but located along the coast. Reportedly, the
complex was the repository of great wealth.[40] Pizarro was already alert to
the growing problem of natives making off with and/or hiding treasure in
the absence of any authority to stop them. Indeed, when Hernando reached
Pachacamac and "asked for the gold...they denied it to me, saying that
they had none. I made some search, but could not find it."[41]

While Hernando was still in Pachacamac, in early February,
Pizarro sent new instructions to his brother, telling him to return, but to go
by way of Jauja, a major city situated on the Inca High Road between
Camajarca and Cusco.[42] He was ordered to find and bring back
Atahualpa's top general, Chalcuchima, who was maintaining an
occupation force there.[43] When he arrived initial attempts to persuade the

---

[38] Prescott; von Hagen, *Conquest of Peru,* 277.
[39] Cieza de León, *Discovery and Conquest of Peru*, 221, emphasis added.
[40] Prescott; von Hagen, *Conquest of Peru,* 264-65.
[41] "Letter of Hernando [...]," in Markham, *Reports on the Discovery of Peru,* 123.
[42] Astete, in Markham, *Reports on the Discovery of Peru,* 84.
[43] "Letter of Hernando [...]," in Markham, *Reports on the Discovery of Peru,* 124.

general got nowhere, but inexplicably and abruptly he decided to accompany Hernando back to Cajamarca. (It turned out that Atahualpa had secretly sent him a message to come to him, so it would appear that Chalcuchima's initial reticence was either a charade, or Atahualpa's message had not yet arrived.)[44] Whether Pizarro was truly concerned with issues of a possible native uprising, or securing gold, the fact was that Hernando and his brothers would be away from Cajamarca for nearly four months, and Almagro would return before they did.

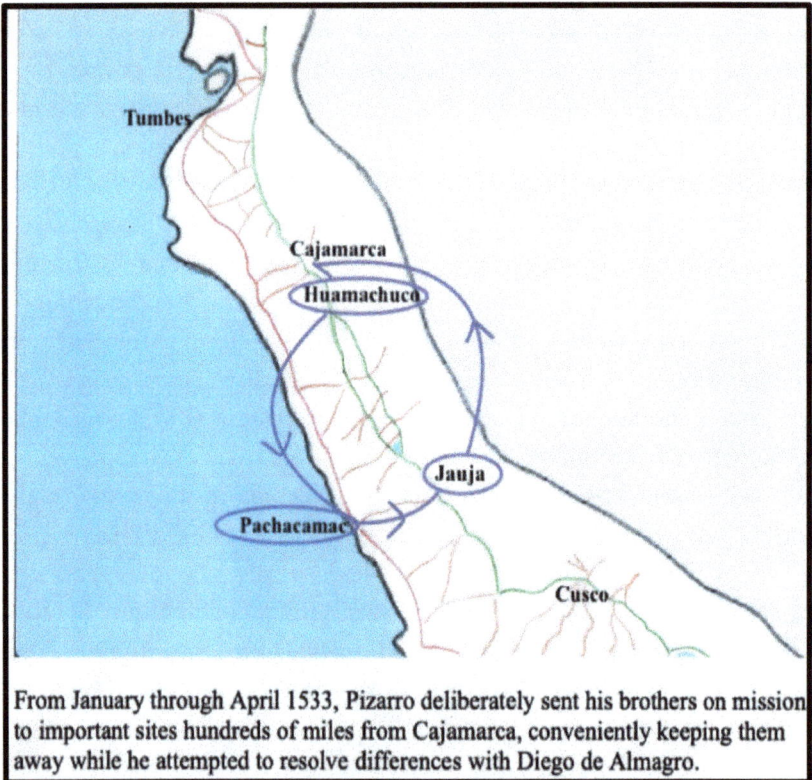

From January through April 1533, Pizarro deliberately sent his brothers on mission to important sites hundreds of miles from Cajamarca, conveniently keeping them away while he attempted to resolve differences with Diego de Almagro.

5.2. Pizarro diverts his brothers

---

[44] Cieza de León, *Discovery and Conquest of Peru*, 231. Hemming, *Conquest of the Incas*, 67-68, thought Chalcuchima had been "deluded by Hernando Pizarro's 'sweet talk'" and had made a "tragic mistake." Betanzos, *Narrative of the Incas*, 272, claims that Hernando had simply "found Chalcuchima drunk and captured him."

It is not clear when Almagro arrived in Cajamarca. Some sources, like Prescott and Kochis, say he arrived in mid-February 1533, while most others, including Xeres, Stirling, and MacQuarrie, say he arrived in mid-April.[45] There is no doubt that he arrived before Hernando and his brothers returned at the end of that month, giving Pizarro enough time to sort out the issue of how the ransom spoils would be divided. If Almagro expected his agreement with Pizarro on equal sharing of treasure to be applied here (their third original partner, Fr. Luque, had died the year before), he would be sorely disappointed. Pizarro told him that only those who had actually participated in the seizure of Atahualpa, the "men of Cajamarca," would receive a share of the ransom.

Almagro was justifiably outraged, having financed and provided a large portion of the men, horses, ships, and equipment for the expedition. After long and rancorous argument, Pizarro agreed to offer his old partner a one-time payment of 100,000 gold pesos off the top of the accumulating treasure, as a sort of quitclaim against it. That settled the matter for the moment, but the continuing arrival of caravans bearing loads of treasure in the form of articles made of gold and silver, as well as jewels, intensified the hardening division between Pizarrists and Almagrists, as the former's "share" continued to grow while the latter's remained fixed. Of course, a fair outcome would have been for Pizarro to cap his side of the ransom at the point when the three rooms were full; and after that, share all additional treasure equally, but that is not what he did.

The antagonism between the two camps only grew when Hernando, Gonzalo, and Juan Pizarro returned to Cajamarca with Chalcuchima in tow. Indeed, upon arrival when the two leaders went out to greet them, Hernando pointedly rode past Almagro's outstretched hand of welcome, ignoring it to move to his brother's side. Their hostility did not lessen after Pizarro entreated his brother to apologize to Almagro and

---

[45] Prescott; von Hagen, *Conquest of Peru*, 278; Paul M. Kochis, *God, Glory and Gold: Journey to the Conquest of the Incas*, vol. 2, *The Quest* (Minneapolis: Mill City Press, 2013), 358; Xeres, in Markham, *Reports on the Discovery of Peru*, 73; Stirling, *Pizarro*, 48; MacQuarrie, *Last Days of the Incas*, 121.

signified how prescient Pizarro had been to send his brothers away before Almagro arrived.[46]

Not only did the antagonism between the two Spanish factions continue to grow and fester, the relationship between them and Atahualpa also changed, due primarily to Pizarro's sleight of hand that revealed an ulterior motive. As the gold and silver articles—vases, goblets, and figurines—began to accumulate in the treasure rooms, particularly after the arrival of a large shipment on January 20, 1533, it seemed that the chambers would be filled quickly. But Pizarro decided to melt down the many large and unwieldy objects into ten-pound bars or ingots, creating more space for more treasure.

Atahualpa thought this deceitful, demanding: "why do you do that?" but Pizarro remained firm in his decision.[47] He ordered the construction of at least half a dozen furnaces, which began melting down the items of silver in early March. (They would not begin the gold melt until May 3.)[48] Distribution of the wealth began in mid-June, a convenient distraction from the more urgent issues under consideration. It may well have been this decision by Pizarro that convinced Atahualpa that the Spaniards would never set him free and that his only way out was by rescue. His reappraisal would be further justified if he also knew that Almagro was soon to arrive with a large force, meaning that the Spanish were there to stay. This may have been the reason he sent his message to Chalcuchima in early February to come to Cajamarca.

The treasure caravans coming to Cajamarca were equaled by the visits of many tribal leaders—*curacas*, *caciques*, tribal headmen—who came to pay homage, offer allegiance, and observe the power of the Spaniards. These men also provided Pizarro with an unparalleled look into the inner workings of the Incan Empire—its politics, military strength, economic system, and culture. Perhaps the most important revelation Pizarro obtained from this intelligence bonanza was that serious questions were being raised about "the legitimacy of Atahualpa's claim to the

---

[46] Reuben Silverman (online), "A Kingdom Set Aflame: Diego De Almagro and the Struggle for Spanish Peru," December 26, 2013, pt. 4, "Almagro at Cajamarca." reubensilverman.wordpress.com.
[47] Hemming, *Conquest of the Incas*, 55.
[48] Astete, in Markham, *Reports on the Discovery of Peru*, 94-95.

Incaship."[49] That, in turn, made him begin to realize that his original idea of seizing Atahualpa and ruling the empire through him was not only too simplistic, but also wrong.

Despite Atahualpa's claims that "in the entire realm…men always fulfilled what he commanded; moreover, not even the leaves on trees moved without his consent," the truth was otherwise.[50] Although he, the Quiteño, had defeated Huáscar, the Cuscoan, in the civil war, factional strife continued. The fact that Atahualpa was forced to maintain large occupation armies in Jauja and Cusco and smaller garrison forces at Vilcashuamán and Bombón were proof enough the people were opposed to the northerners. And Pizarro's conquest of Peru would not be complete until he had captured the Capital at Cusco. This meant that if Pizarro intended to rule Peru through a puppet Inca, Atahualpa was not the man for the job.

The Problem of Atahualpa

All spring and summer while the caravans kept arriving with boundless treasure, Pizarro began receiving numerous reports of plans to rescue Atahualpa by force. This was not surprising, as the Spaniards were constantly on alert for attacks, but it led to heightened vigilance. Whether Atahualpa realized that he would never be freed, regardless of Pizarro's protestations that he would honor their bargain, and had ordered an attack, or not, the nearly constant rumors of Atahualpa's armies coming to rescue their leader offered Pizarro an opportunity to resolve the Atahualpa problem.

The threats seemed real enough. The *curaca* of Cajamarca, for example, had told Pizarro that Atahualpa had sent orders to Ruminavi in Quito to attack and free him. Such reports were taken seriously, and the governor ordered that records be kept, and their veracity vetted with "leading nobles and Indian women." Even an uncle of Atahualpa was consulted. All claimed that the reports were "all true," even to the details of where to place grain to feed the arriving army. Pizarro confronted

---

[49] Kubler, "The Behavior of Atahualpa, 1531-1533," 424.
[50] Cieza de León, *Discovery and Conquest of Peru,* 254.

Atahualpa about it, which he vehemently denied, challenging the governor to "find out whether it is true."[51] But the truth was elusive.

Constant rumors of impending attack formed the backdrop of the debate among the leadership regarding plans to continue the conquest. The debate centered on what to do about Atahualpa. Almagro, the Crown's accountant Alonso Riquelme, and Friar Valverde argued for killing him. They said that releasing him was unthinkable and dangerous, for he would attack as soon as he could. They further argued that to take him along as captive would be equally problematic as it would only open up opportunity for attacks along the way to free him. Almagro had the additional argument that as long as Atahualpa lived, and treasure kept arriving, that wealth would be considered part of the ransom payment, which would be denied to him. He and his followers wanted to march on Cusco, their *El Dorado*, and begin to obtain their own source of wealth.

On the other side of the argument, Hernando Pizarro and Hernando de Soto, in particular, argued for keeping Atahualpa alive and honoring their bargain. So, obviously, did his sister, Quispe Sisa. Pizarro's captains believed that his original plan of ruling Peru through Atahualpa was still sound and believed that as long as they held him they could marshal support from local chiefs. It was also true that both men had spent a considerable amount of time with the Inca over the previous several months and had come to like and respect him, and, perhaps, be influenced by him. Pizarro stood apart from the debate, leaving the impression, as Hemming notes, that he "wanted to keep him alive."[52] But the governor played his cards close to his chest.

In truth, Pizarro had come to realize that in the coming march on Cusco, Atahualpa was no longer an asset, but a liability—and, that he, Pizarro, was on the wrong side in the continuing north-south factional struggle. Privately, he agreed with Almagro, Riquelme, and Valverde that it was dangerous either to release the Inca prisoner or take him along. Marching south to Cusco with Atahualpa at his side would make it difficult to gain allies, as the local people would see him as a conqueror on the side of the Quiteños and decline to provide the help they would need. Indeed,

---

[51] Hemming, *Conquest of the Incas,* 74-75.
[52] Ibid., 76.

the drive south involving several months of travel would absolutely require the assistance of the people to succeed, making a change in his political relationship with them mandatory.

Moreover, there was no time for procrastination. Atahualpa, having delivered over a million pesos of gold and twice that of silver, was demanding his release as part of their bargain. Pizarro agreed in writing that he had satisfied his side of the bargain, but he also stipulated that he would have to continue the Inca's detention until additional reinforcements had arrived. Thus, Pizarro's quandary. It was he who had welched on the bargain with Atahualpa, yet to honor it would be to his peril. His way out was to decide secretly to discard the agreement.[53]

To make the needed pirouette, Pizarro had to find some justification for killing the Inca, locate a Huáscar relative to install in his place, and march south as a liberator not a conqueror *against* the forces of Atahualpa. As Quintana noted, his decision "was at first kept secret, and in the meantime, as some apology for the deed, and to render it less hateful, reports were raised of seditions, of movements among the Indians, and of the projects of their generals to save the prisoner."[54] Finding a replacement was much easier. It just so happened that Huáscar's younger brother, Túpac Huallpa, was hiding out in Pizarro's own rooms. He had come to Pizarro seeking protection from Atahaulpa's murderous proclivity and the governor had safely secreted him in his palace quarters.[55]

The problem for Pizarro was ridding himself of Atahualpa without also alienating his main allies—his brother Hernando, de Soto, and his mistress and Atahualpa's sister, Quispe Sisa. It would be no easy task. To accomplish it, Pizarro adopted the same maneuver that he had used to clear the decks for the negotiation with Almagro. He would move his main allies out of the way before he dealt with Atahualpa.

First, in mid-June 1533, he sent Hernando to Spain with dual purpose. His declared mission was to accompany the royal fifth for delivery to the Crown, report on progress to date, and request certain

---

[53] Prescott; von Hagen, *Conquest of Peru*, 284-85 and Helps, *The Spanish Conquest in America*, 3:392-93.
[54] Quintana, *Lives of Balboa and Pizarro*, 205.
[55] Hemming, *Conquest of the Incas*, 54.

additional grants. He also instructed Hernando to request that the king allot land and a governorship to Almagro beyond that already marked out for Pizarro. Sending Hernando back a few days before the distribution of wealth began suggested that *timing* was the deciding factor, as it removed him from any role in the difficult decision to be made about Atahualpa.[56]

Pizarro also permitted Hernando to take sixty of his men to Spain with him, which suggested that he was not overly concerned about an attack.[57] The attack scare was useful, however, in another way. As reports increased in volume and intensity, Pizarro repeatedly questioned Atahaulpa and tortured his general, Chalcuchima, who denied everything. Cieza claimed that these reports stemmed from the translator Felipillo, who, caught sexually assaulting one of Atahualpa's wives, sought to do him in by manufacturing false troop reports.[58] That Felipillo feared and resented Atahualpa was true enough, but the argument that he somehow controlled the flow of information getting to Pizarro is implausible. By this time, there were several natives in Pizarro's camp who had picked up enough Spanish, in addition to Quispe Sisa and some of her *yanaconas*, and enough of his men who had learned some Quechua, that a monopoly over information flow could not be sustained.[59]

Pizarro's approach to Quispe Sisa was a little different, complaining to her that he suspected Atahualpa of planning his liberation and that his troops were growing restive with worry. She could not completely counter the rumors of impending attack, as the men feared being "caught in a trap." Pizarro told her that he had been "forced to promise his troops that the Inca would be brought to trial…to see if he was in fact conspiring to murder the Spaniards."[60] He thus carefully prepared Quispe Sisa for a trial of her brother, which he claimed was out of his hands because it impacted on the loyalty of the troops.

---

[56] Prescott; von Hagen, *Conquest of Peru,* 281, opined that Pizarro "thought the present a favorable opportunity to remove his brother from the scene of operations, where his factious spirit more than counterbalanced his eminent services."
[57] Quintana, *Lives of Balboa and Pizarro,* 203, says that Hernando returned to Spain with sixty men.
[58] Cieza de León, *Discovery and Conquest of Peru,* 251-54.
[59] Olivares, *Ñusta,* 34.
[60] Ibid., 35-36.

Finally, Pizarro took the opportunity of the budding crisis to maneuver away Atahualpa's other principal supporter, de Soto, whom he sent out on a several days-long reconnaissance mission to determine whether troops were mobilizing or not. Atahualpa, incidentally, read the signs correctly, lamenting that with his "friends" out of the picture he was sure that "fat man" (Riquelme) and "one eye" (Almagro) would conspire to kill him.[61] Indeed, as later writers would conclude, Pizarro had sent de Soto "off on a wild goose chase."[62] But Atahualpa seems not to have suspected Pizarro of treachery, bequeathing his sons to the governor's care, a bequest that he ignored.

De Soto's absence cleared the remaining impediment to Atahualpa's removal. On the evening of July 26, 1533, Pizarro, responding to a handful of panicky reports that troops were marching on Cajamarca, "acceded" to demands from the anti-Atahualpa partisans to hold a trial to determine his guilt or innocence. Less a trial than a Star Chamber proceeding, Pizarro determined that he and Almagro would preside, assigning officers to play the roles of prosecutor, defense lawyer, and jury. A dozen questions were put to Atahualpa, most of which had nothing to do with the main charge of plotting an attack. He was asked: "how many concubines he had," "was Huáscar the rightful heir," "had Atahualpa waged unjust wars," "was Atahualpa an idolater." To Prescott, "these charges were so absurd that they might well provoke a smile" were the matter not so serious.[63]

Acting quickly, indeed, with "chilling speed," Pizarro sentenced Atahaulpa to death for conspiring against the Spaniards and Fra. Valverde affirmed that there had been "ample grounds" for condemnation.[64] His sentence was death by burning unless he converted and became a Christian. Then, he would die by the garrote, which was the death he chose. A dozen of those who attended objected to the verdict on the grounds that Pizarro had no jurisdiction over a foreign king, but he overruled them.[65] Indeed, although Pizarro pleaded that there was nothing

[61] MacQuarrie, *Last Days of the Incas*, 126.

[62] Hemming, *Conquest of the Incas*, 82.

[63] Prescott; von Hagen, *Conquest of Peru*, 288.

[64] Quintana, *Lives of Balboa and Pizarro*, 209.

[65] Astete, in Markham, *Reports on the Discovery of Peru*, 102-03.

he could do once the verdict had been rendered, the truth was that the *Capitulación de Toledo* accorded him plenipotentiary power as governor of Peru, and therefore he could in fact have overturned the verdict had he chose.

Quispe Sisa appealed to Pizarro to spare her brother, to no avail. Pizarro insisted that he could not risk the loyalty of his men by overturning the verdict. After several intense exchanges, she realized that Atahualpa was doomed, so she "gave up and...stepped aside." But she never forgave Pizarro for what she believed was his perfidy. She also claimed that from this point, once she "saw that Atahualpa's situation was futile, [she] decided to become the guardian of the treasure and would not permit the Spaniards...to put their hands on it."[66]

Holding Atahualpa's execution in the middle of Cajamarca plaza that very evening also served Pizarro's purpose of displaying to all in attendance (and who would later spread the news) that he had broken with the northerners. Immediately following his death, he wrote a letter to King Charles on July 29, carefully explaining that "he had been advised that the Inca had 'ordered a mobilization of fighting men to come against [me].'"[67] He had acted, been forced to act, he seemed to say, on bad intelligence, including demands by officers of the Crown.

In fact, as Stirling notes, "Pizarro's motive for ordering the killing of Atahualpa was soon made apparent with his decision to appoint a new emperor to unite the thousands of warriors from Huáscar's defeated armies and from the subject tribes camped in the valley, whom he would need as auxiliaries on his march to Cuzco."[68] Hemming comes to the same conclusion, saying that, "by killing Atahualpa the Spaniards had cast themselves as champions of Huáscar's cause."[69] In truth, Pizarro continued to hew to his strategy of ruling through a puppet emperor—only it was no longer Atahualpa.

---

[66] Olivares, *Ñusta*, 40-41, 25.
[67] Hemming, *Conquest of the Incas*, 80.
[68] Stirling, *Pizarro*, 60.
[69] Hemming, *Conquest of the Incas*, 102.

To Cusco

Pizarro had been in Cajamarca for seven months and now prepared for the march on Cusco, the capital of the empire. His main concern was to reorganize his command to reflect his courtship of the southerners. The first step was to anoint Túpac Huallpa, the young man he had been protecting from Atahualpa, as the new Inca. Túpac Huallpa was the son of Huayna Cápac and younger brother of Huáscar, so he had impeccable credentials. Assembling the many curacas and chiefs in Cajamarca, Pizarro staged the traditional, three-day investiture ceremony, as well as another in which Túpac Huallpa formally submitted his regime to the King of Spain. The chiefs, mostly southerners relieved to be free of northern oppression, welcomed Túpac Huallpa as the ruler next in line of succession. The only jarring note was that Chalcuchima, Atahualpa's general, was included in all of the ceremonies.

Reinforcing this southern orientation, Pizarro now replicated Atahualpa's earlier move in the same direction by taking the dead Inca's principal wife, Cuxirimay, as his mistress. Recall, Atahualpa had earlier taken her as *his* principal wife, even though she was only ten years old, to align himself with Huayna Cápac in order to strengthen his claim to be Inca. However distasteful this may have seemed to some of his men, in retrospect Pizarro's act strengthened his appeal to the Cusco elite. It would have internal repercussions within his household, however.

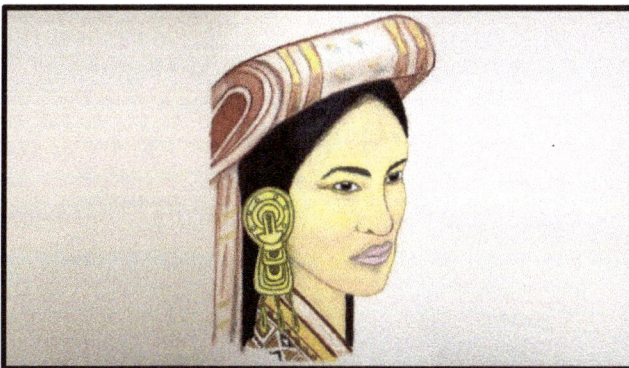

5.3. Cuxirimay Ocllo

Quispe Sisa undoubtedly saw the entry of Cuxirimay into her household not only as a rival for Pizarro's affection, but also as a potential threat to herself. Cuxirimay was a beautiful woman and a descendant of Manco Cápac, the founder of the empire, and thus of higher status than Quispe Sisa.[70] For Quispe, perhaps bearing Pizarro's children was in part a way to strengthen her position within his household, assuaging a concern that Pizarro would eliminate her the way he had eliminated her brother, or in some other way marginalize her to cater to the southerners. (She would give birth to Francisca Pizarro the following summer and to Gonzalo the year after that. As it turned out, the pregnancies only delayed the inevitable, as far as her relationship with Pizarro was concerned. Within three years, the governor would cast Quispe Sisa off, and take up fully with Cuxirimay, who also would bear him two children.)

The march on Cusco would be a major undertaking, the distance to cover being over twelve hundred miles. The cumbersome caravan that set out from Cajamarca on August 11, 1533 stretched out over a mile. In addition to the over three hundred horse and foot soldiers there were: native auxiliaries from the south, Cañari warriors from the north (whom Atahualpa had totally alienated), porters, bearers, herders to manage the flocks of accompanying llamas that served both as beasts of burden and food, women to manage household and cooking duties, men to guard the treasure being brought along from Cajamarca, and those detailed to guard their prisoner, Chalcuchima.

In terms of military strategy, Pizarro had two major concerns. Most importantly, he must avoid entanglement in a two-front conflict, with Ruminavi's army at Quito and Chalcuchima's and Quiz Quiz's armies at Jauja and Cusco, respectively. (Chalcuchima's army was now under the temporary command of Yucra Huallpa.) Secondly, there was the constant problem of possible ambushes at vulnerable places—mountain passes, bridges, narrow gorges, and river crossings—along the route.

---

[70] Jennifer Brooks, *Marriage, Legitimacy, and Intersectional Identities in the Sixteenth Century Spanish Empire* (Macalester College: History Honors Project, Paper 21, 2016), 72, 78. Not only was Cuxirimay of higher status than Quispe Sisa, Pizarro's relationship with her gave him "a higher status among the Inca."

To deal with the two-front problem, Pizarro sent Benalcázar to San Miguel de Piura with a two-fold mission. He was to secure the vital port and the road to the mountains, but he was also to be prepared to intercept and engage Ruminavi's army should it move south. To deal with the ambush problem, Pizarro sent out long-range patrols to scout the route ahead and sought intelligence from friendly local chiefs they encountered. As it turned out the two-front threat would never materialize, as Ruminavi himself would face briefly a two-front threat from Pedro de Alvarado, the governor of Guatemala, who sought to seize Quito for himself and Benalcázar.[71]

It took two months to travel the 680 miles from Cajamarca to Jauja through mostly friendly territory, with only one major incident. Shortly after starting out, Atahualpa's brother, Titu Atauchi attacked the caravan with six thousand men, but was repulsed.[72] After that there were only fleeting sightings of hostile native forces. Moving deliberately and stopping at larger settlements for rest and replenishment for days at a time, Pizarro's initial route took him through the Huaylas Valley where it was warm, stopping at Huamachuco and Andemarca, and then at Recuay where they spent twelve days until mid-September.

From Recuay, the caravan moved upland into the mountains toward Tarma and Bombón, passing through the villages of Chiquian, Cajatambo, and Oyon, which were largely deserted. It was much colder in the mountains and the going was tougher, requiring the company to cross narrow, shaky suspension bridges and to ford rivers that were beginning to flood from thawing mountain snows. The closer they got to Jauja the more evidence they saw of enemy battle preparations, as the Quitan troops pursued a scorched-earth policy. In addition to nearly deserted villages, they found empty storehouses, broken aqueducts, burned bridges, and dead bodies hanging from poles—evidence of Quitan terror and intimidation tactics against the hostile southern population.[73]

Entering the Jauja Valley on October 12, they saw below them, across the Mantaro River that bounded the east side of the settlement, a

---

[71] This story will be discussed in the next chapter.
[72] Astete, in Markham, *Reports on the Discovery of Peru,* 104.
[73] Hemming, *Conquest of the Incas,* 90-91.

large number of soldiers—Chalcuchima's forces, several thousand strong. When the Inca warriors sighted the Spaniards, they began to chant, taunting them to come across, confident they could not as they had burned the bridges. As the Spaniards entered the town, they encountered several hundred warriors attempting to set fire to the thatched roofs of the storehouses in the town, whom they beat off. At this, the inhabitants came out to greet them, thankful for liberation at last from their northern oppressors.

It would be here, at Jauja, where the first large-scale military action since Pizarro had landed in Peru would take place. Almagro's horse cavalry surprised Chalcuchima's forces by fording the river, which had not yet reached its high level with mountain runoff; and charged the Indian squadrons who could not outrun the horses, "pursuing them and killing them for some twelve leagues."[74] Those who managed to escape retreated toward Cusco to join up with Quiz Quiz's forces. Having thus cleared the area, Pizarro decided to make camp and recuperate. He stayed at Jauja for two weeks until October 27.

Jauja was a large town five hundred miles from Cusco, but a vital point on the high mountain road between Quito and Cusco. Pizarro decided to establish Jauja as the Christian capital of Peru and began to construct a fortified town with a town hall, a church, and living quarters for the eighty men and women he left behind to hold it. To give his main force more agility he left the cannon as well as the Cajamarca treasure there and assigned Alonso Riquelme the task of protecting the settlement.

While in Jauja, however, Pizarro suffered a serious blow to his general strategy of ruling through a puppet Inca and his specific plan to gain the support of the southern faction. Túpac Huallpa passed away suddenly and unexpectedly. There was no evidence of foul play in his death, but logic pointed to Chalcuchima, as he had now become a convenient scapegoat responsible for every setback. Of course, the Incan commander denied everything, but Pizarro reinforced his shackles nonetheless, fearing that he would escape to lead his forces against the Spaniards.[75]

---

[74] Stirling, *Pizarro,* 62.
[75] Prescott; von Hagen, *Conquest of Peru,* 303.

In fact, as Pizarro surely realized, the Inca crown was the capstone of the empire and with Túpac Huallpa dead, there was a struggle under way to gain control of it. The Incan Empire had no formal succession mechanism, only a strict custom regarding who could lay a claim to rule. The necessary but not sufficient condition was that a claimant had to be a descendant by blood of Manco Cápac, the founder of the dynasty, and ideally be progeny of a brother-sister marriage. It was also necessary that he have fought his way to the top. Of course, a youthful, inexperienced claimant would need the support of generals, high priests and royal women of the palace, who would engage in a game of high intrigue with no holds barred to promote their respective candidate to the top.

Word came from Quito that Ruminavi was putting forth Atahualpa's brother, Quilliscacha, to replace Túpac Huallpa. And from Cusco, Quiz Quiz put forth one of Huayna Cápac's young sons, Paullu.[76] Promotion of either, of course, would have strengthened the power of Atahualpa's generals who stood behind them. Pizarro resolved to press on with the march to Cusco without naming a new Inca, a decision that sealed Quilliscacha's fate. With no chance of Quilliscacha becoming Inca, Ruminavi sought to rule Quito himself, sending Quilliscacha to his death.

Toward the end of October, the governor began the push to Cusco. He sent de Soto with seventy horsemen out first on a long-range reconnaissance probe to chart the way forward and ascertain the position and strength of the enemy. He was not to venture beyond Vilcashuamán, a junction town some two hundred and fifty miles along the royal road, where a left turn leads directly to Cusco. He was to wait there for Almagro and Pizarro, who departed a few days later; first, Almagro with thirty horsemen, then Pizarro with the foot soldiers and the supply train.

De Soto, traveling fast, met no resistance for five days before catching up to the remnants of Chalcuchima's retreating force at Vilcashuamán. Entering the town at dawn they surprised the inhabitants, mostly women and a few men. The warriors were out hunting and when they learned that the Spaniards had come, they quickly returned to engage them in a two-day fight. The rough terrain gave the Indians the initial advantage, as they manned the heights surrounding the town. In a message

---

[76] Hemming, *Conquest of the Incas,* 96.

to Pizarro for help, de Soto reported that several of his men had been wounded and they had lost one horse, with two others wounded. The Indians had lost over six hundred dead before continuing their retreat to Cusco, but they were learning how best to fight the Spaniards.[77]

De Soto decided to pursue the retreating troops of Chalcuchima and intercept them before they could join up with Quiz Quiz's troops at Cusco. In a message to Pizarro he said that he intended to seize and hold the bridge over the Apurimac River, the last natural obstacle before Cusco. When de Soto's force reached the Apurimac, however, they found the bridge destroyed and were forced to find a safe place where they could ford the river. So, it was not until November 8 that de Soto arrived at the base of the mountain ridge on top of which was the village of Vilcaconga.[78]

This time, Chalcuchima's men would not be taken by surprise. When the bulk of de Soto's men were in mid-ascent, climbing on foot, and some had nearly reached the top of the rise, they were surprised by Chalcuchima's warriors, several thousand strong, who came down on them from the heights. Charging over the hill behind a hail of stones and arrows, they caught the Spaniards by surprise, swarming into them in hand-to-hand combat before they could mount their steeds and get into formation. De Soto tried to maneuver the attackers onto the level ground at the bottom of the defile where his horses would be decisive, but the Indians refused to take the bait.

After hours of battle the two sides withdrew for the night, with the Indians holding the high ground and the Spaniards settling on an adjacent rise nearby. The altitude had tired both men and horses and in the resulting battle the Spaniards had taken unprecedented casualties. They lost five men killed, eleven wounded, and two horses destroyed, with fourteen wounded.[79] Weakened, de Soto feared the worst, expecting an attack at

---

[77] Ibid., 103-04.

[78] Stirling, *Pizarro*, 65, thought de Soto had disobeyed orders in order to be the first to enter Cusco, but the geography—Cusco was two hundred and sixty miles from Vilcashuamán—and the deployment of Indian forces in between makes this a dubious argument. Besides, a few days later, Pizarro sent de Soto along with his half-brother Juan ahead to Cusco to prevent damage by retreating Indians.

[79] Cieza de León, *Discovery and Conquest of Peru,* 290.

dawn, which they would find it difficult to repulse. Debating their options, they decided that they must withdraw to Vilcashuamán and hope to link up with Almagro.

Fortune smiled again on the Spaniards. After midnight, de Soto's men heard the trumpet call of Almagro's fast approaching force, a welcome sound, indeed. The arrival of Almagro's thirty cavalry and ten foot soldiers encouraged both captains to change plans. They now decided to charge the Indians at daylight, but when they advanced the next morning, they found that the Indians had withdrawn, melting toward Cusco. Moving on they decided to stop at the next village, Jaquijahuana, to await Pizarro, who arrived four days later, on November 13.

Two interrelated developments mark Jaquijahuana's place in this history. First, in what was literally a bolt out of the blue, came a young man accompanied by several *orejónes*, and clad in a common yellow tunic. Approaching Pizarro, he told him that he was Prince Manco, one of the many sons of Huayna Cápac and half-brother of Huáscar. He had been on the run evading the assassins of Atahualpa, but now felt safe enough to reemerge to pledge his support against the Quiteños. Pizarro could not believe his eyes or ears. Here was exactly the person he had hoped Túpac Huallpa would have been and he quickly proposed an alliance, which Manco accepted.

Second, Manco also came bearing gifts in the form of evidence incriminating Chalcuchima. He averred that Chalcuchima had been sending messages to Quiz Quiz instructing him on how to fight the Spaniards—what their tactics were and how to counter them. For proof, Manco produced the very messengers whom Chalcuchima had sent, exposing his perfidy. Armed with this information, Pizarro confronted Chalcuchima, who denied everything, but it was no use. Pizarro had had enough, ordering that Atahaualpa's general be burned at the stake that very day.[80]

On November 14, as Pizarro and his men neared the great pass that opens to the capital, they saw arrayed before them on the plain a very large force, numbering over thirty thousand warriors. It was here that Quiz Quiz had decided to make his stand, mistakenly. In the battle that raged

---

[80] Stirling, *Pizarro*, 65.

that day the highly mobile Spanish horse cavalry decimated the Indians. They fought valiantly but unsuccessfully, and were forced to retreat into the city. Pizarro's men camped in the area of the pass, anticipating that the next day would see the final battle in the streets of Cusco.

The next morning, November 15, Pizarro and his men, with Manco at his side, made their way through the pass. In the valley below lay the magnificent Incan capital of Cusco. It was the largest, most impressive city any of them had ever seen. The city, at over eleven thousand feet altitude, was ringed by still higher mountains and sited in the valley between two rivers. At its center were large temples, palaces, plazas, gardens, storehouses, and markets. Thousands of houses surrounded the urban center, supporting a population numbering close to one hundred thousand. Paved, but narrow streets were laid out in orderly fashion, as were aqueduct water and sewer systems. The architecture was mixed with stupendously large, polygonal stone palaces and walls, extensive terracing along the hillsides, and mud brick houses with thatched roofs.[81]

---

[81] For an analysis of the art, architecture and history of Cusco and environs, see Zecharia Sitchin, *The Lost Realms* (New York: Harper, 1990), 120-31.

This 1860 map by E.G. Squier has been overlayed with colors to show some of ancient Cusco's distinct features: its Puma shape with Sacsayhuamán, the temple/fortress complex, as its head; the main plaza, outlined in orange, from where royal roads led to the four segments of the Inca Empire: northeast to Antisuyu, east to Collasuyu, southwest to Contisuyu, and west to Chinchaysuyu; and the two main rivers bordering the city—the Tullumayu on the northern side, and the Saphi on the southern side.

5.4. Layout of Cusco

Pizarro's Fateful Choice

As Pizarro surveyed the majestic scene before him, "some two hundred" local *curacas*, high officials, approached to offer their allegiance.[82] It was not the first time that local elites had welcomed the

---

[82] Stirling, *Pizarro,* 66.

Spaniard as a liberator from the Incan yoke, but this time was different. The appearance of the city's nobles at the gates of Cusco represented a collective plea for freedom, not re-imposition of Incan rule. Here was a genuine opportunity to emulate what Cortés had done in Mexico and build a Spanish colony in Peru based on an alliance of former Incan tributaries and vassals, displacing the Inca entirely. Had Pizarro understood Incan political culture he might have made a different decision. Undoubtedly, he relied heavily upon the advice of his two Incan mistresses, Quispe Sisa and Cuxirimay, who had an interest in maintaining Incan infrastructure, if not hegemony.[83]

Seeing some smoke wafting above the city and fearing that Quiz Quiz intended to torch the city rather than allow the Spaniards to take it, Pizarro sent de Soto and Almagro ahead to attempt to prevent a conflagration. It soon became clear, however, that Quiz Quiz and his men had slipped out of the city under the cover of the morning fog, heading west for the mountains and then north, home to Quito. Pizarro and his men entered the city unopposed and, assembling in the main square, proclaimed victory. Their years-long quest had been completed.

For the next several days, Pizarro allocated temples and palaces to his captains, while allowing his troops to rampage the city, plundering its riches and its women. Pizarro and his men would accumulate more treasure from Cusco than they had garnered in Cajamarca. Their actions resembled the Spanish Sack of Rome just a few years before, in 1527. The nobles stood aside, raising no objection to the pillage because the Spaniards were demolishing the symbols and substance of their oppressors.

But, instead of taking his cue from Cortés and displacing the Inca, Pizarro hewed to his puppet Inca strategy and installed Manco as the new Inca, assuming that he still needed to cultivate the support of the Cuscoan elite.[84] But Pizarro apparently forgot that Atahualpa and his minions had long since eviscerated the Huáscar southern faction in Cusco. The majority

---

[83] Kochis, *God, Glory and Gold,* 2:410-14, discusses their influence and advice.
[84] Michael Wood, *Conquistadors* (London: BBC Books, 2010), 143-44, says "many members of the Inca royal lineages…were prepared to welcome him…. Pizarro, on the other hand, saw the appointment of a puppet king as the best way to normalize Spanish control in Cusco…"

of those who remained were the representatives, hostages really, of vassal states that the Inca had required to maintain a presence in the capital. Cusco, the navel of the world, was the cosmopolitan center of empire to which flowed people, food, clothing, artists, craftsmen, gold, and silver. It was also the repository where the mummies of Incan ancestors were kept. The population consisted of the nobility, representatives of their vassal states, and those who served them.

There was much to be done to pursue and vanquish the remnants of Atahualpa's armies, but the main task Pizarro faced was to make the shift from conqueror to governor of the nation, which may have been why he retained the Inca organization, thinking that he could employ it in governing. But this decision, above all others, would come back to haunt him.

Some perspective is required to understand the magnitude of Pizarro's decision. Geography shaped the structure of the Inca regime. The tribes of the high valley plateaus were separated by nearly impassable mountains. In similar fashion, the coastal tribes were separated by the several dozen rivers and aqueducts that flowed down to the ocean. Arid desert separated them from each other. The result was an atomized population with one tribe separated from the next, each with distinctive history, culture, economy, politics.

The Inca tribe, originating in the region of Lake Titicaca, was "clearly identifiable by their high cheekbones and Asiatic features, in contrast to the flat-nosed and oval-faced coastal Indians whose appearance was more Polynesian."[85] Moreover, they had appeared as a conquering force only within the past century, although they had manufactured a longer history. Their strategy was to concentrate superior force against isolated target tribes, defeat and then integrate them into their growing empire, utilizing the best they had to offer, dispensing with the rest. The empire's main goal thus was to maintain control of an extremely diverse population. The idea of the Incan Empire as a beneficent despotism is well wide of the mark. There is little evidence that compassion played a prominent role in the high-level decision-making process. On the other

---

[85] Stirling, *Pizarro,* 50.

hand, comparison of the Inca political system with contemporary Communist systems has merit.

An extensive road network stretching parallel along the mountains and the coast from Quito to Cusco facilitated their conquest. The road system was not designed to promote commerce but was specifically reserved to insure the rapid movement of troops. It also functioned as a message transmission belt. Rest stops, called *tambos*, stocked with food, clothing, and other necessities dotted the system. Ordinary citizens were prohibited from using the roads without specific authorization, but locals were required to maintain it and keep the rest stops fully stocked as part of a carefully prescribed labor contribution.

Population policy served the same control function. The Inca selected groups of conquered peoples for resettlement to other areas to reduce the likelihood of rebellion. Incan leaders took high ranking women of defeated peoples as their wives or concubines to develop local loyalty. Royalty was defined by bloodline with consanguinity the highest value. Offspring of brother-sister marriages occupied first rank with the purest bloodline. Offspring of an Incan father with a conquered mother was a secondary line of royalty. No other bloodline combination counted, which defined the nature of the Inca system as one in which a narrow political elite ruled over the masses, who had no chance to acquire power.

The Inca created what we would call today a political commissar system of control. They brought selected leaders, *curacas,* to Cusco to educate them in Incan language, culture, and values. Then, they would send them back to their home tribes to administer them. In each conquered tribe they would assign what the Spanish called an *orejón,* distinguished by the gold medallions he wore in his ears, hence the name, which in Spanish means "big-eared." He oversaw the work of the local curaca much as a political commissar does in a communist system. The population was further broken down in decimal fashion from small groups to larger, each managed by a representative of the regime.

Incan language policy served as a further control mechanism. Incan language, Quechua, was taught only to the selected few, not to the many. In effect, it was a secret language of the elite. The reciprocal was that in general no tribe could understand the language of another. The Inca religious policy was designed to serve the same end by incorporating local deities into the Incan pantheon but insisting that the Incan deity of the sun god, Inti, be atop all others.

The Inca thus contrived a political-military hierarchical web that they systematically extended over conquered peoples as a means of control. The problem was that the totalitarian nature of the system produced intense resentment against the Inca. The historical fact that Incan armies were almost constantly at war—either extending their empire or suppressing rebellions within it—is eloquent testimony to the failure of the system. Indeed, as described above, once the last great emperor Huayna Cápac passed from the stage, ironically, just as Pizarro was ascending it, the system began to implode in the civil war over his succession.

When Pizarro strode into the central square of Cusco as the liberator of the Peruvian people, *curaca* after *curaca* offered him their allegiance. But when he put Manco on the throne as the new Inca, he also endorsed and legitimized the continued existence of the Inca organization. Although the system disintegrated temporarily, it would be Manco's ability to revitalize this organization and use it to build a great force of rebellion that would threaten the very existence of Spanish rule in Peru within two years.

Chapter 6

Challenge and Response

Pizarro attempted to stabilize, organize and colonize Peru according to his mandate, but the task proved overwhelming and his approach contradictory. The strategy of attempting to rule Peru through the puppet Inca, Manco, worked so far as the battle between the Inca factions of north and south were concerned. However, the vast majority of the tribes subjugated by the Inca rejected any relations with their former masters and eagerly sided with the Spaniards against them.[1] But Spanish depredations against the population alienated them, leaving them little option but to support the Inca against the Spaniards. The result was that when Manco rebelled against Spanish rule, the formerly opposed subject tribes sustained the rebellion for nearly a year before deserting that cause.

In the end, the Spanish presence in Peru after the conquest was characterized more by battles among the Spanish themselves, than between Spanish and Andean peoples. Pizarro's decisions, aside from enriching himself and those around him, would begin the transformation of Peru from an isolated, totalitarian despotism into an international, market-based regime with all of its good and bad features, as Peru became an integral part of a world system of wealth and commerce. In Spain, it boosted Charles V's dreams of European conquest, and in Europe generally galvanized efforts to defend against and compete with Spain for hegemony.

---

[1] Henry Kamen, *Empire: How Spain Became a World Power, 1492-1763* (New York: Harper Collins, 2003), 113, notes that "Spanish military success was made possible only by the help of native Americans."

Threats—Imagined and Real

Upon entering and taking control of Cusco in November 1533, Pizarro quickly realized that he had little to fear from Quiz Quiz. Had the Incan general wished to defend Cusco there was no better place than the walled fortress of Sacsayhuamán, situated at the northern edge of the capital. That would also be true for himself, if Quiz Quiz decided to attack. No, he concluded, Quiz Quiz was on the run and Pizarro decided to chase him, sending de Soto with fifty horsemen and several thousand hastily formed Incan troops under the "command" of Manco. They engaged Quiz Quiz and his men in the vicinity of the Apurimac River at Ccapi, routing them. But unable to follow due to the fact that Quiz Quiz had burned the suspension bridge and the waters were reaching high flow, they returned to Cusco at the end of the year.

By the time de Soto returned, Pizarro had begun the process of handing out land grants (*encomiendas*) to his men and expropriating and melting down the vast treasure of Cusco; a process that would consume several months and destroy the physical basis of much of Incan culture. The result was a greater total amount of treasure than was accumulated at Cajamarca. (Although the total was greater, the per-capita share was less because there were so many more men involved.) Almagro and his men, however, had received their share in full. Pizarro had also embarked upon the difficult task of reining in the excesses of his men as they rampaged and plundered the capital. He assigned Francisco Beltrán de Castro and his old comrade from Cajamarca, Pedro de Candia, to maintain order.

Two threats, one receding, the other menacing, would shape events for most of the coming year. The first, from scouts trailing Quiz Quiz, was that he and his men had gained the main Inca highway and were heading north. Their destination, thought to be Quito, would however take them first to Jauja, which alarmed Pizarro because the town was vulnerable. Pizarro had left Jauja in the charge of Alonso Riquelme, with eighty men, most of whom were old and infirm, with few experienced fighters, to guard the treasure brought from Cajamarca. To go to Riquelme's aid, Pizarro sent de Soto and Almagro with fifty horsemen, and Manco with twenty thousand warriors, on the highway after them.

The rainy season delayed their departure until the end of January 1534, and their progress was slowed by swollen rivers and cut bridges. By the time they reached Jauja in early March the battle was over, and Riquelme had won, assisted greatly by local anti-Inca tribes. The battle, as Hemming noted, "was really decided by the attitude of the local natives tribes....who provided two thousand auxiliaries for Riquelme's army."[2] It was another of many examples of the reaction of tribe after tribe, who, even after coming to the conclusion that the Spaniards were not the liberators they had hoped for, still hated them less than they hated the Inca tyranny, a classic demonstration of the adage "the enemy of my enemy is my friend."

Beaten off at Jauja, Quiz Quiz took his dwindling army to Bombón where he attempted to establish a stronghold. But he faced growing disaffection among his men who wanted nothing more to do with the uneven battle against the Spaniards and simply wanted to proceed north home to Quito. When harried at Bombón, they began to retreat toward Quito, at which point Pizarro's forces broke off their pursuit. Quiz Quiz's fate would be determined by his own men, who, refusing to continue the struggle against the Spaniards when they arrived in the north, turned on and killed their leader.

The only remaining source of organized Incan resistance was in Quito where Atahualpa's general Ruminavi and his captain Zope Zopahua ruled as warlords over the region. It would be from Quito that the second threat would emerge—ironically, not from Ruminavi, but from abroad. This new peril came in the form of an old conquistador: Adelantado Don Pedro Alvarado, Hernán Cortés's compadre in the conquest of Mexico, and now governor of Guatemala.

Alvarado's interest in Peru was straightforward. When Hernando Pizarro arrived in Panama City in November 1533 on his way to Spain, the treasure he brought with him astounded the people. Hernando attempted to recruit men and women to settle in Peru, displaying the treasure aboard ship as one of his inducements. Word of Peru's fabulous treasure spread quickly throughout Central America and the islands,

---

[2] John Hemming, *The Conquest of the Incas* (New York: Harcourt Brace Jovanovich, 1970), 140.

sparking the beginning of a gold rush to Peru. This portended the depopulation of Spain's other territories—few would choose a hardscrabble existence in the jungles or the islands when they could go to Peru, where the streets apparently were lined with gold. The king hurriedly issued a decree in an attempt to limit the potential stampede, with only moderate success.[3]

Having gone to Guatemala, pilot Juan Fernández, one of Pizarro's men at Cajamarca, "gave Alvarado a full account of the enormous treasures which had been shared."[4] Moreover, the governor was in position to act. On the king's orders, he was readying a large fleet to sail for the Spice Islands (today's Malacca Straits and Indonesia) in the continuing quest to find a shortcut to China. Out of more than curiosity, Alvarado, who, as a governor had access to the king's decrees, took a look at the Capitulation of Toledo given to Pizarro. In point one of the Capitulation he found that the king had licensed Pizarro to an area two hundred leagues "more or less" along the Peruvian coast from Santiago to Chincha, south of present-day Lima.[5]

If the riches of Peru were as great as they were reputed to be, Alvarado decided that he would claim for himself the area outside of Pizarro's remit. Responding to the Audiencia of Mexico's attempt to dissuade him, he said that his commission from the king as *adelantado* of the South Seas "restricted him to no particular course or limit, that it left him at liberty to shape his own plan."[6] So, this man of "peculiar restlessness," according to Helps, set off for Ecuador on January 23, 1534, with a now very large expeditionary fleet of eleven ships and over five

---

[3] Hemming, *Conquest of the Incas*, 144-45.

[4] Manuel José Quintana, *Lives of Vasco Nunez de Balboa and Francisco Pizarro,* trans. Margaret Hodson (Edinburgh: William Blackwood, 1832; repr., Kessinger, 2010), 230.

[5] Text (in Spanish) of *La Capitulación de Toledo: "1529, 26 de julio. Toledo. Real Cédula aprobando la capitulación concedida por Carlos V a Francisco Pizarro para la conquista y población del Perú,"* archived at La Biblioteca Virtual Miguel de Cervantes, www.cervantesvirtual.com.

[6] Quintana, *Lives of Balboa and Pizarro*, 230.

hundred men; and more than a hundred horses with guns, provisions, porters, and slaves.[7]

Pizarro had advance knowledge of Alvarado's general intent as early as December 1533 when his old friend, Gabriel de Rojas arrived to tell him that he was readying an expedition for Peru but did not know his precise plans. (Alvarado had commandeered from Rojas two supply ships Pizarro had commissioned.)[8] He also knew that Alvarado would be coming with a force far superior to his and that "his small and dispersed army of some two hundred Spaniards was no match for the invaders."[9]

Alvarado made landfall at the Bay of Caraquez, near Puerto Viejo and southwest of Quito, on February 25. His plan was "to explore the land beyond Chincha." In other words, he intended to head south toward Chile, sending one of his galleons under Captain Juan Fernández ahead to explore the coastline, equipping him with "special notice" boards that allowed him to stake a claim of possession in the name of the king (and himself). But Alvarado changed his mind after hearing about the "many riches that were in Quito." An "Indian whom he captured," claimed to have "seen them with his own eyes," and "promised to lead them on a safe route to the city."[10]

Pizarro had sent Sebastián de Benalcázar the previous summer with treasure from Cajamarca to take charge of San Miguel de Piura. The port soon became a busy entry point for a growing number of potential settlers seeking their fortunes in Peru; many, like Alvarado, were lured by stories of riches in Quito. Now, Captain Fernández put in at San Miguel on his way south with Alvarado's expedition. When Benalcázar learned of

---

[7]Arthur Helps, *The Spanish Conquest in America and Its Relation to the History of Slavery and to the Government of Colonies,* vol.4 (New York: Harper & Bros., 1868), 15.

[8] Quintana, *Lives of Balboa and Pizarro,* 231-32.

[9] Stuart Stirling, *Pizarro: Conqueror of the Inca* (Stroud: Sutton, 2005), 80.

[10]Pedro de Cieza de León, *The Discovery and Conquest of Peru,* ed. and trans. Alexandra Parma Cook and Noble David Cook (Durham: Duke University Press, 1998), 294-95; 300. Cf. Hemming, *Conquest of the Incas,* 152. As noted earlier, historians differ as to the location of the northern boundary of Pizarro's grant in the *Capitulación de Toledo.* Hemming presumes that "Santiago" referred to either Tumbes or Puna (an island in the Gulf of Guayaquil). In that case, Quito would lie to the north of Pizarro's territory, and Hemming claims it was Alvarado's intent from the beginning to "invade this northern province."

Alvarado's plans, he took it upon himself to assemble some two hundred men—many from among those who had just arrived seeking their fortunes—and sixty-two horses to set out for Quito to get there before Alvarado did.[11] On his departure he sent a message to Pizarro to tell him of his plans.

When Pizarro heard that Benalcázar had left San Miguel undefended, he faced a quandary. He had to secure the port, which was the only means of acquiring reinforcements. But he also knew that Quito was in fact unsettled territory. In the back of his mind there was the niggling concern that Benalcázar, Alvarado, or both might be tempted to lay claim to it before he did.[12] So, he quickly sent Almagro out with a small contingent with the charge to go first to San Miguel to secure the port and then to catch up with Benalcázar and take command of his forces.[13] At this point, the threat from Alvarado and, perhaps from Benalcázar, was greater than the threat either perceived to come from the other.

There was yet another factor in this evolving equation and that was Ruminavi, who, with his captain Zope Zopahua, was in control of Quito. Learning from their own scouts that Benalcázar was heading for them, they decided to mount a defense of their land. Their strategy was to drive a wedge between Benalcázar and the Cañari tribe, who were allies of the Spanish and whose lands lay to the south of Quito. Thus, they intended to engage Benalcázar's forces before they could be augmented with Cañari warriors, who, recall, had been bitter enemies of Atahualpa and his warriors.

Benalcázar, on the other hand, knew that getting to Quito ahead of Alvarado would require first taking on and defeating Ruminavi's forces that held it, and to do that he would need to buttress his small force with Cañari allies. Departing in early March 1534, Benalcázar and his men ascended to the Inca high road and marched north toward the Cañari capital of Tumibamba (hispanicized "Tomebamba"), initially making good progress across the dreary but level high plain. Moving with mounted

---

[11] Hemming, *Conquest of the Incas,* 153. Cieza de León, *Discovery and Conquest of Peru,* 269, says Benalcázar took 140 Spaniards with him to Quito.
[12] Ibid., 329. Cieza de León reports that "there were those who were disgruntled with Benalcázar and...declared that he was a rebel and was intending to join Alvarado."
[13] Stirling, *Pizarro,* 81.

reconnaissance forces in the lead, Benalcázar came upon forward elements of Ruminavi's forces in southern Ecuador, scattering them in disarray and defeating the attempt to prevent a link-up with the Cañari.[14] Nevertheless, Ruminavi was preparing for a protracted encounter all along the road to Quito. It would be, in Hemming's words, "the greatest pitched battle of the conquest."[15]

Defeating Ruminavi, Claiming Quito, Buying Off Alvarado

Meanwhile Pizarro, ever the resourceful commander, continued to place his men in the best positions to address the perceived threat from Alvarado. Having dispatched Almagro to reinforce Benalcázar, he acted to consolidate Cusco, before leaving for Jauja where he would be in position to support his men. His appointed governors, Castro and Candia, had failed to stop the looting and pillage of Cusco which was completely out of control and rapidly alienating the local citizens, native and Spanish alike. So, Pizarro "founded" Cusco as a Spanish city and named Hernando de Soto as temporary lieutenant governor and *corregidor* (administrator or mayor) to replace Castro and Candia.

Putting de Soto in charge was a matter of military expediency, because Pizarro did not trust him completely, but he turned out to be a good manager.[16] This decision helped calm and stabilize the city for the moment, but inflamed Pizarro's own brothers, Juan and Gonzalo, who, having ridden with de Soto had come to dislike him, and felt they were being discriminated against by their older brother.[17] At the moment, this was of little concern to Pizarro, who was focused on larger issues, but the petty grievances of his brothers would grow to be a major problem within months.

---

[14] Hemming, *Conquest of the Incas*, 155-56.

[15] Ibid., 158.

[16] David Duncan, *Hernando de Soto: A Savage Quest in the Americas* (Norman: University of Oklahoma Press, 1996), 188. De Soto "understood that this was a marriage of convenience only, and that Pizarro would push him aside the instant he no longer needed him."

[17] Stirling, *Pizarro*, 84.

The Cusco situation addressed, at the end of March Pizarro, accompanied by Manco, moved with the majority of his forces and his household to Jauja where he could be in position to reinforce against the threat from Alvarado. Founding Jauja as the temporary capital of Peru, he remained there through the summer until the threat had dissipated. As at Cusco, he sought to protect the houses and property of the natives from the predatory instincts of the men to whom he had given *encomiendas*. Concerned about the growing lack of respect for Manco among Spaniards and natives alike, in an act that he would come to regret, he issued a proclamation ordering that "the freedom of the Inca Manco must be preserved and 'his command over the natives must not be taken from him in any way whatsoever.'"[18]

While at Jauja, however, Pizarro experienced the happy moment of the birth of his daughter, Francisca. Both mother and daughter were baptized there, Quispe Sisa taking the name Inés.[19] They also celebrated the rout of Quiz Quiz and his men with a festival of traditional drinking, dancing, and games. During this tense but ultimately peaceful time at Jauja, the crisis of Quito played to its end.

Neither Alvarado nor Almagro would reach the Quito area before Benalcázar. He arrived at Tumibamba, where he rested for a week and negotiated the terms of alliance with the Cañari. They offered Benalcázar some three thousand battle-tested warriors, along with porters and guides, who relished the opportunity to do battle against Ruminavi, their hated enemy. In late April their combined forces moved out of Tumibamba on the great Inca road toward Quito. Going through the fourteen-thousand-foot pass between soaring Riobamba mountaintops he descended onto the road leading to Riobamba, about one hundred miles south of Quito. There, at Teocajas, on May 3, 1534, he would meet the army of Ruminavi.[20]

---

[18] Hemming, *Conquest of the Incas*, 143.

[19] Stirling, *Pizarro*, 83-84.

[20] The best accounts, on which this analysis draws, are: Hemming, *Conquest of the Incas*, 156-61; Cieza de León, *Discovery and Conquest of Peru*, 268-84; and Paul M. Kochis, *God, Glory and Gold, Journey to the Conquest of the Incas*, vol. 2, *The Quest* (Minneapolis: Mill City Press, 2013), 423-29.

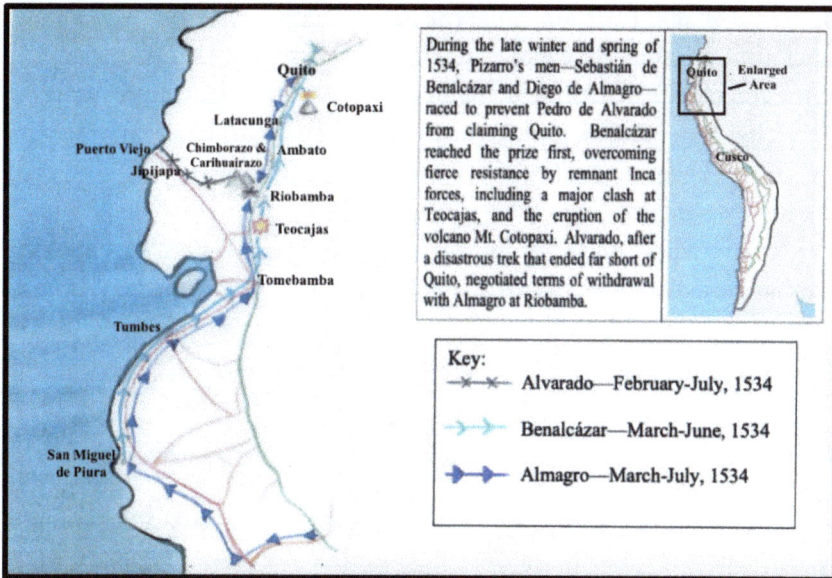

During the late winter and spring of 1534, Pizarro's men—Sebastián de Benalcázar and Diego de Almagro—raced to prevent Pedro de Alvarado from claiming Quito. Benalcázar reached the prize first, overcoming fierce resistance by remnant Inca forces, including a major clash at Teocajas, and the eruption of the volcano Mt. Cotopaxi. Alvarado, after a disastrous trek that ended far short of Quito, negotiated terms of withdrawal with Almagro at Riobamba.

Key:
—✕—✕— Alvarado—February-July, 1534

–>–>– Benalcázar—March-June, 1534

➤➤➤ Almagro—March-July, 1534

6.1. Quest for Quito

Ruminavi had decided upon a strategy of forward defense and attrition. He would not fortify and defend Quito itself, but engage Benalcázar in carefully prepared battlegrounds along the route to Quito. The first battleground was on the plains at Teocajas, south of Riobamba. His battlefield tactic was similar to those the Inca had used against other Indian forces, except that he had devised some new wrinkles to deal with Spanish horses. He would attack, attempt to encircle, then retreat, hoping to lure the Spanish into prepared traps, mine fields, and ambushes. He hoped that staked pits, trip holes, and a new weapon similar to the bolas, or *ayllos*, would enable them to defeat the Spanish cavalry.[21]

At Teocajas, hoping to wear down Spanish numbers, he hurled three successive echelons of forces, each some twelve thousand strong in human wave attacks against the advancing Spaniards and Cañari. Benalcázar's cavalry charges wreaked havoc on the first wave of attackers, soaking the plains in Incan blood. A second attack followed hard on the first, with a similar result. Seeking a respite as the altitude was taking its

---

[21] Cieza de León, *Discovery and Conquest of Peru*, 278, says the Indians "believed that the Spaniards, provoked by them to do battle, would proceed until they fell with their horses into the pits, and thus they tried to incite them into combat in that area."

toll on horse and rider alike, the Spanish turned only to find yet another echelon of warriors descending upon them. Nearing exhaustion but with little choice but combat, the combined Spanish-Cañari force proved equal to the challenge, fighting off Ruminavi's attacks. Afterwards, as night fell, both sides repaired to hillocks within crossbow distance of each other to lick their wounds.

A friendly Indian from Cajamarca warned Benalcázar about the traps and minefields that lay ahead and offered to lead them safely around them, an offer that was gratefully accepted and acted on that very night.[22] Despite their exhaustion from the day's battles, they left quietly with campfires burning, and marched to Riobamba skirting the fortified position of Rumanavi's forces. It was accomplished despite harrying flank attacks by Ruminavi's men, who, belatedly alerted to the Spanish escape, chased after them. Nevertheless, the Indians had managed to kill five men and at least two horses, significant casualties for the numerically small Spaniards. (For reasons unknown, the Indians did not seek to capture the horses and use them against the Spaniards. Instead, in most cases, they killed and dismembered the animals, parading them around like trophies.)

Benalcázar and his men spent a week in Riobamba acclimating to the altitude, recuperating from the battle, and preparing for the road ahead. Advancing from Riobamba, the Indians constantly harassed Benalcázar's columns as they marched, engaging them in battles along the way, trying to maneuver them into prepared ditches and pits. Ruminavi's troops attempted to prevent a crossing of the Ambato River, ambushed Benalcázar's men in ravines and defiles outside of the towns of Latacunga and Panzeleo, all to no avail. They could not stop the inexorable advance of the Spanish-Cañari forces, which, by the middle of June, were within a two-day march of Quito.

As they approached within fifteen miles of the city an event occurred that had an effect on all concerned, but especially the Incans, who were sensitive to signs from nature. Without warning, the 19,000-foot Cotopaxi volcano located thirty miles south and to the east of Quito,

---

[22] Hemming, *Conquest of the Incas*, 158, notes that "they were saved by an Indian from Cajamarca who offered to guide them by a circuitous route to the west of the Incas' prepared position."

erupted in fury, blowing off its cap, and spewing hot ash, debris, and smoke miles into to the air and a hundred miles across the surrounding countryside. The ash blackened the sky with thick, acrid smoke; and molten lava, several feet deep, flowed in scalding rivers down the mountainside, incinerating everything in its path.[23]

Undoubtedly, Ruminavi and his chiefs took the eruption as a sign of the displeasure of their god, Viracocha, but whether it determined what he did next is unknowable. Rather than attempt to defend Quito, he decided to adopt a scorched earth policy, perhaps appropriate considering the circumstances, and abandon it. He would burn as much as he could, destroy its aqueducts, and take as much of its treasure, stores, and people as he could to a remote and defensible forested and craggy redoubt north and east of the city. Those who refused to accompany him, and especially the young virgins, he slaughtered rather than leave for the Spaniards.

Five days later, June 22, 1534, Benalcázar and his Cañari allies entered the burnt-out still smoldering hulk of what had once been the opulent northern capital of the Incan empire. Searching the city, they found only a few elderly persons and children. Their disappointment great, they felt but small satisfaction at arriving before Alvarado. Leaving a contingent to guard the city, Benalcázar set out in search of Ruminavi in hopes of finding him and whatever treasure he had taken with him. He, in fact, encountered and dealt sharp blows to the retreating forces of Quiz Quiz that had reached the end of their journey at Quito. While on the march north of Quito, in early July, Benalcázar learned from advanced scouts that Almagro was approaching Quito, prompting his return.

Their meeting was initially extremely tense and testy, as Almagro had been operating under the misapprehension that Benalcázar intended to claim Quito for himself and set up an independent settlement. It was only after some moments had passed that he realized his error. Benalcázar made it plain that he had acted at all times in the name of the king and in the interests of Pizarro and Almagro. Once their misunderstanding had been cleared up, they turned to face the common danger of Alvarado, who,

---

[23] Kochis, *God, Glory and Gold*, 2:426-27. Cieza de León, *Discovery and Conquest of Peru*, 282, says the Spaniards were in Riobamba when Cotopaxi erupted, which seems unlikely.

scouts said, was himself nearing Quito with a large army. Quito was now Pizarro's, but how would Alvarado react when he discovered that his great gamble had failed? Would he resort to force, or accept the fact that he had been beaten to the punch?

Once again, as it had so many times in this history, fate smiled on Pizarro. By all logical calculation, Alvarado should have reached Quito long before Benalcázar and claimed it. It had taken Benalcázar four months to fight his way from San Miguel de Piura to Quito against the fanatical hordes of Ruminavi. Yet, Alvarado, who began his march at the same time from Puerto Viejo, less than half the distance from Quito, arrived after Benalcázar. Bad advice, bad decisions, cruel treatment of natives, difficult terrain, and terrible weather conditions turned out to be more of a hindrance to Alvarado than Ruminavi's attacks had been to Benalcázar.

Alvarado's first mistake was to trust the captured Indian who offered to lead him to Quito by the shortest route. In fact, this unnamed guide had led Alvarado's men almost directly southward instead of northward, to the region of Jipijapa, thirty miles south of Puerto Viejo. Then, while his men were plundering the surprised natives of several towns of their substantial riches in gold and jewels, the guide disappeared, leaving Alvarado in the middle of nowhere.[24]

Attempting to find the way to the great Inca high road to Quito, Alvarado sent two large parties on reconnaissance missions. The first, led by his brother Gómez, went north; the other, led by Captain Benevides, went east. Both returned with news that the great high road lay just ahead. Alvarado's second mistake was to decide to march east, instead of north. He assumed that the road must lie along the towering mountains he could see in the distance—the massive, twin peaks of the Chimborazo, 20,000 ft; and the Carihuairazo, at 16,000ft. He was perhaps wary of believing captured Indians, who assured him that the shortest route lay north and not east, and that they would guide him.

Winter was approaching, and their route took them through most difficult terrain, dotted with lakes, bogs, and thick forests, which slowed them as they approached the mountains. Coming across villages as they

---

[24] Cieza de León, *Discovery and Conquest of Peru*, 300-01.

marched, they were able to avoid starvation by confiscating provisions from the inhabitants. They treated these natives dismissively, harshly alienating them. As word of the Alvarado party's advance preceded it, natives fled to avoid contact; those who were captured refused to cooperate, despite torture. The resulting isolation and lack of sustenance caused severe losses of men to fever, and cannibalization of their horses and dogs for food barely kept them from reaching the edge of desperation.

The worst was yet to come. Crossing the highest pass in the Andes between the Chimborazo and the Carihuairazo mountains they were hit by sleet, snow, and freezing conditions which took a further heavy toll upon them.[25] They lost a fifth of their expedition, some eighty-five men, many frozen in their sleep, and what remained of their native bearers, horses, and dogs. On top of that the eruption of Cotopaxi rained ash and debris down on them as they descended through the pass to Riobamba and at last reached the great high road. At that point they were still over ninety miles away from Quito. It was a famished, debilitated, discouraged, and bedraggled band that began the trek to Quito. As they were trudging along, they came across hoofprints and horseshoes on the road. With that final exasperating signal, they realized that Pizarro had beaten them to Quito.

Encountering Almagro's scouts, Alvarado sent messages forward and after some posturing of forces and several testy exchanges it was agreed that the *adelantado* should make camp in some ancient ruins outside Riobamba, which Almagro claimed to have established as a Spanish city. The two sides would meet there. Alvarado attempted to bluff Almagro, declaring that he had come with the "permission" of the king to "explore and claim on behalf of his imperial majesty lands to the north and east of the grant to you and Governor Pizarro." He had no intention, he averred, to encroach, nor cause any "ill will," and was willing to work out "honest conditions" of mutual benefit. [26]

Almagro, experienced negotiator that he was, replied affably with the argument that it was plain that there was no place left for Alvarado to

---

[25] Hemming, *Conquest of the Incas*, 161, notes that Alvarado "chose the wrong route to penetrate the Andes, and climbed one of the highest passes, between Chimborazo and Carihuairazo."

[26] Kochis, *God, Glory and Gold*, 2:434-35.

claim. Benalcázar was already in possession of the land to the north. In fact, they had already founded the Spanish cities of Santiago de Quito and Riobamba, with mayors, judges, and notaries.[27] He himself was expecting confirmation of word from the king of his own license of the land to the south beyond New Castile. The land to the east was uninhabited dense forest. Alvarado inquired whether the governor would supply guides, provisions and safe passage for his men to travel there? Almagro replied sadly no; he had no guides for that no man's land.

As the two leaders negotiated, Alvarado's men fraternized freely with their countrymen and heard "such magnificent reports of the wealth and wonders of Cusco that many of them were inclined to change their present service to Pizarro."[28] Indeed, Almagro encouraged their interaction, hoping to gain their allegiance. Two notable defections impacted their negotiation. Antonio Picado, Alvarado's secretary, went over to Almagro; and Felipillo, the translator, went over to Alvarado. The information they imparted clearly gave the advantage to Almagro, for Picado revealed the sorry state of Alvarado's men, while Felipillo reinforced the notion of Pizarro as the successful conquistador that he was.

As the negotiations continued, it was clear to Almagro that Alvarado was looking for a face-saving way out of what had become a disastrous cul de sac. He said that he had spent twenty thousand pesos to outfit his expedition and needed something to show for the hardships he and his men had experienced. Almagro offered to buy him out with a princely sum five times what he said he had spent for all of his equipment, ships, stores, and weapons. The governor of Guatemala would return to his home province with dignity and a profit. The men, Almagro proposed, could return with him or stay on as part of their army with prospects of enriching themselves with future discoveries. Three hundred and forty men would sign on.[29]

It was a deal Alvarado could not refuse. Privately, he knew that a resort to arms was a non-starter. His men would not take up arms against

---

[27] Quintana, *Lives of Balboa and Pizarro*, 240.
[28] William H. Prescott, *History of the Conquest of Peru,* partly abridged and revised by Victor W. von Hagen (New York: New American Library, 1961), 321.
[29] Kim MacQuarrie, *Last Days of the Incas* (New York: Simon & Shuster, 2007), 160.

their fellow countrymen. Besides, the outcome of any conflict between them would only leave the winner vulnerable to attack by the Indians under Ruminavi, who still lurked nearby with a substantial force. After Alvarado had returned to Guatemala, in his report to the king he explained his reason for accepting the buy-out and confessed that Almagro's success in winning over his men was such that "had I persevered in the prosecution of my conquests, not thirty men would have followed me."[30] Hemming also says that Almagro had conducted an *audiencia* while at Riobamba and recorded indictments from Alvarado's men of the cruel and inhuman treatment he had meted out to his own men and natives, alike. This report was sent to the king to discredit the governor.[31]

Their agreement signed on August 26, 1534, a messenger was sent to Jauja where Pizarro ratified it and arranged for the payment to be made at the coastal city of Pachacamac. Pizarro had several reasons for choosing Pachacamac for the signing ceremony. He wanted to keep Alvarado away from Cusco to avoid any temptation to renege on the deal. Thus, the route from Quito to Pachacamac would take the combined force down the mountain to the coast road to San Miguel de Piura, then along the coast road to Pachacamac, bypassing the high road. Besides, Pizarro was planning to explore along the coast to find a suitable place to establish a port city and capital for New Castile, and Pachacamac was close by.

Pizarro named Benalcázar temporary governor of Quito, assigning him some four hundred men. He ordered him to rebuild the city and ferret out and destroy Ruminavi. It would take him several weeks, during which time he established a settlement at Popayan in present-day Colombia, but was ultimately successful, dragging the captured general in chains to the central square of the city where he was executed. Thus ended the resistance of the last of Atahualpa's main generals.[32]

Meanwhile, at Pachacamac Pizarro feted Alvarado as befitting his status as governor of a province and paid him his 100,000 pesos, which amounted to a thousand pounds of gold. It was an impressive affair, persuading Alvarado to make one last try to retain a piece of the action in

---

[30] Quintana, *Lives of Balboa and Pizarro*, 244.
[31] Hemming, *Conquest of the Incas*, 162.
[32] Stirling, *Pizarro*, 83.

Peru. He suggested that the three men form a "league," where all would share in the bounties of their respective conquests. Almagro, undoubtedly mindful of his own past experience with Pizarro and Luque "would not hear of this league," saying that it would be impossible for the three partners to keep the peace (*que seria impossible tener paz tres compañeros*).[33] He may also have been thinking about the future.

Post-Conquest Problems

Pizarro and his partner, Almagro, began to consolidate, organize, and govern Peru, but trouble was brewing as struggles over the spoils intensified. That January 1535, the governor had founded his capital of New Castile on the coast at the Rimac River, which he named *Ciudad de los Reyes*, City of Kings, but which was known as Lima, a Spanish dyslexic mispronunciation of Rimac. Pizarro decided to live in Lima and spend his time turning the capital into a major port and commercial hub to sustain the growing Spanish presence. He also founded another city a few miles to the north of Lima, which he named Trujillo, after his hometown in Spain. His benign neglect of Cusco, however, soon came back to haunt him.

When Pizarro went to Lima, Almagro went to Cusco. Pizarro named him governor, removing de Soto as lieutenant governor but keeping him on as *corregidor*. Almagro began to govern the city as the capital of New Toledo, while awaiting the king's decree formally awarding him title of his governorate to the south of Pizarro's grant, whose southern border was at Chincha. At last, Almagro was to be rewarded for his long, secondary status under Pizarro. The problem was that the border between their domains was undefined and both men claimed Cusco, which lay along it.

Pizarro also had sent Manco back to Cusco, instructing de Soto to mentor him in his efforts to restore some semblance of his reputation to facilitate Spanish control. It was not easy because Inca control had disintegrated under the impact of the Spanish invasion. In addition, the Spaniards in Cusco showed him little respect, which hindered his efforts among the Indians, but that gradually began to change as indiscriminate

---

[33] Helps, *Spanish Conquest in America*, 4:17.

Spanish expropriation of the wealth, women, and land of the natives gradually turned them against their erstwhile liberators and pushed them back toward the Inca. The overbearing Spanish presence created fertile ground for what was about to come.

Almagro now possessed the largest Spanish military force in Peru, over five hundred with the addition of Alvarado's men, changing the dynamic within their fraying partnership. The arrival of this large force in Cusco magnified the problems of governance. If Cusco had been ungovernable under Pizarro's administrators, it became positively chaotic now as Almagro's men, eager for booty, began to run roughshod over the arrangements put in place by Pizarro. Pizarro's brothers, Juan and Gonzalo, a "law unto themselves" in lawless Cusco, opposed Almagro and mobilized most of the eighty-eight *encomenderos* whose lands were being threatened by Almagro's men to resist the bands who roamed the area like packs of wolves.[34]

Within weeks the city was divided with the Almagrists occupying the northern sector and the Pizarrists the city center. De Soto attempted to keep order, which, in practice meant attempting to keep the Pizarro brothers under control, leading to antagonism between them. Confrontations between the two factions began to occur daily in the streets, reaching a flash point in early March. Juan, Gonzalo and their supporters fortified a palace in the city with cannon and marched into the central square determined to have it out with the Almagrists. Attempting to defuse the situation, de Soto was challenged by Juan to a duel and bloodshed was only averted by cooler heads at the last minute.[35]

The crisis in Cusco produced different reactions from Manco and Pizarro. Manco was under growing criticism from the Inca elite because of his supine reaction to Spanish depredations. The Pizarro brothers, especially Gonzalo, treated him disrespectfully, making it plain for all to see that he was a mere puppet, with little but ceremonial power. Almost daily the brothers demanded that Manco reveal the location of hidden treasure and hand over women from his extensive harem for their seemingly insatiable sexual pleasure. The last straw in this process came

[34] Stirling, *Pizarro*, 85.
[35] Duncan, *Hernando de Soto*, 198.

when Gonzalo demanded that Manco give his principal wife, Cura Ocllo, to Gonzalo to be his concubine.

The obvious disrespect of the Pizarro brothers for Manco reverberated within the Inca elite who began to demand that he be replaced by someone who could stand up to the Spaniards. His challenger was a half-brother, Atoc-Sopa, who had rallied the support of a sufficiently worrisome segment of the elite. Manco cleverly struck a deal with Almagro. In return for Almagro's help in eliminating Atoc-Sopa, Manco would assist Almagro with the expedition he was planning to the south to secure his newly awarded patrimony. Thus, Almagro sent several of his men one night to slit Atoc-Sopa's throat, sealing their alliance in blood.[36] In return, Manco supplied Almagro with a 12,000-man force, several thousand porters, and his own half-brother, Paullu, accompanied by the high priest, "Vila Oma," to guide him to what he was told were riches greater than those found in Cusco.[37] Little did he know that Manco was secretly plotting the destruction of all of the Spaniards in Peru.

Pizarro's reaction to the crisis in Cusco was more elegant. Arriving from Lima in late May 1535, Pizarro perceived three major problems. There was the immediate issue of Cusco, which both he and Almagro claimed in the absence of a clearly delineated border. There was the issue of Spanish factional animosity, which threatened total anarchy. And there was the issue of Manco's shift of allegiance to Almagro. Pizarro tried to rebuild his relationship with Manco by bringing the opposing factions together under his leadership, to no avail. The Inca leadership split, with Manco siding with Almagro; and a new challenger, Pacsac, supporting Pizarro.

---

[36] MacQuarrie, *Last Days of the Incas,* 170-71; Kochis, *God, Glory and Gold,* 2:448, 464. Juan de Betanzos, *Narrative of the Incas,* trans. Roland Hamilton and Dana Buchanan (Austin: University of Texas Press, 1996), 279, tells this story differently, without naming the challenger. He claims Manco knew that Pizarro "had with him a young son of Huayna Cápac," and "suspected," he wanted to name him Inca. So, Manco plotted to assassinate him, implicating his brother Paullu in the plot. He called him to his chambers where Paullu and an aide killed him and then told Pizarro that he had been killed in a quarrel with Paullu.

[37] The "Willaq Umi" was the Quechua term for the Inca High Priest. The Spaniards used the title as a proper name for Manco's chief priest, variously written by historians as Vila Oma, Villac Umu, Villaoma, etc.

Pizarro's attempt to reach agreement with Almagro fared much better. Aided by the very able negotiator, licentiate Hernando de Caldera, Pizarro offered Almagro two propositions. First, he proposed to set aside the Cusco question, pending the arrival of the king's decree that Hernando Pizarro was bringing back with him to Peru. Presumably, the king's decree would settle the matter of jurisdiction. Secondly, as Almagro's grant of land south of New Castile was not in question, Pizarro proposed to finance his partner's expedition so that he could establish his control and begin to accumulate the great riches that were reputed to be there.[38] Despite some misgivings among his men, Almagro agreed.

To seal and to revitalize their "partnership" the two men signed a formal agreement, which was duly notarized and consecrated at a church mass, on June 12, 1535. They agreed that from the king's two grants "a new obligation results." They swore to maintain their partnership in a "brotherly way," where "everything will be done openly." All profits would be shared equally "with no fraud, cunning, or any deceit in it." They promised that "neither one of us will slander or attempt anything that can result in or cause harm and injury to the honor, life, and estate of the other." They vowed to maintain a joint and respectful approach to the King and that neither "will issue a private report" to him intended to "harm and injure the other."[39]

If honored, their agreement would offer positive but different kinds of returns for each man. For Almagro it would constitute an insurance policy against the possibility the expedition would produce little treasure. Then, at least, he would still be able to claim half of Pizarro's treasure in New Castile. For Pizarro, on the other hand, the agreement constituted a futures bet on any possible treasure Almagro would find. For both, it presumed restraint with regard to Cusco, pending the arrival of the

---

[38] Stirling, *Pizarro*, 89. In a *Capitulación* dated May 21, 1534, King Charles had granted Almagro permission to conquer and govern an area stretching 200 leagues from the southern border of Pizarro's territory, toward the Magellan Strait. For the Spanish text, see "Capitulación que se tomó con el Mariscal Don Diego de Almagro, para descubrir doscientas leguas del Mar del Sur hacia el estrecho. Año de 1534," in República del Perú, Ministerio de Relaciones Exteriores, *Colección de los Tratados, Convenciones, Capitulaciones, Armisticio* [...] Tomo Primero (Lima: Imprenta del Estado, 1890), 39-44.

[39] See Cieza de León, *Discovery and Conquest of Peru*, 378-81, for the entire text.

king's decree. They recognized that it was a last attempt to hold together a partnership under tremendous outside pressure of conflicting interests. It would fail before the ink was dry on the parchment.

The flies in the ointment were Pizarro's brothers. Almagro pleaded with Pizarro to send them back to Spain, but he demurred. Although he chastised them for their behavior, it was pro forma. As soon as Almagro departed on his expedition, Pizarro named Juan acting governor of Cusco and the two brothers openly flaunted their power as soon as their elder brother returned to Lima. The first casualty was Hernando de Soto, who, sorely disappointed by being passed over for governor of Cusco, appealed to Almagro to name him second in command of his expedition. Almagro, too, declined, naming Rodrigo Orgóñez to the post. Thoroughly disillusioned, de Soto decided to return to Spain.[40]

De Soto's departure in early July headlined a substantial exodus of veterans from Cusco. Along with the departure of Almagro's large expedition, several others had also left, heading north. According to Garcilaso de la Vega, whose numbers seem high, Alonso de Alvarado took a force of 300 to Chachapoyas, Juan Porcel took 250 to Bracamoros, and Captain [Sebastián] Garcilaso de la Vega took 250 to the Cauca Valley in Colombia.[41] In addition, fifty-two of Pizarro's original "men of Cajamarca" had departed for Spain and only three of the "Gallo Thirteen" remained, Pedro de Candia, Nicolás de Ribera, and Juan de la Torre.[42] Whatever restraint Pizarro had imposed at the outset was now gone with their departures and the most recent arrivals "who had missed the great riches of the first conquistadors, were often the most brutal toward the natives."[43]

Manco and the high priest, Vila Oma, completely disgusted with Spanish oppression, decided that the time was ripe for rebellion. The

---

[40] Duncan, *Hernando de Soto*, 199. De Soto would have an illustrious career after Peru, exploring and discovering the vast American south from Florida to the Mississippi River where he met his end at age 42.

[41] Garcilaso de la Vega, *Royal Commentaries of the Incas and a General History of Peru*, abridged; trans. Harold V. Livermore; ed. Karen Spalding (Indianapolis: Hackett Publishing Co., 2006), 119.

[42] Kochis, *God, Glory and Gold*, 2:463-64.

[43] Hemming, *Conquest of the Incas*, 178.

Spanish were soon to be "scattered out over the land," Almagro was soon to be gone, and only a small number of settlers would remain in Cusco. Calling a secret meeting of chiefs from the four corners of Tawantinsuyu, they crafted a plan for general insurrection. Manco's first objective was to reestablish Inca control over the former tribes and states of the empire. Thus, in his speech he was at pains to point out how beneficent Inca rule had been, with the people enjoying "tranquility and perpetual peace." It was the Spanish invasion compounded by greed and duplicity that had destroyed all that. "Furthermore, they have drawn the yanaconas and many mitamaes [who have become traitors] to them." [44]

He also revealed that their plan was already in motion. He disclosed to the chiefs that Paullu and Vila Oma were with the "other usurper, Almagro [and]…are encharged to effect an uprising to kill them." Their mission was to "go with Almagro to Chile and…lead him down a path that has no escape" and through the barren lands "where there is no food." After setting them on this course, Vila Oma would return. "The Indians of Chile and Copayapo will attack them and kill them all. If they do not kill them, we will finish them off when they return." Their plan was that when Vila Oma returned to Cusco, Manco would steal away and join him at their headquarters in Calca outside the capital. They would direct the attack and "kill all of them in Cusco. Afterward, we will descend [to Lima] and kill the Macho Apo [Pizarro]…and the rest of them in the entire country." [45]

While Manco and Vila Oma would put this plan into action, initial missteps forced a delay of several months until the spring of 1536. When Almagro's expedition had reached Tupiza, more than 800 miles from Cusco, in October, Vila Oma quietly slipped away from it and headed back to Calca. When he did so, Manco attempted to sneak out of Cusco and make for their headquarters at Calca, but was caught on the way and brought back to Cusco. Shackling Manco, Juan and Gonzalo attempted to extract information about the rumors of rebellion then rife. Various torture

---

[44] For the text of the speech, see Cieza de León, *Discovery and Conquest of Peru*, 406-08. Yanaconas were the servant class in Inca society and the Mitamaes were subject peoples resettled in other provinces.

[45] Betanzos, *Narrative of the Incas*, 280-81.

means were used on him, including burning his eyelids, expectorating and urinating on him, all to no avail.[46]

In the meantime, Vila Oma decided to commence with hostilities. It was not yet the full-scale rebellion they planned, but a form of guerrilla warfare with attacks against individual Spanish settlers. Most of the Spanish *encomenderos* lived clustered in the settlements and only occasionally rode out to inspect their holdings. The Indians began to attack them on the roads, killing over thirty of them, more than had been lost in the entire conquest to date. Juan and Gonzalo marshaled a posse of horsemen to carry out reprisals against them. Toward the end of the year, with the help of friendly yanaconas, they caught up with a substantial grouping of Indians at a fortified rocky outcropping called Aconcagua. In a fierce struggle, the Spaniards carried out a merciless slaughter in which some eight thousand were killed with many committing suicide rather than submit to the Spaniards.[47]

Meanwhile, in December 1535, Hernando Pizarro had returned from Spain after a two-and-a-half-year absence. Reuniting with Francisco in Lima they poured over the king's decrees. Hernando had done exceedingly well in augmenting the terms of the original Capitulation. The right to import slaves for the mines, and to name top officials to lifetime appointments in new towns and settlements, along with tax breaks, all served to strengthen the Pizarro family hold on New Castile. Hernando, of course, invested his considerable treasure wisely in Spain. The king had awarded him a knighthood, made Francisco a Marquis, and awarded Friar Valverde the Bishopric of Cusco.

On the crucial question of Almagro's governorate, however, Hernando had been less successful. He had hoped to avoid the issue of awarding Almagro his own land grant, but the latter's friends in court pressed the case and the king complied. He awarded Almagro lands of two hundred leagues length "beginning at the southern limit of Pizarro's

---

[46] Kim MacQuarrie, *The Last Days of the Incas* (New York: Simon & Schuster, 2007), 185-87 and Hemming, *Conquest of the Incas*, 179, 185. Proceeding on a very difficult path, when Almagro reached Copiapo, some thirteen hundred miles from Cusco, all of the Indians supplied by Manco fled, leaving the Spanish in the lurch.
[47] Stirling, *Pizarro*, 95.

territory."[48] The question, it was seen, was to whom would fall the prize of Cusco. The king's disposition was that it would go to Pizarro, whose land was "increased to 270 leagues, instead of the 200 of the capitulation, including the caciques of Chepi and Coli."[49] The king's decision showed, according to Prescott and Quintana, that Cusco "now fell, without doubt, within the newly extended limits of his own territory."[50]

Notwithstanding the views of later scholars on this question, Pizarro was sufficiently concerned about its continuing ambiguity to send Hernando forthwith to Cusco with authority to take control of the city. In January 1536, when the posse returned to Cusco, Juan and Gonzalo found that their brother, Hernando, had arrived and was already taking steps to strengthen Cusco by organizing the *encomenderos*. But his approach to Manco alarmed them because he had promptly released him. He explained that "one of the principal injunctions which had been forced upon his attention at the court of Spain was to look to the good treatment of the Inca."[51] Thus, despite growing evidence of unrest, especially in Collao to the south where several Spaniards had been killed, Hernando attempted to court Manco and "win his friendship."[52]

Through the first few months of the year Hernando's friendly approach seemed to be working, as Manco and Hernando frequently dined together and discussed ways of improving the Inca's status. It was but a deception. Manco and Vila Oma were quietly bringing together several hundred thousand men from around the "four corners" and waiting for the

---

[48] Prescott; von Hagen, *Conquest of Peru*, 326. See preceding note 38 for reference to the Spanish text. A Spanish *legua común* as used in the 16th Century was 3.46 miles. Dr. John D. Worth at the University of West Florida has created tables for converting basic colonial measures here: https://pages.uwf.edu/jworth/jw_spanfla_measures_conversions.html#Common_Leagues

[49] Rafael Varón Gabai, *Francisco Pizarro and His Brothers, The Illusion of Power in Sixteenth-Century Peru*, trans. Javier Flores Espinoza (Norman: University of Oklahoma Press, 1997), 301, citing Rául Barrenechea Porras, *Cedulario del Peru, Siglos XVI, XVII y XVIII* (Lima: Ministerio de Relationes Exteriores, 1944-48), I:179, 191.

[50] Prescott; von Hagen, *Conquest of Peru*, 334. Quintana, *Lives of Balboa and Pizarro*, 260-61, concurs, saying "Cusco would be comprehended in the seventy leagues now added to his government."

[51] Helps, *Spanish Conquest in America*, 4:25.

[52] Hemming, *Conquest of the Incas*, 186.

end of the rainy season before commencing the rebellion. By April they were ready and Manco boldly asked Hernando's permission to travel to the Yucay Valley where his father Huayna Cápac was buried to celebrate his passing. He promised to return with a life-size, pure gold statue of his father that was hidden there. Unsuspecting, Hernando agreed and Manco and Vila Oma departed Cusco April 18, 1536.

The Great Inca Rebellion

Manco's strategy was to recapture control of the Inca heartland of Central Peru by surrounding and isolating the scattered Spanish settlements there and concentrating overwhelming forces against each one. The time was ripe to strike, as the Spanish presence was stretched thin across the land. Almagro's force, the largest in Peru, was over a thousand miles away in Chile and the expectation was that it would be severely weakened if not destroyed by the hostile tribes of the south. In any case, it would not be a factor.[53]

The Spanish presence elsewhere was sprinkled over a handful of settlements. The two largest were Cusco and Lima. There were two hundred Spaniards in Cusco with a thousand Indian supporters and eighty-six horses; Pizarro had two hundred Spaniards in Lima with over a thousand Indian supporters and a hundred horses. There were several dozen in Jauja, and fewer in Trujillo, Puerto Viejo, and San Miguel de Piura. The forces of Benalcázar, Alvarado, Porcelo, and Garcilaso de la Vega were between fifteen hundred and two thousand miles to the north and were deemed to be too far away to be a concern. For Manco and his generals, therefore, the critical field of battle was in the form of a scalene triangle whose points were Jauja, Cusco, and Lima.

---

[53] Betanzos, *Narrative of the Incas*, 280-81.

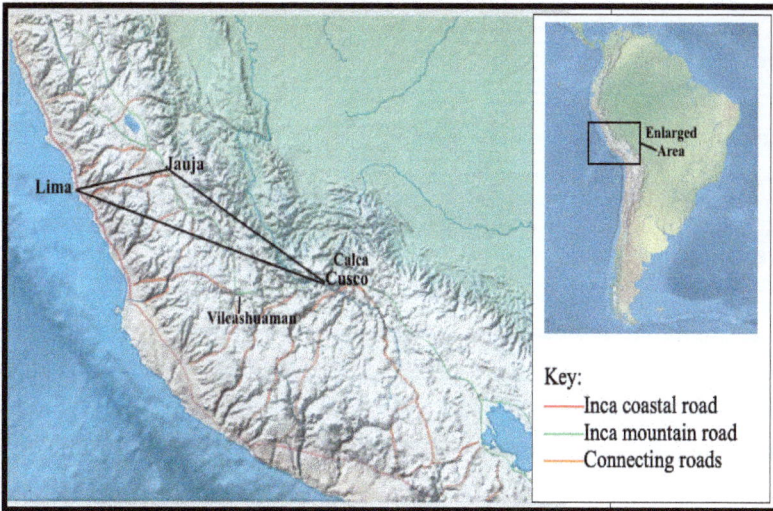

6.2. Inca rebellion's strategic triangle: Lima-Jauja-Cusco

Their plan was to seize Cusco first and then attack Lima, but crucial to accomplishment of both objectives was control of the high road between Jauja and Cusco, which would enable them to isolate the two targets from each other. Manco put Vila Oma in charge of the Cusco attack and Quizo Yupanqui in charge of controlling the high road to Jauja and preventing reinforcements from getting to Cusco. Later, he would command the assault on Lima.

The attack on the first target, Cusco, began with a diversion. Manco anticipated that the Spanish would come after him this time the way they had the first, which is what happened. In late April, a humiliated Hernando, finally convinced by his yanaconas that Manco was in revolt, sent Juan with seventy horses, nearly all that he had in Cusco, on a mission to the Yucay Valley to recapture him. Reaching the ridge overlooking the valley, some fifteen miles from Cusco, Juan saw several thousand troops gathered on the other side of the river that runs through the valley at Calca. With the bridge destroyed and the Indians taunting the Spaniards, as was their wont, Juan and his men forded the river and went after the sling throwers who were pelting them with stones. Rather than put up a fight, however, the Indians retreated up the hillsides, allowing Juan and his men to occupy Calca.[54]

They spent four days searching for Manco in and around Calca, finding a substantial amount of treasure, but no Inca. The Indians harassed them at night but made no attempt to drive them out. As MacQuarrie notes, "given the warriors' great numbers, the Spaniards were surprised that the natives didn't attack. The Inca commanders seemed strangely content to allow the Spaniards to remain virtually unmolested in Calca."[55] On the fourth day a messenger came charging in from Cusco to urge their immediate return because tens of thousands of Indians were massing for an attack on the capital. Juan hurriedly sought to return, but now the Inca hordes expended considerable effort to delay their march. They managed to fight their way back to the city to the relief of Hernando and the rest of the beleaguered inhabitants.

In a brilliant, secret mobilization, Vila Oma had surprised the Spaniards by surrounding Cusco with over a hundred thousand warriors. When the buildup on the slopes around the city was complete, on May 6, 1536, the Indians invaded the city, accompanied by a massive barrage of arrows, lances, and stones. As they ran through the streets, they used slings to hurl hot coals onto the thatched roofs of the houses, setting them ablaze. While Cusco burned and acrid smoke hung low over the city, the forces engaged in fierce hand-to-hand combat. At the same time teams of Indians constructed barricades to consolidate their advance and block off parts of neighborhoods. They diverted water from the aqueducts into the fields to hinder horse movement and dug pits for them to trip into. Spanish auxiliaries worked feverishly to undo these measures.

Hernando, sending the first of several messages to Pizarro for help, organized his defense around the cavalry. Under the leadership of Gonzalo, Hernán Ponce de León, and Gabriel de Rojas they each used a dozen horses to charge and disrupt Indian formations. Even though killing large numbers, the cavalry charges through the narrow streets were not as

---

[54] Hemming, *Conquest of the Incas*, 190; MacQuarrie, *Last Days of the Incas*, 199. Prescott; von Hagen, *Conquest of Peru*, 336-37, differs, claiming that there was a major engagement here.

[55] MacQuarrie, *Last Days of the Incas*, 199.

effective as on the plains, as Indians began to walk the walls of the houses to avoid the crushing power of the men on horseback. Battles raged neighborhood by neighborhood against seemingly inexhaustible numbers. After a week, Manco's forces were in possession of most of the charred remains of Cusco. The Spanish eventually retreated to two large palace complexes in the north of the city, Hatun Cancha and Suntur Huasi.

Barricading themselves in the two palace complexes, Hernando realized that they had gone from the frying pan into the fire. Situated high above them was the fortress of Sacsayhuamán, which they had left unguarded and the Indians now occupied. Vila Oma had taken it for his headquarters and his men, invulnerable to attack, were raining down hot coals, arrows, and lances onto their position. Superb leader that he was, Hernando decided that their only hope of defeating the attack and saving themselves lay in gaining control of the fortress. But how? It seemed impregnable, but Pascac, the Inca half-brother of Manco who had sided with Pizarro, told them that although the fortress was impregnable from the city side, with its nearly perpendicular walls, it was vulnerable from the north.[56]

Hernando devised a two-pronged plan. He saw that the Indians had brought their women and servants with them to cook and manage the camps to which they retired every night. He decided to disrupt their camps, sending his cavalry charging into them, killing all the women he could and cutting the hands off the servants. This not only forced the Indians to defend the camps, it demoralized the attackers. While carrying out these disruptive tactics in what was a no holds-barred conflict, on May 13, Hernando sent Juan with fifty horsemen to find the back way into the Sacsayhuamán fortress. Juan charged through the Indians guarding the northwest gate to the high road leading to Jauja. But after riding for a time, he wheeled around and in a broad flanking movement made for the high plain where three very large walled terraces bounded the fortress on the north side.

---

[56] Hemming, *Conquest of the Incas*, 197.

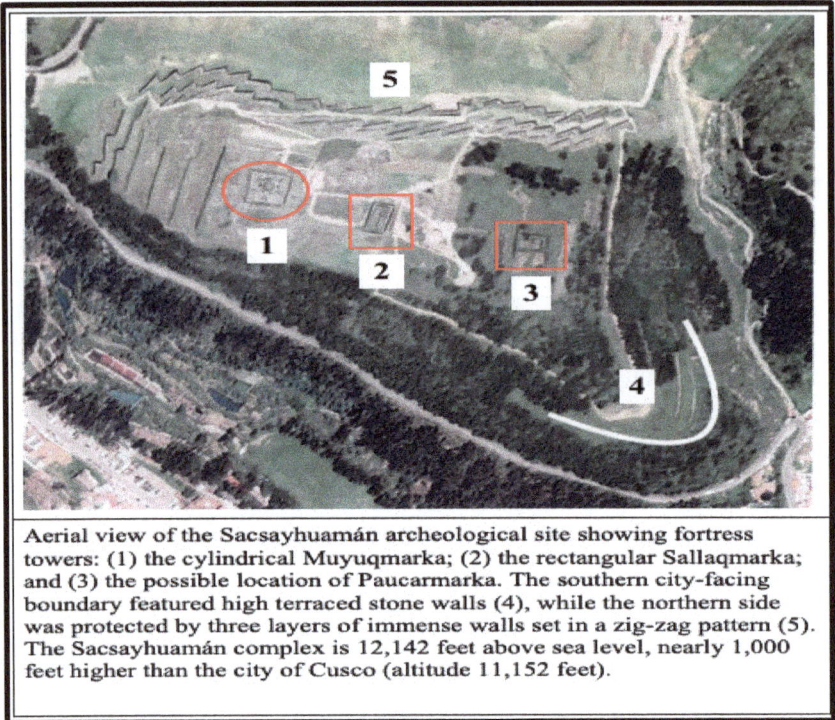

Aerial view of the Sacsayhuamán archeological site showing fortress towers: (1) the cylindrical Muyuqmarka; (2) the rectangular Sallaqmarka; and (3) the possible location of Paucarmarka. The southern city-facing boundary featured high terraced stone walls (4), while the northern side was protected by three layers of immense walls set in a zig-zag pattern (5). The Sacsayhuamán complex is 12,142 feet above sea level, nearly 1,000 feet higher than the city of Cusco (altitude 11,152 feet).

6.3. Aerial view of Sacsayhuamán

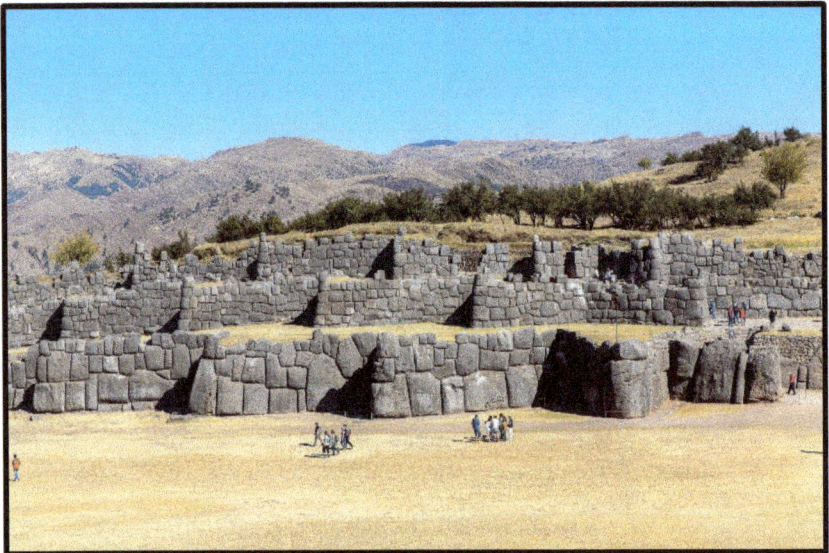

6.4. Zig-zag walls at Sacsayhuamán. Vitaly Markov/Alamy Stock Photo

Thus began the battle for Sacsayhuamán, which would determine victory or defeat for either side. The polygonal walled terraces were designed in a jagged, zig zag fashion which enabled supporting defensive attacks from two directions against an assault anywhere along its length. But Hernando, realizing the significance of the battle, decided to risk all and virtually denuded the defense of the city to send Cañari, Chachapoya, and Huari reinforcements to support the Spanish assault on the terraces. After a ferocious struggle, with attack followed by counterattack over the course of two weeks, the Spanish/allied force managed to muscle their way up the terraces.

The major casualty in the attack on the first terrace was Juan Pizarro, who, fighting without a helmet because of a previous injury to his jaw, was hit by a stone slung from above and immediately felled. He would languish and then expire after two weeks, the first Pizarro casualty. Hernando assigned Gonzalo to his leadership post and the battle continued. Using hastily improvised scaling ladders, the Spanish and their Indian allies climbed the highest terrace and then assaulted the fortress on top with its commanding towers. The Indians fought fiercely, but ran out of ammunition stones and arrows, forcing Vila Oma to steal silently away to Calca to plead for reinforcements. By the time he returned the Spanish were in control of Sacsayhuamán and were able to defend their position in Cusco itself. Manco's men kept pressure on Cusco with periodic attacks and guerrilla-style strikes for most of the summer, hoping to starve the inhabitants out, but the city remained in Spanish hands. Indeed, as Flickema notes, "the overall intensity diminished significantly after May of 1536."[57]

When Pizarro learned of the rebellion in early May he acted quickly to consolidate his position at Lima, send reinforcements to Cusco, and call for assistance from other colonial outposts in the Americas. He sent messages to all of the settlements to congregate in Lima, but with no contact he was operating blindly, had no knowledge of the scope of the rebellion, but had to assume the worst. Some settlers stayed where they were, some were fearful, wanting to depart, but Pizarro sent every ship in

---

[57] Thomas Flickema, "The Siege of Cusco," *Revista de Historia de América*, no. 92 (Jul-Dec 1981):25-26.

the harbor at Callao away to bring back reinforcements and supplies. He assumed that Lima might be the last outpost and was determined to hold on until reinforcements arrived, but he knew that it would take weeks, if not months, for the ships to return.

His first decision was to send Juan Morgovejo de Quiñones with thirty horsemen to the high road to take control of the major road junction at Vilcashuamán, about two hundred and sixty miles west of Cusco. This would enable him to control movement along the road between Jauja and Cusco. Then, he sent Gonzalo de Tapia with seventy horsemen to reinforce Cusco, but he sent them along the coast road for a hundred miles before climbing up to the high road leading to Cusco.[58] But Manco's general Quizo Yupanqui, whose mission it was to control the high road between Cusco and Jauja, was already in place and ready with plans to thwart them.

Quizo's plan was to trap the Spanish in the many narrow passes, ravines, defiles, and gorges that make up the Andes, and bombard them with boulders from on high. Disabling them they would then descend and attack, killing and beheading most, including the horses, while taking a few prisoners. Both the Morgovejo and Tapia contingents were taken in this way, the severest single clash defeats of the conquest. And there were more. Moving on the road to Jauja, Quizo's forces saw and trapped Diego Pizarro's sixty-man force heading for Cusco. The result was the same. Arriving at Jauja, Quizo's men surprised and slaughtered the two dozen or so *encomenderos* who were unaware of the danger. One escaped to Lima, but not in time to warn Pizarro.[59]

As news filtered back to Pizarro about Manco, he decided to name a new Inca to play on the divided loyalties of the Indians. Hastily crowning Manco's brother Cusi Rimac as his new Inca, he intended to send him to Jauja to establish his court there. He assigned Alonso de Gaete with a twenty-horse contingent to escort him and his substantial retinue. After they had left, the lone Jauja survivor arrived, warning Pizarro of the loss of Jauja. Pizarro quickly sent Francisco de Godoy with thirty horsemen to assist, but this entire scheme collapsed. Cusi Rimac had been collaborating with Manco all along, and led Gaete into a devastating ambush in which

---

[58] MacQuarrie, *Last Days of the Incas*, 233-34.
[59] Ibid., 236-38.

eighteen of his twenty men were killed. Two escaped, encountering Godoy's men on the road, and they returned to Lima together.[60] Quizo controlled the high road.

Lima, Do or Die

By June 1536 Manco had concluded that he could not take Cusco. Despite his large force, the close confines of the city meant he could not overwhelm the Spaniards with numbers; and where he could use numbers on the open ground, the Spaniards devastated them with horsepower. The best estimate of total Spanish killed at Cusco was less than twenty, as opposed to several thousand Indians.[61] Moreover, the Andean people were not solidly behind the Inca as large tribes and vassals supported the Spaniards with men and provisions against the Inca tyranny. It was also clear that he could not maintain his large force around Cusco for much longer, because his fighters were mostly farmers who would soon begin to return to their fields for planting season.

His choice was to revert to guerrilla war, where his men had already had considerable success. He could always concentrate superior forces against smaller targets and make the roads unsafe, but the failure to take Cusco insured that he could not marshal another sizable army for another try. Therefore, Manco broke camp at Calca, which was too vulnerable to attack. He moved his headquarters to Ollantaytambo, a massive and truly impregnable mountain fortress nine thousand feet above sea level overlooking the Urubamba River, twenty-five miles west of Calca.[62]

Finally, Manco may have realized that he had committed a strategic blunder by attacking Cusco first instead of Lima. Attacking Cusco first had a superficial plausibility to it as it was the Inca capital. But logistics was the essence of success and as long as Pizarro controlled the port of Lima, the Spaniards ultimately could count on an inexhaustible supply of men, weapons, horses, and provisions. Even though no ships had

---

[60] Ibid., 239-40.
[61] Flickema, "The Siege of Cusco," 32.
[62] For an astute analysis of the significance and purpose of monumental architecture of the Andes, see Zecharia Sitchin, *The Lost Realms,* (New York: Harper/Collins, 1990).

arrived since the outbreak of the rebellion, they were coming. It was only a matter of time. Only by seizing Lima and shutting down the supply line would he have a chance for victory.

Thus, Manco ordered General Quizo to attack Lima as soon as it was possible. Lima was a very different place to attack compared to Cusco, for there could be no surprise. Located twelve miles in from the coast, rolling hills ringed the city on three sides, but a large plain lay between them and the city itself, which was also linked to its port of Callao by the Rimac River.

6.5. Sacred Valley of the Incas

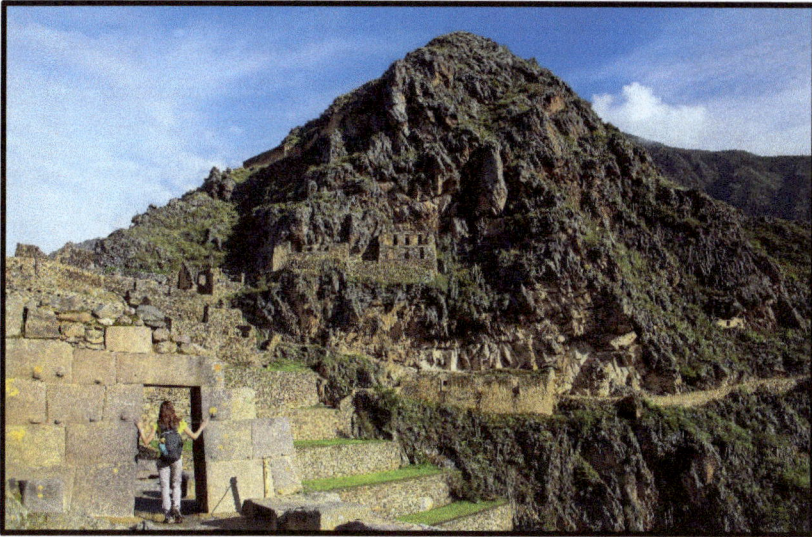

6.6. Ollantaytambo. Don Mammoser/Alamy Stock Photo.

Pizarro's earlier recall of his forces to Lima saw Alonso de Alvarado return from Chachapoyas with fifty men and thirty horses. Gonzalo de Olmos came in from Puerto Viejo with seventy men and horses and Garcilaso de la Vega arrived from San Mateo Bay with eighty men.[63] Thus, although Pizarro had lost close to two hundred men and a hundred horses to Quizo's guerrilla attacks in the Central Highlands, he had gained roughly that many back with the return of his scattered forces. Not all had responded to his call for assistance. As far as the record shows, neither Sebastián de Benalcázar, nor Pedro de Alvarado provided assistance, even though in the latter case, a desperate Pizarro offered to withdraw entirely from Peru if only he would help to save it.[64]

By early August, Quizo had marshaled a force fifty thousand strong and was staging them in the hills beyond the city. The moment that Pizarro had dreaded had come. To gauge their strength, Pizarro sent Pedro de Lerma with seventy horses to carry out a spoiling operation. In what was a "sharp engagement," Lerma's men punished Quizo's forces, but suffered one dead and several wounded.[65] Lerma's attack offered lessons

---

[63] Hemming, *Conquest of the Incas,* 208-09.
[64] Helps, *Spanish Conquest in America,* 4:55-56.
[65] Hemming, *Conquest of the Incas,* 210.

to both Quizo and Pizarro. It persuaded Quizo that the best way to assault Lima was to attack from three directions simultaneously to dilute the Spanish ability to respond with their cavalry. Thus, he positioned one group between Callao and Lima to cut off any possibility of escape by sea, and the other two in the hills northeast and east of the city.

Pizarro drew a different lesson from Lerma's operation. He realized that his forces could easily be overwhelmed if attacked from three sides at once and so reverted to the same plan he had used at Cajamarca— to funnel the Inca into the city and then attack them in its close confines. Although this discomfited his captains, who preferred to operate in the open plain, Pizarro chose the plan that would allow him to utilize all of his weapons—cannon, arquebus, cavalry, and auxiliaries— in a combined and concentrated defense.

Pizarro trained his guns on the approach to the city and hid his horsemen in two echelons in side streets on either side of the city gates, with foot soldiers further back. When Quizo's troops reached the gates of the city, Pizarro gave the signal to fire his guns. The barrage ripped through the front ranks, stopping them in their tracks.[66] The cavalry came next pushing them back into the plain where they were followed by the foot soldiers and auxiliaries, who dealt heavy blows, driving the attackers back into the hills.

Quizo and his commanders retired to the safety of the hills and prepared for their next assault. It would be five days of anxious waiting for the citizens of Lima. While they awaited the next assault, Pizarro sought help from the Huaylas community of his "wife" Doña Inés (Quispe Sisa). She agreed to ask her mother Contarhuacho to send troops, but on one condition. It appears that Doña Inés saw an opportunity to rid herself of a perceived competitor for Pizarro's affections, one princess Azarpay. Azarpay had been betrothed to Túpac Huallpa, whom Pizarro had named Inca. But when Túpac Huallpa died suddenly on the road to Cusco, Azarpay disappeared to avoid being handed over to one of Pizarro's

---

[66] Hemming, Cieza de León, Kochis, and others all fail to mention Pizarro's use of guns in defense of Lima, but recent discoveries prove otherwise. MacQuarrie, *Last Days of the Incas*, 254 does. See also Lucy Odling-Smee, "Early Gunshot Victim Uncovered," *Nature*, June 20, 2007, who notes recent archeological evidence showing conclusively that Pizarro's forces utilized muskets in the defense of Lima.

captains as a concubine. When the rebellion broke out, she went to Lima for protection and was living in Pizarro's household.[67]

Doña Inés accused Azarpay of harboring spies for Manco among her servants and demanded that Pizarro execute her, or she would not ask her mother for assistance. After a brief interview, Pizarro promptly had Azarpay garroted. It seems unlikely that Doña Inés issued such an ultimatum, given the fact that her own life was at stake. In any event, Contarhuacho did send troops, and they proved important to the defense of the city.[68] But there must have been something to the story because shortly after the siege was broken, Pizarro parted company with Doña Inés, passing her off to one of his pages, Francisco de Ampuero, while he took up the company of the third Incan princess living in his household, Cuxirimay.

While the household drama was being played out in Lima, Quizo sent his report of the battle by *chaskis* to Manco with a request for further orders. There can be no doubt what those orders were. They were to do or die. Quizo transmitted these orders to his men, saying "I intend to enter the town today and kill all the Spaniards who are in it....Those who accompany me must go with the understanding that if I die, all will die, and if I flee, then all will flee." They all agreed.[69] The second attack on Lima suffered the fate of the first but was far worse. Quizo and his captains were all killed leading their forces in the first assault. With their commanders dead, the troops became disorganized, as Spanish cavalry, foot soldiers, and auxiliaries slaughtered large numbers while forcing them back into the hills in disarray.

Pizarro's Victory

Pizarro's defense of Lima in August and Hernando's preemptive nighttime attack against forces marshaling outside of Cusco the following

---

[67] For different accounts of this episode, see Varón, *Francisco Pizarro and His Brothers*, 186; Hemming, *Conquest of the Incas*, 211; and Stirling, *Pizarro*, 137.

[68] Thomas Ward, *Decolonizing Indigeneity: New Approaches to Latin American Literature* (Lexington: Lexington Books, 2016), 192, says that Contarhuacho sent troops to protect her daughter, countering the notion of a quid pro quo over Azarpay.

[69] MacQuarrie, *Last Days of the Incas*, 255.

month effectively ended the Inca Rebellion.[70] Moreover, the Inca Empire was no more, reduced now to its Quechua core and a handful of allies. Even though Hernando was unable to drive Manco out of his mountain redoubt at Ollantaytambo, Manco saw that his dream of driving the Spaniards out of Peru had ended, as he began to contemplate leaving his country entirely.[71] Supply ships were streaming in to Callao, bringing in men, horses, weapons, and provisions. The Spaniards were here to stay.

One would have to conclude that the final months of 1536 were the most satisfying of Pizarro's life. He had defeated the Inca challenge and Manco was a man on the run. He had firmly reestablished Spanish rule, although he would have to deal with nuisance attacks periodically. And he had revitalized his personal life, settling in Lima with his new paramour, Cuxirimay (Doña Angelina).[72] But all was not sweetness and light. While the serious threat of native rebellion had ended, just over the horizon a new threat of rebellion arose—from none other than Pizarro's old partner, Diego de Almagro.

---

[70] There is some confusion about the Inca rebellion, its duration, demise, and even its description. The term "siege" is misused. The definition of "siege" involves surrounding a town, preventing supplies from entering, and forcing the surrender of its inhabitants. Thus, strictly speaking there was neither a siege of Cusco, nor Lima, but there obviously were attacks. Further, the Indians were never able to surround either city and prevent supplies from getting in, or prevent Spanish food forays and attacks. At most, the siege of Cusco lasted three weeks, until the recapture of Sacsayhuamán at the end of May. There was no siege at Lima. Rebellion there certainly was, and it did continue in guerrilla form after its initial defeat. Manco disbanded his army around Cusco to allow his warriors to leave for the planting season. They never returned. The failure to distinguish between the Inca and many opposing tribes is also unfortunate, for it assumes wrongly that rebellion was generalized among the population when it was not. There was as much of a conflict of natives against the Inca, as there was of Inca against the Spaniards.

[71] Kochis, *God, Glory and Gold*, 2:509-10.

[72] Stirling, *Pizarro*, 174-75.

Chapter 7

Whom the Gods Would Destroy, They First Make Mad

A form of insanity now descended on Peru as the factional struggle between the Pizarrists and the Almagrists driven by their base instincts of greed, lust, and depravity precipitated the near destruction of the colonial enterprise. It would take over a decade before the Crown was able to stabilize its Peruvian colony, and at great cost. Years of subsequent effort by the Crown, the council of Indies, the clergy, and its partisan historians would not be able to erase the indelible stain of Spanish blood spilled on the Andean nation.

As Helps saw it, the preoccupation with treasure "destroyed almost every person of any note who came within its influence, desolated the country where it originated, prevented the growth of colonization, and changed for the worse the whole course of legislation for the Spanish colonies. Its effects were distinctly visible for a century afterward."[1] All but one of the dramatis personae met violent ends; the single exception, Hernando Pizarro, escaped only by virtue of being imprisoned in Spain for over twenty years. The rest, except Juan, and including Francisco and Gonzalo Pizarro, Francisco Martín de Alcántara, Diego de Almagro and his son, Diego II known as *El Mozo* (meaning "the younger"), and Manco Inca all died violent deaths at the hands of Spaniards.

The madness, if that is what it was, began at the top with King Charles, who was constantly at war, especially with France in Italy, and with the Ottoman Empire in Hungary and in the Mediterranean; and

---

[1] Arthur Helps, *The Spanish Conquest in America and Its Relation to the History of Slavery and to the Government of Colonies,* vol. 4 (New York: Harper & Bros., 1868), 12.

preoccupied with internal rebellions in Castile, Ghent, and the Frisian Islands. Charles was also in perennial debt, dependent upon the growing stream of silver and gold coming from America, yet perpetually worried that this seemingly infinite source of collateral would dry up. In 1535, he was negotiating the largest loan from international bankers ever arranged, some 800,000 ducats, which would be substantially financed through future revenues from America.[2] The eruption of conflict between Pizarro and Almagro therefore caused great concern in that regard. It led the king to become overly involved in an attempt to resolve their differences, only to precipitate the very turn of events he hoped to forestall.

Almagro's Delusion

In Peru, the madness first touched Diego de Almagro. By virtue of the recently negotiated agreement to share equally all of their treasure, Almagro could have claimed half of what Pizarro had and enriched their partnership. Instead, he perceived an opportunity and concocted a scheme to displace his erstwhile partner and take it all. The Inca rebellion with its threat to disrupt silver shipments to Spain offered him the opportunity. If Almagro could blame the Pizarros for the rebellion, bring peace, restore the alliance with Manco, and ensure continuity of silver shipments to Spain, he stood a chance of replacing Pizarro and assuming the governorship of both New Castile and New Toledo. It was a breathtaking idea, born of the terrible ordeal of his southern expedition.[3]

---

[2] Sergio Sardone, "Forced Loans in the Spanish Empire: The First Requisition of American Treasures in 1523," *Economic History Review* 72, no.1 (May 2018):7.
[3] See Paul Kochis, *God, Glory and Gold: Journey to the Conquest of the Incas,* vol. 2, *The Quest* (Minneapolis: Mill City Press, 2013), 512-26.

7.1. Almagro's expedition into Chile, 1535-1537

The four thousand-mile trek into Chile, lasting a year and a half, was a catalog of crises, conflicts, and disappointments. Within weeks of departure from Cusco, Almagro's expedition began to suffer native defections—including their guide Vila Oma, the Incan High Priest; hostile encounters with native tribes, extreme privation, and no treasure. They took the Inca high road south along the towering cordillera from Lake Titicaca through deep penetrating snow and freezing temperatures past the towns of Tupiza, Chicoana, and Copiapo. Penetrating as far as the Maule River, south of present-day Santiago, they encountered the fiercely hostile, and invincible, Araucanian tribes of southern Chile when they decided to return.

Except for the natives they chained, the rest deserted them, leaving the five hundred and seventy men to their own devices. Many froze to death in their saddles attempting to make their way through high mountain passes. Their only recourse was a resort to brute force to compel native assistance along the way. Diverging to what they thought would be a more temperate route on the way back, they were forced to cross the high Atacama Desert, the driest non-polar region on earth, five thousand feet above sea level with daytime temperatures exceeding 100 degrees F. Only by fashioning water bags from llama bladders were they able to traverse the region from one dank water hole to the next.

In January 1537, they emerged from the desert into the pleasant mountain region of Arequipa, at 7,500 feet elevation and situated at the base of the Misti Volcano, rising to 19,000 feet. Food and water were abundant and temperatures mild. While they attempted to recover from their ordeal, they received news from Cusco of the great rebellion then nearing its end. The revolt raised the distinct possibility that Pizarro's hold on Peru had weakened, leading Almagro and his men to conjure up ways to reclaim what they felt was rightfully theirs.[4]

It was in Arequipa, embittered by the privations of the journey, where Almagro and his chief lieutenants, especially Rodrigo Orgóñez and Gómez de Alvarado, conceived and began to execute their plan to seize power in Peru from Pizarro. Underlying all they did was the belief that they had been given a raw deal—by the king, who they thought had allotted worthless territory; by Pizarro, who had "purposely tricked" them into going on a wild goose chase in Chile;[5] by the hated Hernando, who had withheld the king's decision from them in Cusco; and by the Indians who promised that they would find riches in Chile immeasurably greater than there were in Cusco.[6]

The origin of their disaffection began on the expedition itself when Almagro's man, Juan de Rada, delivered the Crown's warrants officially granting Almagro's land of New Toledo and Pizarro's extension

---

[4] Reuben Silverman (online), "A Kingdom Set Aflame: Diego De Almagro and the Struggle for Spanish Peru," December 26, 2013, pt. 6, "Failure in Chile and the Struggle for Cusco," reubensilverman.wordpress.com.

[5] William H. Prescott, *History of the Conquest of Peru,* partly abridged and revised by Victor W. von Hagen (New York: New American Library, 1961), 354.

[6] The road not taken. One can only imagine how different this history would have been had Almagro acted on reports that there were large silver deposits at a place called Potosí just to the south and east of Lake Titicaca.

to New Castile. Pizarro had declined to forward the authorizations to Almagro when Hernando first brought them from Spain, wanting to remove any temptation for his partner to return immediately to Cusco. So, he "gave time for the Adelantado to become more and more distant, and that the royal warrant might reach him at so remote a point, and probably find him so involved in difficulties…as to render it impossible for him to return."[7]

As Almagro and his men chewed over the terms of the warrants, they noticed two points that offered them hope. The first was that nowhere in either man's warrant was there reference to the city of Cusco itself. Second, they saw that there were several "ways of reckoning the [extended area] which had been assigned to Pizarro." Thus, it is clear that they knew and understood that the king had enlarged Pizarro's realm by an additional seventy leagues beyond his original two hundred, but they disputed that it included Cusco. As they saw it, depending on whether the distance was measured by the "royal road," "as the crow flies," "north to south," "east to west," or along the sinuous coastline, one could arrive at a different result for each. [8] The ambiguity of the warrants was sufficient to encourage Almagro to lay claim to Cusco; but Cusco was simply a pretext to take the first step in a larger design.

From Arequipa, Almagro sent two letters, one to Manco and another to Hernando. To Manco he donned the mantle of peacemaker, offering an alliance and proposing a meeting to work out the details. Based

---

[7] Manuel José Quintana, *Lives of Vasco Nunez de Balboa and Francisco Pizarro,* trans. Margaret Hodson (Edinburgh: William Blackwood, 1832; repr., Kessinger, 2010), 261.

[8] Helps, *Spanish Conquest in America,* 4:64-65, characterizing Pizarro's newly extended grant as "two hundred and seventy-five leagues." Others, citing official documents, record that the king had increased Pizarro's *gobernación* to two hundred and seventy leagues, instead of the two hundred included in the 1529 *Capitulación.* See Rafael Varón Gabai, *Francisco Pizarro and His Brothers, The Illusion of Power in Sixteenth-Century Peru,* trans. Javier Flores Espinoza (Norman: University of Oklahoma Press, 1997), 301. Kim MacQuarrie, *The Last Days of the Incas* (New York: Simon & Shuster, 2007), 270, differs on who knew what, saying "Almagro was unaware of the fact that the King had already extended the southern boundary of Pizarro's realm, [thus] he believed that there was still a good chance Cusco actually lay within the northern boundary of his own governorship."

on their past friendship and claiming to be acting on behalf of the king, he said that Pizarro had provoked the rebellion and that the king would recognize Manco's "just" war in response and pardon him. Their combined forces would be powerful enough to take control of Cusco and strengthen both their claims against Pizarro.[9]

Almagro's second letter was to Hernando and struck an entirely different chord. He had come as an ally. He avowed that he had returned from Chile as soon as he had heard of the rebellion and the attacks on Cusco, which he claimed as his city by virtue of the king's recently received warrant. As governor of New Toledo, he was coming to Cusco with his army to "punish the rebellious Indians." Therefore, "there was no need to worry," nor should his arrival "cause any concern."[10] But Almagro did not go to Cusco. Instead, departing Arequipa he marched directly north to the small town of Urcos, some twenty-five miles southeast of Cusco, and waited.

Hernando was, of course, not fooled by Almagro's blandishments, nor had he forgotten their long history of personal antagonism and conflict over Cusco. He knew there was no longer a threat to Cusco from Manco and that Almagro's professed intent to "punish the rebellious Indians" was a cover for a more insidious objective of seizing Cusco for himself. Spies, ubiquitous in Peru, had informed Hernando of Almagro's letter to Manco. He had also noted that the Indians previously encamped around the city had withdrawn, indicating possible cooperation with Almagro.

Hoping to inject a sliver of doubt into Manco's thinking, Hernando sent his own letter to Manco in Ollantaytambo. He made it plain that Pizarro was the king's representative in Peru, not Almagro, who was his subordinate and therefore without authority to make offers of any kind. He also said that Almagro was deceiving Manco into believing that he wanted him as an ally. In fact, Hernando averred, Almagro intended to kill him, replace him with Paullu, as Inca, and take credit for ending the rebellion.[11]

---

[9] Kochis, *God, Glory and Gold*, 2:518-19.

[10] Pedro Cieza de León, "Guerra de Las Salinas," *Guerras Civiles del Perú* (Madrid: Libraria de la Viuda de Rico, 1899), 27, as quoted in MacQuarrie, *Last Days of the Incas*, 270.

[11] Stuart Stirling, *Pizarro: Conqueror of the Inca*, (Stroud: Sutton, 2005), 105.

Hernando's letter combined with Almagro's troop movements created intense anxiety in Manco's mind. Could he trust Almagro, with whom he had once had a close relationship, but who had spent the past year and a half with his brother Paullu? Were they plotting against him, as Hernando claimed? Why, he wondered, had Almagro moved half of his troops from Urcos around Cusco and into Calca in the Yukay Valley? There could be no question of any relationship with Hernando, but were the two of them colluding against him? Disquieting was the fact that his scouts had witnessed a meeting of their soldiers a few days before. For insurance, Manco deployed five thousand men to the environs of Calca.[12]

To determine whether Almagro was sincere, Manco brought the two Spaniards' emissaries before him, demanding that Almagro's man chop off the hand of Hernando's messenger. He complied, but neatly chopped off only a single digit. Apparently satisfied, Manco sent the messenger, minus a digit, back to Hernando. Then, he sent Almagro's messengers back with his agreement to hold a meeting in Calca. But no sooner had the messengers left than yet a third emissary arrived in Ollantaytambo to try his skill as a negotiator.

Rui Díaz, one of Almagro's men who had been friendly to Manco, arrived to plead Almagro's case. Manco received him amicably but insisted that he demonstrate Almagro's hostility to Hernando by lopping off the heads of four of Hernando's scouts he had captured. When Díaz protested that he could not murder a fellow Spaniard, Manco had him tied to a stake, his hair and beard shorn, and pelted with sticky guava fruit before releasing him to return to Almagro. The die was cast. Manco would trust none of them. There would be no alliance and he ordered his troops around Calca to attack Almagro's forces there.[13] The attack signaled that

---

[12] William H. Prescott, *History of the Conquest of Peru*, vol. 2 (New York: Harper & Bros., 1847), 90; and Kochis, *God, Glory and Gold*, 2:520.

[13] The Rui Díaz episode is replete with contradictions in the literature. Quintana, *Lives of Balboa and Pizarro*, 282, says Almagro sent him; John Hemming, *The Conquest of the Incas* (New York: Harcourt Brace Jovanovich, 1970), 226, says that he was attempting "personal diplomacy." Kochis says the four scouts were in Almagro's custody while MacQuarrie says that Manco had them; and as for the subsequent attack on Almagro's forces, Kochis blames Almagro for provoking them, while MacQuarrie, sees it as Manco's decision after ruling out an alliance: Kochis, *God, Glory and Gold*, 2:520-21; MacQuarrie, *Last Days of the Incas*, 266-69.

the first part of Almagro's plan, the alliance with Manco, had failed. He would henceforth insert Paullu into the role planned for Manco, while he pressed on with his second step, the seizure of Cusco.

For Manco, there was no alternative but to retreat, Ollantaytambo being too close to the enemy's positions. His own fighters were withering away, and "the bearded ones" were increasing in number. In addition to Almagro's forces at Urcos and Calca, and the garrison at Cusco, there was yet another even larger Spanish contingent at Jauja, within a few days' march. This was the large expeditionary force under Alonso de Alvarado, whom Pizarro had sent the previous November to control movement along the high Inca road. Manco and his trusted Inca core of supporters repaired to Vitcos, in Vilcabamba on the eastern side of the mountains at the edge of the Amazon forest, thinking he would be safe there, but he would be a hunted figure for the rest of his life.

Almagro Seizes Cusco and Wants More

Meanwhile, Hernando had responded to Almagro's letter (and no doubt contacted Pizarro for help). Hoping to buy time, he pleaded with Almagro to maintain the peace because only the Inca would profit from a conflict between them. He offered to welcome him into the city, saying that his "own quarters were prepared for him." He proposed they send a message to Pizarro "so that he might come and settle matters amicably." Almagro's response was an "evasive reply," while his forces moved closer, pitching camp "a league's distance from Cusco" on April 18, 1537.[14] There can be little doubt that the last thing Almagro wanted was to wait for the arrival of Pizarro to "settle matters."

Hernando sent a second message inviting Almagro to enter the city "as a friend," but he replied "haughtily," saying that he would enter Cusco only to occupy the governor's, that is, Hernando's, quarters, and none other. Hernando sent yet a third message pleading for amity "until the marquis should arrive." But Almagro replied that Cusco was his by authority of the King's grant and he meant to take it, moving his

---

[14] Helps, *Spanish Conquest in America*, 4:66.

encampment to within a crossbow's shot of the city. An attack seemed imminent.[15]

Hernando now called together the city council and enjoined them to send a delegation to Almagro to demand that "if he had powers from his majesty, he should present them before the council." To this Almagro assented, sending a messenger with the king's warrant. After studying it, the council observed that the warrants made no mention of the city and the line between the two men's lands was not clearly defined. Therefore, as Pizarro "had occupied the city of Cusco and held it as part of his government," the issue would have to be settled by "pilots," who could establish the exact beginning latitude of Pizarro's territory. Once that line was established and if "the city should fall within the limits of Almagro's government, they would be ready to receive him as governor." [16]

It would, of course, as Almagro well knew, take months to complete the task of surveying the land and he ordered his men to prepare to attack the city forthwith. It was now, he concluded, "an affair which arms or stratagem must decide." He would employ both. Amid growing tension, a second delegation of the council arrived hoping to arrange a peace, but the best they could obtain was a short extension of the truce during which time, Almagro said, "he wished to prove how Cusco fell within his limits." But this was a "stratagem" to put Hernando off guard. That very midnight of April 19, 1537, in a driving rain, Almagro's men under the command of his general, Rodrigo Orgóñez, charged into the city, surrounding the large palace where Hernando and Gonzalo were sleeping. The brothers with a dozen supporters defended themselves until the building was set on fire, at which point with the roof about to collapse, they surrendered.[17]

Almagro proclaimed Cusco the capital of New Toledo and named the able and neutral Gabriel de Rojas as mayor. The city council, several of whose members were sympathetic to Almagro, promptly recognized his

---

[15] Ibid.

[16] Ibid., 68-69 and Prescott, *History of the Conquest of Peru*, 2:91-92. (In the sixteenth century the means of establishing longitude had yet to be discovered.)

[17] Helps, *The Spanish Conquest in America*, 4:68-69. Prescott, *History of the Conquest of Peru*, 2:93-94, describes the same sequence of events happening ten days earlier.

"title" to the city. He also set about reassigning *encomiendas* and *repartimientos* to his followers, as well as reaffirming the grants to those inhabitants of the city who now professed their allegiance. Those who had sided with the Pizarros he imprisoned along with Hernando and Gonzalo, whom he locked in one of the towers at Sacsayhuamán. Orgóñez demanded that Almagro kill both men, but Almagro decided he would be better served to keep them alive as hostages.[18]

The only two immediate threats to his new realm were Manco in Vitcos with his depleted forces and Alonso de Alvarado in Jauja with a powerful seven hundred-man force, where he had been since the previous November. (The defense of Cusco had been accomplished without any assistance from Alvarado, which underscores the view that the danger to the city had already passed by the time he reached Jauja and certainly by the time that Almagro arrived at Arequipa in January of 1537.) Almagro determined to deal with the greater threat first. He entered into an exchange of messages with Alvarado, hoping to confuse him about the true state of affairs. Indeed, he invited Alvarado to join him, while he moved his troops into position to attack.[19] He would meet Alvarado at the Abancay River (likely the Pachachaca River on today's maps).

Alvarado, having learned about the Cusco coup, had already begun the five hundred-mile march to the city. Pizarro sent orders "not to move on to Cusco," hoping not to provoke Almagro, but it was too late.[20] By the end of the first week of July, he had reached the Abancay River, about one hundred and twenty miles west of Cusco, where he halted and prepared to meet Almagro's forces. He set a strong force at the bridge and a smaller one below where the river could be forded. Unfortunately for Alvarado, he assigned Pedro de Lerma to oversee the force at the ford. Lerma had been insulted by the fact that Pizarro had named Alvarado over him as commander and decided to defect to Almagro.

Thus, when Almagro's forces drew up at the bridge across the river from Alvarado's, they knew that Lerma would permit them to ford

---

[18] Prescott, *History of the Conquest of Peru*, 2:95-96, says that he declined to kill them because "he had still an attachment for his old associate, Francisco Pizarro."
[19] Quintana, *Lives of Balboa and Pizarro*, 289.
[20] Helps, *Spanish Conquest in America*, 4:76.

the river and circle around to attack Alvarado's forces from below. The attack commenced late on the night of July 12, ably assisted by ten thousand men under Paullu, who kept Alvarado's men preoccupied from the heights with rock throwing and hostile shouts. The battle ended quickly, with much confusion and few casualties on either side, but many prisoners.[21] Almagro threw Alvarado into the same cell with Gonzalo, but now put Hernando in separate confinement.

With the defeat of Alvarado and the incorporation of many of his men, Almagro believed that he was strong enough to strike directly at Pizarro's capital at Lima, which he now claimed as also falling within his jurisdiction! But before undertaking that task, at the end of July, Almagro sent Orgóñez with three hundred men after Manco, to ensure that when he mounted the offensive to conquer Lima, there would be no attack from behind. Orgóñez nearly captured Manco at Vitcos. But he was distracted while accumulating substantial treasure, including a highly venerated golden idol of the sun; and Manco was able to escape capture with only a few of his closest advisers, including his wife Cura Ocllo. They moved further through the dense forest and into the mountains to establish a state in exile in Vilcabamba, out of reach of Orgóñez' forces, but they were weakened sufficiently to be no longer a concern for Almagro.[22]

The outcome of the battle of Abancay, which changed the balance of forces in Almagro's favor, persuaded Pizarro to try to reach a settlement with him. He would need time to build up his forces, which were now arriving in response to his earlier calls for assistance. Importantly, the Crown was also troubled by the confrontation and sent mediators. These included Friar Francisco de Bobadilla, Provincial (supervisor) for the Order of Our Lady of Mercy in the Indies.[23] King Charles evidently realized that he had made a mistake by not explicitly including Cusco as

---

[21] Prescott, *History of the Conquest of Peru*, 2:96-97. Both Helps, *Spanish Conquest in America,* 4:72, and Quintana, *Lives of Balboa and Pizarro*, 291, say Lerma went over to Almagro's forces before the battle had begun. Kochis, MacQuarrie, and Stirling make no mention of Lerma. Hemming, *Conquest of the Incas,* 229, stresses the role Paullu's men played in the battle, while also omitting any mention of Lerma.

[22] MacQuarrie, *Last Days of the Incas*, 286-90.

[23] Stirling, *Pizarro,* 109. Varón, *Pizarro and His Brothers*, 154-55 notes that the Mercedarians "had a long-standing connection with the Pizarros."

part of Pizarro's territory. Rather than issuing another *cédula* to clarify his intention, he would allow a third party to "adjudicate" the matter in favor of Pizarro. It would be a long, tortuous process.

Negotiations were initiated by Pizarro, who sent a group of respected emissaries to speak with Almagro in Cusco. The delegation included Gaspar de Espinosa, a friend to both men and their silent partner in the original enterprise to explore the South Seas. If anyone could reconcile the two antagonists, it would be their old friend and benefactor. Espinosa appealed to Almagro's grander instincts, declaring that surely there was room enough in Peru for the two men to extend their authority without doing what will "irritate Heaven, offend the King, and fill the world with scandals and disasters." But Almagro held firm to what he believed were his rights to Cusco. Exasperated, Espinosa warned that what would come to pass was foretold by the old Castilian proverb: "*El vencido vencido, y el vencedor perdido,*" which, loosely translated, meant: "the conqueror will be conquered, and the victor ruined." Unfortunately, there was no opportunity for this wisdom to sink in, as Espinosa suddenly and unexpectedly expired.[24]

Espinosa's death stalled the mediation effort and cleared the way for Almagro to press on with his plan to attack Lima. The defeat of Pizarro would confer command of all Peru to him. With Orgóñez as his captain-general, Almagro moved off with his forces across the mountains toward Lima, but two developments forced a deferral of this plan. The first was news that Gonzalo and Alvarado had escaped and were bound for Lima. Seeking an explanation, Almagro discovered that opportunists had perforated his Cusco base. Captured prisoners, bribing their captors, were slipping away "twenty by twenty and ten by ten," most of whom made their way back to Pizarro's camp.[25]

One of his officers, Lorenzo de Aldana, had conspired to bring about the release of Gonzalo and Alvarado. Aldana had demanded that Almagro award him a bonus for joining the march on Lima, but he declined. Staying behind, in revenge or pique, Aldana took bribes from Gonzalo and Alvarado instead, freeing them. The Aldana episode

---

[24] Helps, *The Spanish Conquest in America*, 4:76-77.
[25] Silverman, "A Kingdom Set Aflame," pt. 6.

indicated that Almagro's hold on the loyalty of his men was weakening. Still, Almagro had Hernando in custody, taking him along under close guard wherever he went. Even though Orgóñez repeatedly demanded that Hernando be killed, Almagro preferred to hold him as hostage, knowing that Pizarro would do nothing to jeopardize his brother's life.[26]

The second development was much more serious. It was intelligence regarding Pizarro's dramatic increase in strength, the result of his many calls for help from abroad during the Indian attacks on Cusco. Men and weapons in great numbers were streaming in to Lima from Panama, Mexico, Nicaragua, and even from Spain and Flanders. Pizarro's forces now stood at a thousand men and over a hundred and fifty guns. Eighty of the guns were newly developed arquebuses brought from Flanders. These guns delivered wire-shot projectiles—chain-linked ball shots that divided when fired and cut a swath of devastation. The wire shots were fairly effective at two hundred yards but devastating at close range. Pizarro had specifically ordered them from his agents in Seville.[27]

The information about Pizarro's greatly increased strength was enough for Almagro to suspend temporarily the plan to attack Lima, because the balance of forces was no longer in his favor. He was now outnumbered one thousand to eight hundred in men, and heavily outgunned. He realized that he, too, would have to strengthen his forces to match Pizarro's. Thus he redirected his men one hundred and twenty-five miles south of Lima to Chincha, where he proceeded to build a port through which he could receive reinforcements. All through the summer, with the help of Paullu's Indians, they constructed docks, piers, and fortifications for defense. Indian guards were deployed in the mountain passes to detect any hostile movements from Pizarro. He renamed his new port "Almagro."

---

[26] Ibid.

[27] Paul Stewart, "The Battle of Las Salinas, Peru, and Its Historians," *The Sixteenth Century Journal* 19, no. 3 (Autumn, 1988):416, and Kochis, *God, Glory and Gold*, 2:528-29.

The Roads to Las Salinas

By the fall of 1537, there had evolved a standoff between the two sides, as each attempted to build forces for the inevitable showdown for control of all Peru. Each now was interested in buying time to build up strength, and amenable to a proposal for arbitration. They agreed that Friar Bobadilla would be the arbiter of the dispute, and that he, "with the assistance of 'pilots,' should fix the limits of the respective governments of New Castile and New Toledo." Bobadilla set up his office in the Indian town of Mala, midway between Chincha/Almagro and Lima; and after his "pilots" had come to conclusions about boundaries, he called both parties to meet with him there on November 13, 1537.[28]

By agreement each leader was to bring only a dozen men with him, but suspicions were rife. Gonzalo heard that Almagro had brought more than the allotted dozen, and sought to do likewise, positioning a "body of crossbows" in the reeds nearby. When Pizarro and Almagro sat down with Bobadilla, they immediately traded barbs, each charging the other with acting illegally and violating the king's warrant. Pizarro demanded that Almagro relinquish the city to him, but Almagro replied: "Cusco is mine…. It belongs to my government, and I will keep it till the King commands me to restore it."[29]

At that point, an attendant, discovering Gonzalo's men in the reeds, quickly alerted Almagro to the danger by singing a little ditty:

> Tiempo es, caballero,
> Tiempo es ya de andar de aquí
> (Time it is, oh cavalier,
> Time it is thou were away).

Hearing the song and understanding its meaning, Almagro abruptly left the room, mounted his horse and sped away.[30] Almagro refused to return, but two days later his lawyers were summoned by Bobadilla to hear the verdict. He declared that "Cusco was within the two hundred and seventy-

---

[28] Helps, *Spanish Conquest in America*, 4:80.

[29] Quintana, *Lives of Balboa and Pizarro,* 311-12. Stirling, *Pizarro*, 109, claimed that Gonzalo had brought seven hundred armed men.

[30] Helps, *Spanish Conquest in America*, 4:81; and Quintana, *Lives of Balboa and Pizarro,* 311n2 say the song came from a remorseful member of Pizarro's camp, and reinforced a warning signal given to Almagro by one of his own men.

five leagues which the Emperor had assigned as the extent of Pizarro's government and...[Almagro] should quit that territory."[31] Furthermore, said the judge, Almagro must turn over to Pizarro all of the gold and silver that constituted the king's fifth. When Almagro's lawyers protested and said they would appeal this decision to the king and the Council of the Indies, Bobadilla replied "there could be no appeal" because both parties had agreed to him as arbitrator.[32]

Bobadilla's decision created a furor among Almagro's men who adamantly refused to give up their city. It appears that it was Pizarro who suggested to the judge a way to break the deadlock. Bobadilla was heard to remark that if empowered to settle the issue, he would rule that "Almagro's [territory] should commence with the new city bearing his name and include half the territory from thence to Lima." Hearing of this, Almagro decided that the prelate might be reasonable after all, and he authorized the resumption of negotiations.[33]

In essence, the settlement that emerged was a trade of Cusco for Hernando, which supports the notion that it was Pizarro's scheme to gain his brother's freedom. Almagro would retain Cusco "till the king should command otherwise," and Hernando would be set free upon his pledge to depart for Spain immediately. Almagro would evacuate Chincha, but Pizarro would provide him with a ship to assist in building a new port at Zangala, a few miles further south. Both men got what they wanted. Almagro gambled that freeing Hernando would lead to a reconciliation, but Orgóñez foretold disaster if Hernando were freed.[34] He was right. Hernando would return to Spain, but not before he had played an instrumental role in destroying Almagro.

Unfortunately, as the details of their agreement were being implemented over the next month, the king once again inserted himself into the proceedings. No sooner had Almagro released and delivered

---

[31] Helps, *Spanish Conquest in America,* 4:81-82.
[32] Quintana, *Lives of Balboa and Pizarro,* 313.
[33] Quintana, Ibid., 315, says probably Pizarro prompted Bobadilla to make this favorable assertion in order to mislead Almagro, who fell into Pizarro's trap.
[34] Ibid., 316; Helps, Spanish Conquest in America, 4:82-83; and Kochis, *God, Glory and Gold,* 2:537.

Hernando to Pizarro's camp, than a messenger arrived with a dispatch from the king. Intended to confirm their agreement, it had the opposite effect. The dispatch read that "each of the governors should retain whatever they had conquered and peopled until any other arrangement should be made by his majesty." [35]

Each leader interpreted this dispatch as supporting his position. When Pizarro went to Chincha to oversee Almagro's evacuation, he handed the dispatch to him. Almagro read it and replied that the "orders were in *his* favor, for from where *he* was to Chincha *he* had conquered and peopled the country, and, accordingly, he it was who was within the limits of his own government, and he begged that Pizarro would move out of it." As Helps notes, "there is no doubt that both sides now believed themselves to be wronged and affronted."[36] This was the war starter.

Thus began a series of moves and countermoves as each side maneuvered to get in a favorable position for the climactic battle. In January of 1538, when Pizarro sent his troops from Chincha along the royal road, his first challenge was to gain control of a snow-driven, 11,000-foot mountain pass at Huaytará, the first of several passes along the winding road to Cusco that offered natural places for ambushes as part of an attrition strategy. Although the pass seemed well defended, Hernando had personally led a small group ascent at night, surprising its defenders, who fled in seeming disarray. But it had been too easy.

Smelling a trick, Pizarro took his men back down the mountain to the nearby Ica Valley, where under much more temperate conditions they camped and assessed their options. He either sensed intuitively or received information from the many spies that abounded in both camps, that Almagro was attempting to lead him away from Lima so he could seize it for himself. Pizarro certainly understood the importance of maintaining control of Lima. It was not only his capital, but also his source of supply and reinforcements. So, he made the decision to turn command of the Cusco force over to Hernando, with Gonzalo as his second in command, while he returned to Lima to secure its defense against surprise attack. (Many scholars say that he returned to Lima because he was getting too

---

[35] Helps, *Spanish Conquest in America*, 4:84.
[36] Ibid., 85-86, emphasis added.

old to campaign, which may be true, but the strategic issue was paramount.)[37]

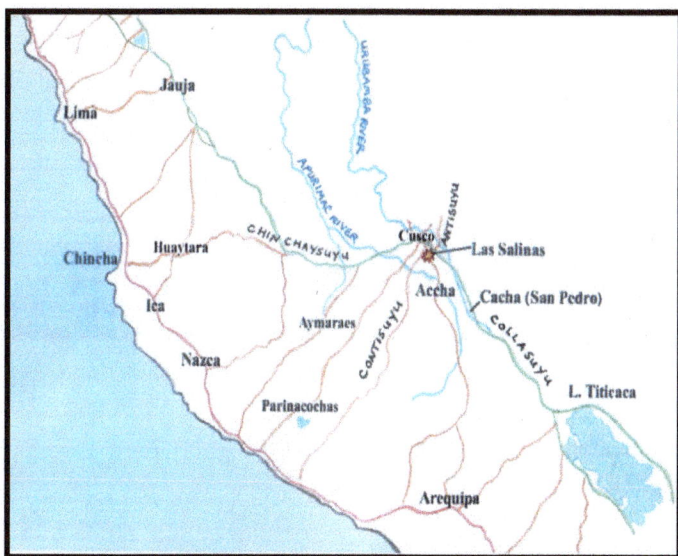

7.2. Area approaching the battlefield at Las Salinas

In fact, this very issue was being actively discussed in Almagro's camp. Orgóñez argued that they should *let* Pizarro take Cusco, while they streaked for Lima.[38] It would enable *them* to strengthen their forces while cutting Pizarro's off from new supplies. But Almagro, supported by most of his captains, decided to make a defense at Cusco. Paullu argued that the best defense was to catch Hernando's men in the passes. Volunteering to take on this task even without Spanish assistance, he declared that "in the passes I will defeat Hernando Pizarro and kill the greater part of his men," but Almagro rejected this course, too.[39] He and his men reasoned that the battleground should be a plain outside the city where their cavalry would dominate. Almagro assigned command of his army to Orgóñez, but he

---

[37] Prescott, *History of the Conquest of Peru*, 2:108, for example, says Pizarro speaking to his men "now declared that, as he was too old to take charge of the campaign himself, he should devolve that duty on his brother."

[38] Quintana, *Lives of Balboa and Pizarro*, 322-23.

[39] Hemming, *Conquest of the Incas*, 234.

relinquished his authority for a different reason than Pizarro. Almagro was being racked by syphilis, which had reached an advanced stage, affecting both his body and mind. He could travel only by litter and obviously could not lead his troops in battle.

In planning a defense, however, Orgóñez decided against a contest of cavalry charges even though he had superior numbers. Orgóñez had 680 men, three hundred cavalry, only a handful of arquebuses and a few small cannon. Pizarro had 650 men, two hundred and eighty cavalry, and some cannon, but he also had between one hundred and ten and one hundred and thirty arquebuses, which would be devastating on the open plain to man and horse alike, unless they could be protected with thick armor plate. So, as soon as they returned to Cusco, he ordered the fabrication of armor plate for coslets, helmets, and cladding for horses out of silver and copper, the only metals available.[40]

Whether based on intuition or secret intelligence, Hernando did not retrace the route north from the Ica Valley to proceed on the Chinchaysuyu royal road to Cusco. Instead, he decided upon a long enveloping movement, taking his forces in the other direction along the coastal road until he reached Nazca. From there, they marched inland northeast across the mountains, perhaps passing through the Accha district on the Contisuyu road, and then turning right across precarious terrain to access the Collasuyu road, which approached Cusco from the south.[41]

Pizarro's advantage in arquebuses dictated Orgóñez's strategy. While he fortified Cusco, he had no intention of attempting to defend the city because he knew that if he did Hernando would attack Sacsayhuamán

---

[40] Helps, *Spanish Conquest in America*, 4:92.

[41] Helps, Ibid., 91-93, says Hernando took his men first to Lanasca (Nazca) and then advanced "slowly to Cusco," having "to make long circuits, for it was winter, and the rivers being swollen, they were obliged to ford them high up in their streams....Having arrived at a place called Acha, he rested there five days for his men to recover from their fatigue." The term "winter" probably refers to Peru's rainy/wet season, which runs from December to March. Stewart, "The Battle of Las Salinas," 416-418, says that Hernando decided on a circuitous route from Nazca in order to foil Almagro's expectations, but "Almagro's men soon learned of it." According to Stewart, Hernando's army stopped at Parinacochas (Flamingo Lake) and Aymaraes, and then left the highway to "travel by uncertain roads, which would enable them to cross by the Caccha Bridge where Almagro would not expect them. On the other side of the river they could find the Collasuyu Highway to Cuzco."

and dominate the city from the fortress heights the way Manco had. Instead, he deployed his forces a few miles outside the city, where the Collasuyu royal road bisected swampy salt pans and where there were rolling hills on one side with some ruined houses and the river (Huatanay) on the other. "Orgóñez reckoned that if Pizarro's army came by that road, it being very narrow by reason of the salt pits which were on one side and on the other, he could easily destroy them."[42] He could also protect his men and cavalry behind the hills and ruined houses until the right moment when Hernando's arquebusiers had run out of ammunition. But Hernando's army left the main highway and approached over the plain that paralleled it.[43]

It was the morning of April 6, 1538. Orgóñez opened fire with his cannon while hastily attempting to reposition his men, but Hernando's "arquebusiers threw themselves forward, passed the swamp, and, taking up a position in the river, discharged their weapons at the enemy." Orgóñez tried to take his men "behind a little hill on the skirt of the sierra," but, "their fire was fatal."[44] Then, Hernando crossed the swampy salt pits with fifty cavalry, drawing Orgóñez and his cavalry out from behind the hill. It was a trick. As they prepared to charge, Hernando's "arquebusiers had now a good mark to fire at the large body of Almagro's troops advancing…"[45] Almagro, observing the battle from a nearby hilltop, as were thousands of Paullu's whooping Indians, realized the game was up and he hurriedly mounted a mule and made his way back to Cusco.

The arquebus had been the critical weapon determining the outcome of the battle, the second time in the Americas that these guns had proved a decisive complement to the man on horseback. The first time had

---

[42] Helps, *Spanish Conquest in America*, 4:94. This battle area lies in what is now a suburb of Cusco called San Sebastian, where a salty river called Cachimayo meets the Huatanay. The Incans built salt works there, causing the Spaniards to name it *Las Salinas*. See Hiram Bingham, *Inca Land: Explorations in the Highlands of Peru* (Boston, N.Y., Cambridge: Houghton Mifflin,1922; Project Gutenberg EBook, July 10, 2004), 148.

[43] Stewart, "The Battle of Las Salinas," 419, and Helps, *Spanish Conquest in America*, 4:96.

[44] Helps, *Spanish Conquest in America*, 4:98.

[45] Ibid., 99.

been in the defense of Lima. (This evolution in military technology was already well under way in Europe, and even in Asia, especially in Japan.) Orgóñez, losing his steed, had been "hit by a chain-shot from an arquebus, which, penetrating the bars of his visor, grazed his forehead, and deprived him for a moment of reason." Before he regained his senses, he was set upon by several foot soldiers who chopped him down while he was attempting to surrender.[46]

The arquebus volleys had broken and disorganized the defending forces, turning the battle into a melee, as the "cavalry on both sides were now mingled in hand to hand encounter." According to Helps, "Gonzalo Pizarro's charge had been the turning point of the engagement," forcing Orgóñez's men out of their "shelter amid the ruins," and chasing them down as they fled to Cusco. The battle of Las Salinas was over in two hours. Several hundred men lay dead or dying on the battlefield, most of them Almagro's. It was noted that "almost all of the wounds received this day were in the face, for so completely were the Spaniards [armored] that it was difficult to get at any man except in the face."[47]

The Madness Spreads

Although Hernando Pizarro's victory over Almagro at Las Salinas ended his role in this history, it did not end the factionalism, either Spanish or Incan, which proliferated and intensified. The hatreds spawned by the civil war continued to fester among the Spaniards, as "have-nots" resented the riches of the "haves." A similar fractionation occurred within Incan ranks, as Paullu, for whom Las Salinas demonstrated Spanish invincibility, "abruptly switched sides" in mid-battle and allied with Hernando.[48] Manco drew a different lesson from Las Salinas, believing that Spanish disarray provided an opportunity to reclaim power. He began to plot a new insurrection.

Entering Cusco, Hernando's troops found Almagro and imprisoned him in the same cell in which he had incarcerated Hernando

---

[46] Prescott, *History of the Conquest of Peru*, 2:117.
[47] Helps, *Spanish Conquest in America*, 4:100-01. Stewart, "The Battle of Las Salinas," 425, discusses the probable historical exaggeration of Gonzalo's role in the battle.
[48] MacQuarrie, *Last Days of the Incas*, 299.

and Gonzalo. The question was: how to deal with him? He was, after all, an officer of the king, a governor of New Toledo, and *adelantado*, and had to be treated with due deference. On the other hand, he had committed aggression, if not treason, by virtue of his attack on Pizarro and seizure of Cusco. Initial thinking was that as an officer of the Crown he should be sent back to Spain for trial. Informed of the victory at Las Salinas, Pizarro—the "marquis" as he was now called—set out for Cusco. He stopped in Jauja, presumably so as not to be involved directly in the proceedings against his old partner. While directing Hernando to send Almagro's son El Mozo to Lima, his orders regarding Almagro were that Hernando should "act so that he shall give us no further trouble."[49]

Hernando promised Almagro that he "would be kindly treated, and justice well considered in his case." Indeed, setting his personal feelings of animus aside, Hernando permitted him considerable latitude in his imprisonment, until it was discovered that he was communicating with his followers. At the same time, Hernando initiated formal proceedings against him, calling on anyone who held a grievance to record it, a dossier amounting to two thousand pages.[50] The proceedings, which took over three months to complete, not concluding until the first week in July 1538, provided the basis for charges pressed against Almagro.

In the meantime, there were over a thousand soldiers in Cusco. Half of these were vanquished and disgruntled Almagrists, who were left with nothing. They demanded that they be given the opportunity to amass wealth for themselves. The solution decided upon was to authorize a number of "expeditions" around the country to provide that opportunity. Hernando sent Alonso Mercadillo with several hundred men to Jauja; Pedro de Vergara to Bracemoros; Alonso de Alvarado to Chachpoyas (for the second time); and Pedro de Candia to the high Andes of Antisuyu, the easternmost region of the Inca Empire. There were others, but the overall effect was to relieve the stresses on Cusco, while providing opportunities for the men in the field to obtain some wealth.

---

[49] Stirling, *Pizarro*, 115.
[50] Quintana, *Lives of Balboa and Pizarro*, 332.

Candia's expedition became the focus of trouble, as over three hundred and fifty of Almagro's men joined it, secretly planning to free their leader. After proceeding some two hundred miles across treacherous terrain, these men persuaded Candia to return to Cusco because their quest for El Dorado had been unsuccessful. Informants conveyed their plot to Hernando, concerned about Candia's loyalty, relieved him of command.[51] At the same time, there were some two hundred Almagrists in Cusco who also were clamoring for Almagro's release. Hernando had learned that they had posted men at several of the passes along the Chinchaysuyu road to Lima in case a decision was made to send him there, pursuant to dispatching him to Spain for trial.[52]

It was clear that as long as Almagro lived, he would represent an alternative to all of those who were disaffected, dissatisfied, and discontented with the Pizarros. The threat of a revolt to seize Cusco and free Almagro "forced Hernando's hand," prompting him to summon the city council whose authority could be dispositive and quick.[53] He informed them of the impending danger, observing that he had insisted that the initial looting done by his own troops upon entering Cusco be stopped and everything taken "should be returned to the owners," an order that greatly angered his men.[54] The result was that some of these men had joined with the Almagrists and were bent on taking violent action.

The question was: what was to be done? Hernando claimed that he "would rather err upon the opinion of all than succeed upon my own," even though his preference was clear. Deliberating the issue, the council concluded that "they saw no other remedy for pacifying the land but passing sentence upon Almagro, who, for his notorious crimes, deserved to die, and whose death would prevent many other deaths." Hernando agreed. "If this thing were not done the land would be lost." The council concluded that the death sentence for Almagro would be the "lesser evil."[55]

---

[51] Stirling, *Pizarro*, 117.
[52] Helps, *Spanish Conquest in America,* 4:104-05
[53] Silverman, "A Kingdom Set Aflame," pt. 6.
[54] Helps, *Spanish Conquest in America,* 4:102.
[55] Ibid., 106-07.

Almagro was stunned when Hernando informed him of the city council's decision. He objected to the charges of treason and rebellion brought against him, insisted that the council did not have the authority to decide, but in the end pleaded for mercy based upon his old friendship with the marquis. Hernando declared that there would be no mercy and no appeal and demanded that he confess to the charges. Almagro refused to confess but did not deny the charges. Hernando revealed "he would not have sentenced him [to death] but would have sent him to the emperor had not the conspiracies of his partisans been such as to prevent that course."[56]

Almagro, realizing that he had no recourse, dictated his will, crafting it ingeniously as a last act of revenge against Pizarro. As governor of New Toledo, he had the authority to name his own successor and named his son, Diego II (El Mozo), to whom he also left a million pesos, which he calculated was his share of the old partnership with Pizarro. He named Diego de Alvarado as his son's legal guardian until he came of age (a curious step as El Mozo was eighteen years of age and an adult according to Spanish law). He also left his entire estate to the king, expecting that the Crown's involvement also would bring scrutiny to the finances of the Pizarros.

On July 8, 1538, the day of execution, Hernando, concerned that there would be a last-minute attempt to free Almagro, decided to garrote him in his cell rather than carry out a public beheading in the main square. To insure against any violence, he deployed a company of arquebusiers in the square with their guns trained on the quarters of the Almagrists.[57] After he was dead, Almagro's body was brought into the square, beheaded, and his head was placed on a pike for all to see. If the Pizarros thought that executing Almagro would remove further incentive for disaffection, they would be incorrect, for resentment continued to fester among the core of his followers.

Shortly after the execution, Francisco Pizarro arrived in Cusco to a grand reception accompanied with all of the pomp and circumstance of a king. Pizarro was now ruler of all Peru, or at least he thought so. The

---

[56] Ibid., 107.
[57] Prescott, *History of the Conquest of Peru*, 2:127.

crocodile tears he shed upon the news of Almagro's death contained no remorse. So, it was in this frame of mind that he received Diego de Alvarado, executor of Almagro's will and El Mozo's guardian. Alvarado "made a formal intimation to the marquis that the government now belonged to *them*, and they required him to quit that country." It was an audacious and brazen attempt to snatch victory from defeat, but it was met by an equally arrogant and dismissive reply. "The marshal," Pizarro said, "by his rebellion, had forfeited all claims to the government."[58] Then, he said, "my government has *no* limit, but extends from the straights of Magellan to Flanders."[59]

Francisco Pizarro's astounding claim that his "government" stretched from Peru to Europe indicated that he, too, had become tinged with the madness. It was madness laced with suspicion, as he sought to expand and consolidate his hold on Peru. He authorized more expeditions to explore and claim more territory, even from those who he himself had appointed. He had heard, for example, that Sebastián de Benalcázar sought to be named governor of Quito, so he commissioned Lorenzo de Aldana to "proceed to Quito, and cautiously deprive Benalcázar of the authority which had been delegated to him…and send him well guarded, to Lima."[60] But Benalcázar was not to be found. He was on his way to Spain to seek the authority of the king for his claim to Popayan in Colombia, which would be granted. Pizarro would send Gonzalo to Quito, eventually naming him governor in 1541, and Pedro de Valdivia into Chile.

Manco, on the other hand, once again stoked the fires of rebellion—against both the Spanish and those non-Inca Indians who supported them. The rebellion this time would not involve all-out attack, but small-scale, guerrilla-style hits against Spanish travelers along the high royal road and against isolated settlements. Manco also directed his ire at the many tribes and peoples who reviled the Inca and cooperated and collaborated with the Spaniards. Guerrilla attacks would not overthrow Spanish rule, but they would become a worrisome irritant, provoking the Spanish to search out and eventually bring the rebellion to an end. (Manco

---

[58] Helps, *Spanish Conquest in America,* 4:109, emphasis added.
[59] Quintana, *Lives of Balboa and Pizarro*, 338, emphasis added.
[60] Ibid., 339.

himself would meet his end in 1544 at the hands of Spaniards he had welcomed as Almagrists persecuted by the Pizzarists. But they, hoping for a pardon for killing the hitherto uncatchable Inca, were themselves caught by Manco's men and killed.)

Pizarro, in dealing with Almagro's followers, ignored Machiavelli's dictum that "men ought either to be well treated or crushed, because they can avenge themselves of lighter injuries, of more serious ones they cannot; therefore the injury that is to be done to a man ought to be of such a kind that one does not stand in fear of revenge." While lavishing land, slaves, and wealth on his brothers and followers, Pizarro was strangely insensitive to the needs of the natives and treated the followers of Almagro with "undisguised contempt." He confiscated their estates and turned them over to his supporters, but left the victims free. The Almagrists, in turn, refused to accept any handouts from the Pizarros and retreated to the mountains to nurse their grievances, but not for long.[61]

Many Roads to Madness

News of the battle of Las Salinas and especially of the execution of Almagro, a Crown governor, had set alarm bells clanging in Seville. The king's concerns only grew as reports began to filter back from Amalgrists who had returned to Spain, especially from Diego de Alvarado, who charged Hernando with the deliberate murder of Almagro. On top of this, reports of Pizarro's increasingly king-like behavior raised fears that he might be tempted to declare his independence from the mother country. Certainly, his remark regarding the span of his government reaching from the Strait of Magellan to Flanders did not go unnoticed. Finally, the increasing flow of treasure in gold and silver from Peru persuaded the king that it was time to strengthen the imperial hold on his fractious colony.[62]

---

[61] Prescott, *History of the Conquest of Peru*, 2:135-136.

[62] R. Trevor Davies, *The Golden Century of Spain, 1501-1621* (London: Macmillan & Co., 1961), 299, Appendix II: Total Bullion Imports from America, 1503-1660. Davies's figures illustrate the dramatic upsurge in Spain's bullion imports from America beginning around 1536. Upon docking in Spanish ports, officials confiscated all treasure, issuing interest-bearing bonds, or notes, in return. Nevertheless, a substantial amount managed to find its way past the officials.

Pizarro on the other hand, now the sole ruler of all Peru, was determined to expand and consolidate his hold. In the summer of 1538, he sent Hernando and Gonzalo on a major expedition supported by Paullu and fifteen thousand Indian troops into New Toledo. The objective was to incorporate Almagro's old territory into his own. Their route south from Lake Titicaca took them through the fertile pampas of the Bolivian altiplano where their cavalry was most effective. According to Stirling, "the slaughter of the Indians ...[there] far exceeded the losses of any other Indian war."[63] Their expedition continued southward into the Charcas region, where, discovering several silver mines, they established the foundation of what would soon become the city of La Plata (Silver City). Hernando would claim one of these mines, at Porco, as his personal fiefdom that would become a major contributor to his wealth.

By the end of the year, Hernando had come to the conclusion that he had to return to Spain to face the charges being raised against him regarding the death of Almagro. His intent had always been to return home, but now he had added incentive, believing that the considerable fortune he had amassed could be put to good use in his defense. So, he returned to Cusco, leaving Gonzalo to finish the conquest of the region of Cochabamba and Chuquisaca.

Gonzalo was very successful. "One by one [the tribes] surrendered and paid homage to King Charles," as the Spaniards established settlements, distributed *encomiendas*, and organized the management of the mines and agricultural lands.[64] Gonzalo subdued the tribes of the region and received the surrender of the leader of the guerrilla war in the south, Tiso Yupanqui, Manco's uncle. Triumphant, he returned to Cusco on March 19, 1539.

In April, as Hernando was preparing to leave for Spain, he expressed a prescient warning to Pizarro regarding the Almagrists. The "men of Chile," he said, "are still free from any shame for their treason against you. Do not allow even ten of them to be gathered together. They

---

[63] Stirling, *Pizarro*, 118.
[64] Hemming, *Conquest of the Incas*, 247.

will try to kill you to avenge Almagro and their hardships."[65] Pizarro scoffed, saying that they were of little concern to him. He would be wrong.

After Hernando's departure, Pizarro himself set out for the southern region on a very long journey of several thousand miles, reinforcing the work done by Hernando and Gonzalo the previous year. (This grueling trip belied the notion that the *marquis* had lost his zeal for the campaign.) While heading for Arequipa where he intended to establish a port, at Quilca on the coast, he received word that Manco was offering to negotiate peace, prompting him to turn back toward Cusco; ending the Inca guerrilla war was an important objective.

Pizarro had come close to capturing Manco, but each time the Indian had eluded his traps. Earlier in the year, he had sent Gonzalo to his base at Vilcabamba and once again they had come up empty. Manco managed to escape, but his wife, Cura Ocllo had been caught. Thus, when Pizarro received news that Manco was interested in negotiating peace, it was clear that Cura Ocllo would be part of the bargain, if not its inspiration. Pizarro took her with him to Ollantaytambo and sent messengers laden with gifts to arrange for a meeting.

But now the madness engulfed Manco as well as Pizarro. Perhaps incensed by reports of the brutal treatment of his wife, Manco inexplicably killed the messengers and despoiled the gifts, including killing a horse that had been part of the package, sending its head back to Pizarro. Pizarro, too, seemed to have snapped at what he considered a senseless act of defiance.[66] He vented his anger on Cura Ocllo, ordering that she be brutally tortured and killed, and that her mangled body be floated down the Vilcanota River in a basket so that Manco would be sure to find her. That was not all. When he returned to Cusco, still in a rage, he burned alive sixteen Indian chiefs in custody, including Vila Oma, who had also just surrendered, and Tiso Yupanqui.[67]

Manco remained at large, but his war began to simmer down by the end of the year. There continued to be sporadic incidents of terror, but fewer. As a result, Peru began to experience a rare period of tranquility,

---

[65] Kochis, *God, Glory and Gold*, 2:568.
[66] Ibid., 573-74. Kochis says that both men simply "snapped."
[67] MacQuarrie, *Last Days of the Incas*, 329-30 and Stirling, *Pizarro*, 123.

and Pizarro busied himself with developing the infrastructure of Lima and other towns. There was a need to accommodate the influx of Spaniards to Peru, whose population by the end of 1539 exceeded four thousand, and was growing. This same growth in prosperity, centered as it was on the treasure shipments to Seville, prompted King Charles to take measures to strengthen the Crown's control of its rich and thriving colony.

In Spain, it seemed at first that Hernando would be able to explain satisfactorily his actions with regard to Almagro, despite the charges of Diego de Alvarado, who was very influential at court. Indeed, fearing that Hernando would escape punishment entirely, Alvarado challenged him to a duel; but Alvarado suddenly and mysteriously dropped dead—a death, according to Quintana, "so opportune, the dark character of his adversary being considered, could hardly be unattended by suspicion."[68] After a year, by early 1540, the king seemed to have come to a decision regarding both Hernando and Francisco Pizarro.

In the spring of 1540, the king ordered Hernando detained, but the wheels of Spanish justice being what they were, he was not actually incarcerated until the following June of 1541. At the same time, the king decided to send Cristóbal Vaca de Castro, an eminent judge, to Peru as a "special investigator" to conduct an inquiry into the events. The judge, renowned for his integrity and wisdom, was also authorized to "assume the government himself, in case of that commander's death," a remarkably prescient contingency provision.[69] Sailing in November of that year, Vaca de Castro arrived in Panama in January 1541. The voyage had taken its toll and the judge became ill, requiring a recuperation of several months. In the meantime, events took a disastrous turn in the capital.

The Almagrists, many scattered around the countryside, gradually began drifting in to Lima, and by mid-year 1541 there were some two hundred in the capital, with El Mozo's house the gathering place. To a man, their lack of fortune rankled, seeing Pizarrists in some cases occupying *encomiendas* they once held; and believing that but for the murder of their chief, their fortunes would be reversed. Pizarro had not

---

[68] Quintana, *Lives of Balboa and Pizarro*, 342.
[69] Prescott, *History of the Conquest of Peru*, 2:202.

participated directly in Almagro's death, but since he was the principal beneficiary, the Almagrists' ire was directed at him.[70]

Their original plan was to put their complaint before Vaca de Castro, believing that he was coming to investigate and adjudicate the case of Almagro. They even sent one of their number to San Miguel de Piura in hopes of lobbying before he arrived at Lima. But the judge had been delayed in Popayán, Colombia. Then rumors began to circulate that he had only come to conduct an inquiry, not to adjudicate the case, which prompted the Almagrists to consider taking measures into their own hands.[71] In yet another manifestation of the madness that had descended on Peru, as Stirling notes, the Almagrists decided that only the killing of Pizarro would serve justice. That they could "imagine that such an act would ever be pardoned by the licenciate or by the Crown, in hindsight appears unbelievable."[72]

Rumors of violence against the marquis were becoming rampant, and Pizarrists and Almagrists jeered at each other openly in the streets. One morning three nooses were found hung in the city square, one each for Pizarro, his secretary Antonio Picado, and the judge, Dr. Juan Velázquez. Pizarrists, on the other hand, had paraded through the streets a "life size effigy of the Adelantado on a donkey." One of the priests had passed on to Pizarro the gist of a confession he had heard revealing a plot to assassinate him at a Sunday mass. Pizarro ordered extra precaution, but publicly displayed no concern. He had called the presumed ringleader, Juan de Rada, questioning his intentions directly. Rada denied all.[73]

The bare bones of the assassination of Francisco Pizarro are well known, but the details surrounding the event are still in dispute. A group of Almagrists stormed the marquis' home, overcoming his two companions, one of whom was his half-brother, Martín de Alcántara, and two pages who attempted to defend him, and slew them all, Pizarro the last. Beyond that there is some disagreement: on the date it occurred, on

---

[70] Kochis, *God, Glory and Gold*, 2:582-84.

[71] Quintana, *Lives of Vasco Nunez De Balboa and Francisco Pizarro*, 348-49.

[72] Stirling, *Pizarro*, 140.

[73] Stirling, *Pizarro*, 139. Quintana, *Lives of Balboa and Pizarro*, 349-50, says that Juan de Rada professed the Almagrists' belief that Pizarro was planning to destroy them and kill the judge, which the marquis denied.

the number of Almagrists who took part in it, who was their leader, and whether there had been a plot, or a panicked reaction to expected arrest. There is general agreement among historians that the assassination occurred on June 26, 1541, but one says it occurred on July 26.[74]

Most scholars estimate that between eighteen and twenty men took part in the assassination, although one says only seven were involved, while another claims there were forty.[75] Quintana says that "the conspirators, though firmly resolved on the governor's death, had neither fixed on the hour nor the day."[76] Helps takes the same view.[77] Prescott, Hemming, MacQuarrie, Thomas, Stirling, and Kochis, on the other hand, say that they had set Sunday, June 26, when Pizarro was exiting the church from mass, as the date and hour for the assassination. Most say that Almagro's son, El Mozo, was the mastermind; but Prescott claims that he was "too young" for such a task and states further that "there is no good evidence of his having taken part in the conspiracy." He names Juan de Rada as the chief conspirator.[78]

Pizarro did not attend mass at the church that day but celebrated it in the private chapel on his property. If the conspirators had a plan, it was disrupted by Pizarro's absence. Assuming by his absence that their plot had been discovered, they panicked. Some argued that their arrest was imminent, and they should flee; while others, the majority led by Rada, said that they had no choice but to invade Pizarro's home and carry out their plan. Helps says it was common among conspiracies that indecision delayed action "until some imminent peril to the conspirators hastens the result and determines the hour of the deed." Thus, in this version, the conspirators had decided "to strike a blow in order to protect themselves against a pressing danger."[79] Quintana says the danger was their imminent arrest. One of the Almagrists had burst into their quarters exclaiming "we

---

[74] Prescott, *History of the Conquest of Peru,* 2:176; Hemming, *Conquest of the Incas,* 262; MacQuarrie, *Last Days of the Incas,* 339; Thomas, *Golden Empire,* 283; and Kochis, *God, Glory and Gold,* 2:585, all say June 26; Stirling, *Pizarro,* 139, says July 26.

[75] Stirling, *Pizarro,* 139, says seven; Thomas, *Golden Empire,* 283, says forty.

[76] Quintana, *Lives of Balboa and Pizarro,* 352.

[77] Helps, *Spanish Conquest in America,* 4:129.

[78] Prescott, *History of the Conquest of Peru,* 2:176.

[79] Helps, *Spanish Conquest in America,* 4:129.

must act. Treasurer Riquelme has ordered our arrest. We have only two hours."[80]

And so ended the life of Francisco Pizarro, a man who lived by the sword and died by one. He was a singular historical figure even in his own time, whose constancy of purpose over several decades brought fulfillment and riches to himself and to the many who followed him, as well as glory and untold wealth to the Crown. At the moment, however, his death precipitated an upheaval as the Almagrists claimed power and set about overturning most if not all of the political and economic arrangements the marquis had put in place.

Crown and Colony: The Years of Madness

The death of Francisco Pizarro removed all restraints on the madness that afflicted Spanish Peru. For the next seven years, Spaniard fought Spaniard, relative against relative, for and against the king. Of three emissaries sent by the Crown, one would be deposed, another killed, and a third would vanquish the last Pizarro in Peru, Gonzalo, who was killed. Only then could the Crown begin to reaffirm control over its increasingly wealthy colony. Ironically, the main responsibility for this carnage lay with the king himself, who, in an effort to counter adverse trends and strengthen positive ones, attempted to impose completely unrealistic laws upon the Indies, which predictably exploded in Peru.

Revenge may have been the professed motive of the Almagrists in killing Pizarro, but the result was their ascension to power. They coerced the city council into agreeing to name El Mozo governor of all Peru, and he quickly sent messengers with notices to all of the settlements demanding their allegiance, with mixed results. Many submitted, but Pizarrists fled into the northern mountains, there to await the opportunity to join in the inevitable counterrevolution.[81] Employing all of the resources of the state, and the confiscated wealth of the Pizarrists, the Almagrists quickly assembled a substantial armed force and prepared to defend their gains from the court-appointed governor, Vaca de Castro,

---

[80] Quintana, *Lives of Balboa and Pizarro*, 352.
[81] Kochis, *God, Glory and Gold*, 2:586.

who, informed of the course of events, began to move southward from Popayán to Quito toward Lima with his own hastily assembled army.

In short, there now emerged in Peru dual power, with the rebel Almagrists moving to Cusco, claiming it as their rightful land; and the Pizarrists in Lima, with Vaca de Castro there too, supported by royalist troops sent from Panama. This condition of divided rule would last in Peru for over a year, until the two sides clashed in a climactic battle at Chupas, outside of Cusco, on September 16, 1542. This single battle, in which each side gave no quarter, pitted one Spanish army against another and saw over three hundred Spaniards killed—more than during the entire preceding period of the conquest. Vaca de Castro's forces triumphed over the Almagrists, and El Mozo was quickly captured, tried, executed, and buried next to his father in Cusco.

A month before the battle of Chupas, in August 1542, Gonzalo Pizarro returned from an eighteen-month-long expedition into the lands east of Quito in the Amazon. Pizarro had sent him to locate the valuable cinnamon trees reported to grow in the rainforest. The expedition confirmed the existence of the trees but could not bring any of the bark out due to the extreme conditions experienced. Out of provisions and on the edge of starvation, Gonzalo had sent his second-in-command, Francisco Orellana, down the Napo River in search of food. After not hearing from him and assuming he had either perished or deserted his quest, a dispirited Gonzalo returned to Quito with the eighty men who had survived from the original 220. (Gonzalo did not know until long afterward that Orellana had little choice but to follow the strong current of the Amazon River to the Atlantic, the first to have done so. At the time, Gonzalo was embittered by Orellana's failure to return to his expedition and vowed retribution.)

In Quito, Gonzalo discovered that his world had literally been turned upside down. News of Francisco's murder devastated him, and he was stunned to find a new governor in charge. He offered to join forces with the royalist army in his determination to avenge his brother's death. Vaca de Castro, a lawyer, not a military man, was politically astute. He realized that Gonzalo had a strong claim to succeed his brother. He also understood that including Gonzalo's forces with his would guarantee military victory over the Almagrists, but the downside was that Gonzalo's presence would further polarize the colony, perhaps causing more problems after victory. So, Vaca de Castro dismissed Gonzalo as governor of Quito, declined his offer of assistance, and encouraged him to "retire" to his estate in Charcas, a proposal to which he reluctantly acceded.

The governorship of Vaca de Castro reached its height during the initial months that followed the defeat of the Almagrists. Free to concentrate on his main task, as Varón notes, he sought "to limit the power the conquerors had and eventually push them aside, as had already happened to Christopher Columbus and Hernán Cortés in Mexico."[82] In the process of consolidating his position as governor, the beginnings of the dilemma that would shortly engulf him were already becoming apparent. One of his mandates was to improve the lives of the natives, which he attempted to do by limiting *repartimientos*, and improving the roads and *chaski* messaging system, but the *encomienda* system was the guts of the Spanish presence in Peru and resistance to change was evident.[83]

Vaca de Castro acted as other Crown authorities had before him. He built loyalties by awarding land and natives to those who would support him, receiving kickbacks in return. It was a common practice throughout the colonies. He was also busy limiting and sorting out the vast estate of Pizarro, a task made easier by the fact of the marquis's death and the disruptive but not legally binding actions of the Almagrists. But this peaceful time did not last. In Spain, the king and his court were pondering the impact of Spanish rule and the promise of vast riches.

King Charles, his court advisers, the Council of the Indies, and the clergy had been immersed in discussions about developments in Peru. The factional battle between the Pizarrists and Almagrists was the incipient concern, but there were larger issues in play. The general decision was to continue the process of gradually phasing out the conquistadors and replacing them with Crown officials. The dispatch of Vaca de Castro had been the first step.

An adverse underlying trend was what might be termed the labor/demographic scissors. The Crown recognized that there was an

---

[82] Varón, *Francisco Pizarro and His Brothers*, 96.
[83] Helps, *Spanish Conquest in America*, 4:139.

alarming rate of depopulation occurring throughout the Americas. The Indies had lost almost all of its natives, and population decline was already apparent in Mexico and Peru. The king was pressed to allow the importation of African slaves as replacements. At the same time, there was occurring a change in the nature of riches extracted, especially from Peru. Early treasure shipped from Peru was mostly gold, silver, and jewels that had been looted from the Inca, but increasingly, its composition was shifting to silver from newly discovered mines.

The question was how to prevent or at least limit the precipitous decline in labor without which the treasure could not be acquired. There was a growing belief that the forced labor method applied by the Spaniards in the mines and fields was at least partly responsible.[84] There were also persistent demands from Fr. Bartolomé de las Casas and other Spanish clerics, who adamantly opposed enslaving the natives, and demanded that they be treated like human beings, not animals. These diverse concerns dovetailed into a major decision issued on November 20, 1542 termed the "New Laws."[85]

The New Laws removed the very basis of the conquistadors' position in all of the Americas, but especially in Peru. They phased out the *encomienda* system by prohibiting a settler from passing on his *encomienda* to his heirs. Upon his death, his entire estate would revert to the king, who would become guardian of his natives. Surviving widows and children would receive "a portion of the usufruct for their sustenance." All officials who held *repartimientos* "were obliged to renounce them." All "personal service" by the Indians was to be "abolished altogether." Any labor that the Indians would perform had to be explicitly defined, "so that the [*encomendero*] might be unable to overtask them." This was devastating enough, but the worst was yet to come. Anyone implicated "in

---

[84] Andrés Reséndez, *The Other Slavery: The Uncovered Story of Indian Enslavement in America* (Boston: Houghton Mifflin Harcourt, 2016), provides a recent exposition of this thesis.

[85] For a brilliant treatment of the formulation, implementation, and revocation of the New Laws, see Geoffrey Parker, *Emperor: A New Life of Charles V* (New Haven: Yale University Press, 2019), 362-72.

the rebellious and fractious proceedings of Pizarro and Almagro, should be deprived of their *encomiendas*." [86]

It would be months before the official sent to enforce this decree arrived in the Americas, but word of the king's decision traveled quickly across the Atlantic. Fueled by speculation, the effect was devastating. All incentive for a Spaniard to risk life and fortune in the Americas was removed. Inheritance was abolished. The settler could not pass on his hard-won gains to his family. Slavery was repealed. The Indians were now free agents who would be paid for work. Crown officials were impoverished. Anyone who had ever held an official position, even a minor one, would be forced to give up his native workers. Worst of all, practically everyone in Peru had been on one side or the other of the deadly feud between Pizarro and Almagro. The Crown, in short, was positioning itself to confiscate the wealth of the settlers.

The New Laws were a calculated risk couched in humanitarian guise that contained within them the idea that the natives could be enticed by better treatment to become wage-earning workers and that the settlers would accept peaceably the new terms of their existence. It was assumed that the king's viceroy would be obeyed; that he could gradually phase out the *encomenderos*, and, above all, strengthen the Crown's control over the productive processes of the colony—especially its silver production, in which native labor and expertise were indispensable. Unfortunately, the assumptions upon which the reforms were based were incorrect. The settlers rose up against the New Laws and the man sent to implement them. Moreover, Indian lives were not improved and they could not be enticed to work in the mines. The resulting chaos nearly precipitated the loss of the richest colony on earth.

The First Viceroy of Peru

Since the victory at Chupas, September 16, 1542, Vaca de Castro had accomplished a great deal. For over a year he had maintained peace and stability in the colony, as well as fostering economic growth. Governing equitably, he had also established generally good relations with

---

[86] Helps, *Spanish Conquest in America*, 4:148-49.

the Indians, overseeing Paullu's conversion to Christianity, granting him a palace residence in Cusco, with an *encomienda*. Indeed, he stood as godfather at Paullu's baptism.[87] However, word of the New Laws descended upon Lima like a thunderclap. Recognizing the incompatibility between the conditions in the colony and the requirements of the New Laws, Vaca de Castro decided to slow-walk their implementation. All through 1543 he reported progress to the Crown, while allowing things to go on as usual.

Meanwhile, in the year since the New Laws were announced, reports filtering back to Spain indicated that they were not being enforced anywhere, and a stream of letters was arriving requesting exceptions. The king, determined to see the laws enforced, named Blasco Núñez Vela to be the first viceroy of Peru. An experienced official, formerly the Inspector General of the Castilian Guards, Núñez Vela was a loyal, obedient, literal-minded servant of the Crown. But his inflexibility and lack of diplomatic skill would trigger crisis in Peru and lead to a tragic end for himself. Sailing from Spain on November 1, 1543, he arrived at Panama City in late January 1544. Accompanying him as part of his entourage were four royal auditors, who would constitute the Lima *Audiencia*.[88]

In the few weeks he spent in Panama, his officious attitude and unflinching determination to implement the New Laws offended and antagonized every *encomendero* he met. Strictly and immediately enforcing the law prohibiting slaveholding against the advice of the accompanying auditors, who advised a go-slow approach, he forced *encomenderos* to free the local Indians and black slaves and send back to Lima the imported "service" Indians. Like a bull in a China shop, Núñez Vela destabilized the Panamanian society and economy in the brief time he stayed there.

Eager to reach Lima, Núñez Vela left Panama without waiting for his auditors to accompany him. But, instead of sailing directly to Lima, he decided to put in at Tumbes and travel the rest of the way by land.

---

[87] Stirling, *Pizarro*, 148.
[88] These judges were: Diego Vázquez de Cepeda, Pedro Ortiz de Zárate, Pablo Lisón de Tejada, and Juan Álvarez.

Proceeding down the coast, he aroused furor and consternation wherever he went, like a malevolent pied piper taking *encomiendas* from settlers and "freeing" Indians. By the time he reached Lima in May, the citizens were in a panic. When leading citizens attempted to remonstrate with him, he peremptorily declaimed that he meant to carry out the king's will, come what may, and no matter how prejudicial the results.

As word spread of Núñez Vela's high-handed, dictatorial policies, settlers began increasingly to turn to Gonzalo Pizarro to intercede. Four city councils in the south agreed to name him Procurator with authority to present their grievances to the viceroy. Gonzalo agreed, and as he traveled to Cusco, supporters soon began to gather around him. Before long he was the leader of a substantial armed force. He named Francisco de Carvajal, an old veteran and political/military genius, as his master of camp. He would become Gonzalo's chief strategist and field commander.

It was a volatile and tempestuous time as a new dual power emerged. Settlers were torn, maddened as they attempted to decide whether to side with the royalists or with those who were now regarded as rebels. Consequently, double-dealing and defections to and from both camps occurred regularly, affecting the balance of forces between them. But as months passed, it became apparent that the advantage was accruing to Gonzalo. A Lima official, Illan Suarez, had been in secret contact with Gonzalo's camp. Núñez Vela intercepted a ciphered letter to him, which, when decoded revealed the growing strength of Gonzalo's army and his plan to move on Lima. Núñez Vela charged Suarez with treason and in a rage killed him, claiming in his defense that Suarez's death had driven him "almost mad," but justified his actions because of his "insolence."[89]

Seeing the balance going against him, Núñez Vela made one bad decision after another, sharply undercutting public confidence. He decided to "suspend the New Laws for two years," but the relief generated by this sensible decision was vitiated by his accompanying declaration that he would reimpose them as soon as he had "pacified the country." He then issued a death warrant against Gonzalo, promising to reward his killer with

---

[89] Helps, *Spanish Conquest in America*, 4:163-64.

Gonzalo's vast estates. Public confidence plummeted at what was a declaration of war.

He moved to strengthen Lima's defenses against attack, but in the midst of building fortifications, reversed himself. He now decided that defeat at Lima was unavoidable, and adopted a scorched earth policy, destroying everything of value in the capital and abandoning it.[90] His new plan was to march to Quito where he would be closer to reinforcements coming from Panama. Lima's leading citizens, along with the auditors, who had by now arrived at Lima, opposed this decision. They demanded that he either reverse it or face arrest. When the auditors made their demand public, virtually all of Núñez Vela's forces either deserted him, or stood aside. Conceding defeat, he surrendered to the auditors. They put him on a ship to Spain, assigning one of their number, Juan Álvarez, to accompany him. At sea, however, Álvarez switched sides. He let Núñez Vela disembark at Tumbes, from whence he proceeded to Quito and north to Popayán. There he would assemble a new army, assisted by Popayán's governor, Sebastián de Benalcázar.[91]

Gonzalo, meanwhile, at the end of October 1544, entered Lima with twelve hundred men, one of the largest armies ever assembled in Peru. Brandishing a hundred arquebuses, he "persuaded" the auditors to name him governor of Peru, pending a decision by the king. Throughout, Gonzalo thought of himself as a loyal subject and resisted advice to declare himself king of an independent state of Peru. Instead, he sent an emissary to Spain to plead his case to the king. He believed that as the king had named Francisco governor with the power to extend his patrimony "for two lives," that is, through two generations, he was the natural successor.

His plan of action consisted of a two-pronged approach. He tasked Hernando Bachicao to take several brigantines and secure the coast, while he marched north to battle Núñez Vela. Sailing from port to port, Bachicao secured the coast against reinforcements going to Núñez Vela. Then, in a surprise move, he sailed into Panama City harbor and took control of the entire fleet lying at anchor, some twenty-eight ships. At one stroke,

---

[90] Ibid., 166-67.
[91] Stirling, *Pizarro*, 155-59.

Gonzalo now controlled all access to Peru. Gonzalo named a trusted ally, Pedro de Hinojosa, governor and commander of the fleet.

Before engaging Núñez Vela, Gonzalo sent Carvajal to put down an uprising in La Plata where Diego de Centeno had raised the royal banner. In a long-developing pursuit, Gonzalo used the deployment of Carvajal's force to the south to lure Núñez Vela into thinking that the contingent confronting him was weak and vulnerable to attack. Núñez Vela took the bait and advanced on Gonzalo's army, only to learn too late that he had been tricked. On January 18, 1546, on the outskirts of Quito, in a mountain valley called Añaquito, Gonzalo's stronger force defeated the viceroy, beheading him on the field of battle. Carvajal, meanwhile, had pursued and routed Centeno's forces, defeating him in battle but failing to capture the royalist leader and his captains, who went into hiding. One of several owners of the newly discovered silver mines at Potosí, Centeno would reemerge a few years later to play a role in the ultimate demise of Gonzalo Pizarro.

With all of Peru at his feet, the notion that Gonzalo should proclaim himself king of an independent Peru became more compelling. Carvajal was among many who supported independence. His view was that having killed Charles' viceroy, Gonzalo could expect no quarter from Castile. His only choice therefore was "to seize the government yourself without waiting for another to offer it to you." He urged him to "Crown yourself king...die a king...and not a vassal." But Gonzalo, attracted as he was to the idea, decided to await the king's decision, governing Peru as a de facto monarch in the meantime.[92]

When Gonzalo's envoy reached Spain, a council immediately was convened under the king's son, Phillip II, who was Regent of Spain while Charles V was in Germany attempting to deal with the rebellious Protestants. They agreed that the rebellion must be suppressed, but it quickly became apparent that sending an army across the Atlantic was both a financial and logistical impossibility. Finances were stretched thin, as the upheaval had disrupted the flow of treasure, and Gonzalo's control of Panama and Nombre de Dios made an approach to Peru impossible. Then,

---

[92] Kochis, *God, Glory and Gold*, 2:658 and Stirling, *Pizarro*, 161.

even if an army should gain access, it would be forced to fight experienced and well-armed Spaniards, not warlike but poorly armed Indians. The decision, therefore, was that Peru would have to be reconquered "by gentle means" (*por buenas medias*). [93]

Pedro de la Gasca and the Reconquista of Peru

The council chose fifty-year-old lawyer/cleric Pedro de la Gasca to solve the problem of Peru. A protégé of Francisco de los Cobos, La Gasca was a brilliant strategist, experienced in difficult negotiations. He was involved in the defense of Valencia against the Turks and the French; and was a legal adviser to the Pope. He was a striking intellect, with an equally striking physical deformity, though this is not evident in images of the man. His condition possibly was a subtype of what is known today as Jarcho-Levin syndrome. Affected individuals are developed normally from the neck up and the waist down, but with a disproportionately short trunk and neck. Despite La Gasca's physical disability, his natural disposition was "as well composed as his body was ill formed."[94]

7.3. Pedro de la Gasca

---

[93] Helps, *Spanish Conquest in America*, 4:187.
[94] Ibid., 190.

La Gasca agreed to take on the challenge, declining either salary or compensation. Not yet aware of the fate of Blasco Núñez Vela, the task at hand was for him to mediate between Gonzalo and the viceroy, reinstating him to office along with the *Audiencia*. La Gasca demanded and was given a blank check for his mission. He was authorized to have "all the men, money, ships, and horses that he might require," have command of "all the offices of government in Peru," have the power to authorize "new expeditions," the "plenary power" to pardon any whom he thought ought to be pardoned, the authority to relieve the viceroy if it seemed appropriate, and after he had pacified the country, he would be permitted to "expend any portion of the royal estate" for its rehabilitation.[95]

In the powers extended to La Gasca there was no mention of the New Laws because the king already had abolished them by an ordinance dated October 20, 1545, although knowledge of that decision had not yet been disseminated to the *encomenderos* of the New World. La Gasca would wield this knowledge to great effect in his plan to pacify the country. Setting sail on May 26, 1546, he stopped first at Santa Marta, where he learned of the demise of Blasco Núñez Vela. Though grieving for the viceroy, La Gasca thought his death an advantage, noting that "it is often better to deal with three enemies than with one perverse ally."[96]

La Gasca traveled under the unprepossessing title of President of the Lima Audiencia and he sailed, unarmed, with only a small group of aides, arriving at Nombre de Dios on July 26. His strategy to reconquer Peru was the epitome of the axiom that the pen is mightier than the sword, as success depended upon conveying to the supporters of Gonzalo that there was literally no reason to be in rebellion against their own country. And his main means of communicating to them was by smuggling letters to every town and settlement in Peru. He anticipated that many of the letters might fall like seeds on barren ground, but the majority would take

---

[95] Geoffrey Parker, *Emperor: A New Life of Charles V* (New Haven: Yale University Press, 2019), 364-65; and Helps, *Spanish Conquest in America*, 4:188.

[96] Helps, *Spanish Conquest in America*, 4:191.

root among the settlers, whose main interest was in retaining their hard-fought gains.[97]

Arriving at Nombre de Dios on July 26, his first objectives were to regain control of the isthmus and the Pacific fleet. He quickly persuaded the commander of Nombre de Dios, Hernán Mexía, of the rightness of his mission; and of his authority to pardon all offenses against the Crown and to enforce the repeal of the New Laws. As these had been the objects of the rebellion, continued resistance was pointless. Mexía was convinced and proceeded to escort La Gasca and his group across the isthmus to Panama City where he arrived on August 11.[98]

In Panama, where La Gasca would spend the next nine months, he could engage in face to face discussions with governor Hernando Hinojosa, a loyal supporter of Gonzalo's, and the ship captains. To Hinojosa in particular, he emphasized that if it came to war, the first battle would be between Panama and Mexico, whose viceroy, Antonio de Mendoza, was committed to the Crown. He also noted that continued support for the rebellion would forfeit all possibility of pardon.

Hinojosa wanted to know if La Gasca had come with the king's decision to acknowledge Gonzalo as governor of Peru. Declining a direct answer, he said only that those who supported the king would "not only be preserved in their houses and estates but would be favored as those persons were accustomed to be favored who served his majesty." Writing to Gonzalo, Hinojosa shrewdly interpreted this reply as a "no."[99] Winning control of Panama and the fleet were of utmost importance, and La Gasca would take his time discussing his brief with Hinojosa and the captains of the fleet. Hinojosa was a staunch supporter of Gonzalo, so La Gasca decided to concentrate on winning the captains over one by one, until the only one left to convert was Hinojosa.

La Gasca's strategy toward Gonzalo and Peru was designed to remove the grounds for rebellion. He smuggled dispatches, carried by monks traveling on ships from Panama, to every leading *encomendero*, prelate, and soldier, to make sure that everyone knew and understood that

---

[97] Prescott, *History of the Conquest of Peru*, 2:352.
[98] Ibid., 350.
[99] Helps, *Spanish Conquest in America*, 4:193.

the objectives of their rebellion had already been achieved. The king had revoked the New Laws and was willing to pardon anyone who would proclaim his loyalty to king and country. He was also willing to consult with all of the leading citizens of the towns and settlements of Peru as to what would best promote "the service of God, the good of the country, and the welfare of the colonists."[100]

In a dispatch to Gonzalo himself, La Gasca included a letter from the king, which, without promising him the governorship, specifically made clear that he would "keep in mind the services which had been rendered both by the Marquis Francisco Pizarro and by Gonzalo himself." The king also offered Gonzalo a way out, viewing the "disturbances" in Peru as developments that did not manifest a spirit of rebellion as regarded his regal authority, but had reference only to the rigor of that viceroy [Blasco Núñez Vela, now deceased]. La Gasca pointed out that the king had sent no army because he wished to spare the country the shedding of more Spanish blood. If Gonzalo were to persist in his rebellion "now that the New Laws were revoked, it would make the inhabitants of Peru think that he did this for his own interest and not for them..."[101]

Gonzalo, perhaps consumed by the "madness," declined this offer, determined to remain the ruler of Peru. Unable to stop the flow of smuggled dispatches, he increasingly began to suspect everyone around him of disloyalty, executing anyone found with one of La Gasca's manifestos. He also attempted to prevent La Gasca from leaving Panama, bringing together mayors and leading persons from around the country to sign a petition requesting that La Gasca not come to Peru. At the same time, he sent a delegation to Spain with a reply to the king's letter, attempting to justify his actions.

The leader of the delegation was Lorenzo de Aldana, one of Gonzalo's strongest supporters, who arrived in Panama on November 13, 1546. In conversation with Aldana, La Gasca explained the extraordinary concessions being offered by the Crown, the result of the colonists' successful but desperate venture. The colonists, he said, had won and

---

[100] Ibid., 198.
[101] Ibid., 198-200.

therefore "had nothing more...to demand." Aldana, though devoted to Gonzalo, "did not feel bound by any principle of honor to take part with him, solely to gratify his ambition, in a wild contest with the Crown that must end in inevitable ruin." He therefore "abandoned his mission to Castile," and announced his support for La Gasca. Even more importantly, Aldana's conversion led quickly to Hinojosa's. Scarcely a week later, on November 19, 1546, the governor along with Aldana and his ship captains proclaimed their oaths of allegiance to Castile, with full pardons and restitution of all their estates.[102] For the time being, however, La Gasca kept their conversions secret.

Having regained control of Panama and the fleet, La Gasca was now prepared to begin the decisive phase of his campaign to reconquer Peru. He ordered the fleet to make ready for action and sent word to the officials in Mexico and Guatemala to provide the needed men and provisions for the army. He also sent word to Benalcázar in Popayán to make ready all available forces when he made landfall at Tumbes, for a subsequent rendezvous at Cajamarca, and he called Governor Pedro Valdivia from Chile.

La Gasca's first concrete step was to send Aldana to Lima in mid-February 1547 with four ships, and orders to welcome aboard anyone who wished to embrace the royal cause. Aldana was also to convey a last offer to Gonzalo to put down his arms. On his way, Aldana put in at Trujillo where he received messages from loyalists offering to join the campaign. They, too, were instructed to proceed to Cajamarca, the rendezvous point.[103] La Gasca was marshaling an army superior to Gonzalo's.

Gonzalo, meanwhile, upon receiving the message from Aldana and realizing that he had lost control of Panama and the fleet, summoned his advisers to consider the king's offer. He also called Carvajal from Potosí where he was supervising silver mining operations. The old cavalier immediately expressed the view that La Gasca's flood of messages were "more to be dreaded than the lances of Castile," and recommended accepting the offer of clemency. But Diego Vázquez de Cepeda, the young

---

[102] Prescott, *History of the Conquest of Peru,* 2:361-62.
[103] Ibid., 365.

auditor who had become influential with Gonzalo in Carvajal's absence, urged that they reject the offer.[104]

Gonzalo decided against the advice of Carvajal, believing that he no longer had any choice but to fight for control of Peru even though the situation was becoming desperate. La Gasca's message campaign was now beginning to show results, as uprisings were reported in the north at Puerto Viejo, Trujillo, and Chachapoyas. In May, in the south, Diego de Centeno reemerged after a year in hiding to lead a surprise, night attack on Cusco, securing it for the royalists. In June, as desertions mounted, news came of La Gasca's flotilla of eighteen ships and over eight hundred men putting in at Tumbes.[105]

With formidable armies to the north and to the south, the appearance in early March of Aldana's squadron off Callao, Lima's port, threw Gonzalo into a panic. With nothing to oppose La Gasca (Gonzalo had burned his only four ships over Carvajal's objections), and fearing the defection of Lima's citizens, he assembled them in the central square and demanded that they proclaim their fealty to him. Should anyone "violate this pledge, he should pay for it with his life."[106] Gonzalo was right to be concerned. Reading La Gasca's smuggled dispatches, many began to steal away to Aldana's ships. Indeed, as soon as Gonzalo's forces left Lima the citizens opened the gates to Aldana, who secured it for the royalists.

The decision to leave Lima had been a product of Gonzalo's madness, as he once again went against the advice of Carvajal. Carvajal wanted to defend the capital, but Gonzalo decided to abandon it, destroying all of value within it and to retreat into Chile with his small, but well-trained force of five hundred men.[107] Attempting to march south, however, Gonzalo found his way blocked by Centeno who deployed a thousand-man force to command the mountain passes south of Lake Titicaca. Thus thwarted, Gonzalo and his men headed toward the coast and Arequipa to ponder their options.

---

[104] Ibid., 367.
[105] Stirling, *Pizarro*, 163.
[106] Prescott, *History of the Conquest of Peru,* 2:375-76.
[107] Stirling, *Pizarro*, 163-64.

There, Gonzalo and his captains realized that they were slowly being drawn like a blade to the smithy into a hammer and anvil end game. La Gasca's large army was marching from Cajamarca to Jauja, and thence to Cusco, along the high Inca road, while Centeno stood blocking his path into Chile. Their decision was to attack Centeno's blocking force, which would enable them to get through the passes, escape the pincer, and march into Chile. Sending scouts to create a diversion, Gonzalo took his force quickly to Huarina, a small town on the shore of Lake Titicaca that had been a sacred site for the Incas. The town was located some three hundred miles east of Arequipa, on the southeast corner of the lake.

It was not long before Centeno deciphered Gonzalo's move and deployed his army into the area. The field of battle was a large plain that lay between the lakeshore and the Andes. Centeno's forces were numerically superior and supremely confident. Of his thousand men, two hundred and fifty were cavalry, one hundred fifty were arquebusiers, and the remainder hastily assembled levies serving as not well-trained foot soldiers and pike men. Gonzalo's force was half that size, but the majority were arquebusiers, three hundred and fifty of them, with only eighty-five cavalrymen, and fewer than a hundred pike men and foot soldiers.[108]

It was October 26, 1547. Unbeknownst to Centeno, Carvajal had prepared a grim surprise. He had carefully observed the desertions from his forces and made sure that his remaining men collected all of the weapons left behind, especially the arquebuses, amounting to nearly a thousand guns. Preparing for the battle, he had ordered these guns to be pre-loaded and given to the arquebusiers, who now had three or four each. His plan was to prod Centeno's force into a frontal attack, which he would meet with his guns, firing in repeated volleys.[109]

Unfortunately for Centeno, he had fallen ill and could not command his men. He was forced to observe the proceedings from a distant hill on a litter. He had informed La Gasca that he had Gonzalo trapped and intended to finish him off, a plan that La Gasca approved. It would be one of the biggest mistakes of his career. After some initial clashes, Centeno's men were incited to charge the positions of Carvajal's

---

[108] Prescott, *History of the Conquest of Peru,* 2:386-87.
[109] Helps, *Spanish Conquest in America,* 4:219.

men. The latter waited until their adversaries reached point-blank range, then opened fire, instantly killing a hundred charging men and wounding more. Centeno's superior number of cavalry, nearly three to one, almost saved the day, but well-trained pike men and foot soldiers were able to protect the arquebusiers while their rifle fire devastated horse and horsemen alike.[110] Centeno, seeing the battle lost, escaped and made his way to Lima.

Gonzalo had won an extremely bloody but gratifying victory over a numerically superior, but outgunned Centeno. The way was opened to proceed into Chile, but he reconsidered. Perhaps affected by the madness of "victory disease," he decided on a change of plan, now rejecting the advice of both Carvajal and Cepeda. Cepeda thought the moment was right to negotiate on the basis of the victory at Huarina, but Carvajal thought they should proceed into Chile and overextend La Gasca's forces, the easier to defeat him.

Gonzalo decided to re-take Cusco and prepare for a showdown with La Gasca. He had never lost a battle, perhaps coming to believe in some divine plan for his quest to rule Peru. He was encouraged by the sharp accretion of new recruits to his forces, including many of the vanquished Centeno's army. His reentry into Cusco only strengthened his resolve, as he was greeted like a king, with royalist officials hanging from the gallows.[111] Over the next several months, he armed and trained his men, and fortified the city. Once again, however, there arose a policy dispute with Carvajal over where to fight.

Gonzalo wanted to defend Cusco, while Carvajal believed that La Gasca's army was too strong to overcome in a head-to-head showdown. He argued for adopting a scorched-earth scheme, much as Gonzalo himself had done at Lima, and retreat to the forests to fight. In his view, the recent adherents to his army from Centeno's defeated force, some three hundred men, were unreliable and Gonzalo would be better off disbanding them and fighting with a smaller but more dependable corps. But Gonzalo,

---

[110] Prescott, *History of the Conquest of Peru*, 2:390-94.
[111] Stirling, *Pizarro*, 164.

supported by several of his youthful captains, decided to "hazard all on the chances of a battle." [112]

Meanwhile, La Gasca was disheartened by Centeno's defeat, but determined to continue. He called for Aldana to strip all the cannon from his ships at Lima and send them to him.[113] Then, he continued to march his army slowly, leaving Jauja at the end of the year and bivouacking at Andahuaylas, about two hundred miles west of Cusco. They remained there three months through the rainy season, which was just beginning. While waiting, additional reinforcements arrived: Centeno from Lima, Benalcázar from Popayán, and Valdivia from Chile. La Gasca chose Hernando Hinojosa, Diego de Alvarado, and Pedro de Valdivia to command the most formidable Spanish army in Peru, some two thousand strong.

When the rains eased, they decided to continue their advance. Two major obstacles stood in their way: the natural barriers of the Abancay and Apurimac Rivers. All expected Gonzalo to mount defenses at the possible crossing points where bridges, long-since destroyed, would have to be rebuilt. Oddly, however, Gonzalo declined to defend them forcefully. Although he sent a small detachment to disrupt the reconstruction of the suspension bridge across the Apurimac, it arrived too late. Crossing the rivers was a major undertaking; but having accomplished these feats, La Gasca's army now stood overlooking the valley at Jaquijahuana, some fifteen miles to the northwest of Cusco.[114]

In Cusco, the argument over the best place to defend was resolved by the appearance of La Gasca's army. Gonzalo was now willing to abandon Cusco and move his force to Jaquijahuana to meet it. Carvajal objected once again. Having fortified the city, he argued for its defense; but if defense was to be elsewhere, he counseled a retreat to Urcos, thirty miles southeast near the forests.[115] It was a strange debate. Cusco offered the best defensive position in the country, as noted repeatedly in this history, but perhaps not against cannon. Nevertheless, referring to the

---

[112] Prescott, *History of the Conquest of Peru*, 2:412.
[113] Helps, *Spanish Conquest in America*, 4:224.
[114] Stirling, *Pizarro*, 165.
[115] Helps, *Spanish Conquest in America*, 4:231-32.

victory at Huarina, Gonzalo adamantly rejected a retreat and selected the eastern end of the Jaquijahuana valley where it narrowed. He believed his flanks would be protected by the river on one side and steep mountain heights on the other. It was there that he deployed his nine hundred-man army, supported by a large force of Indians. It was April 8, 1548.

As the opposing armies stood poised for what promised to be the final battle for control of Peru, a strange thing happened. Gonzalo's army began to crack, the first desertion being the Auditor Cepeda, who, feigning an advance, spurred his horse into a gallop across the plain to the opposing side. His act triggered others, and soon Gonzalo's entire army was abandoning their positions and fleeing in disarray—toward La Gasca's forces, back to Cusco, or into the mountains.[116]

It was over with hardly a shot fired, an anticlimactic end to what had threatened to be the greatest, bloodiest battle ever fought by opposing Spanish armies in Peru. Gonzalo, seeing his army literally disappear before his eyes, realized that it was over. Observing the spectacle, he turned to one of his aides and said, "I believe they are all deserting me." He then turned his horse toward La Gasca's lines and slowly rode over to surrender. Carvajal, attempting to flee, was caught when his horse stumbled into a gully. Both men were beheaded the next day on the field of battle, thus bringing to a precipitous end the last of the conquistadors, and the end of an era.[117]

---

[116] Stirling, *Pizarro*, 167.
[117] Kochis, *God, Glory and Gold*, 2:675.

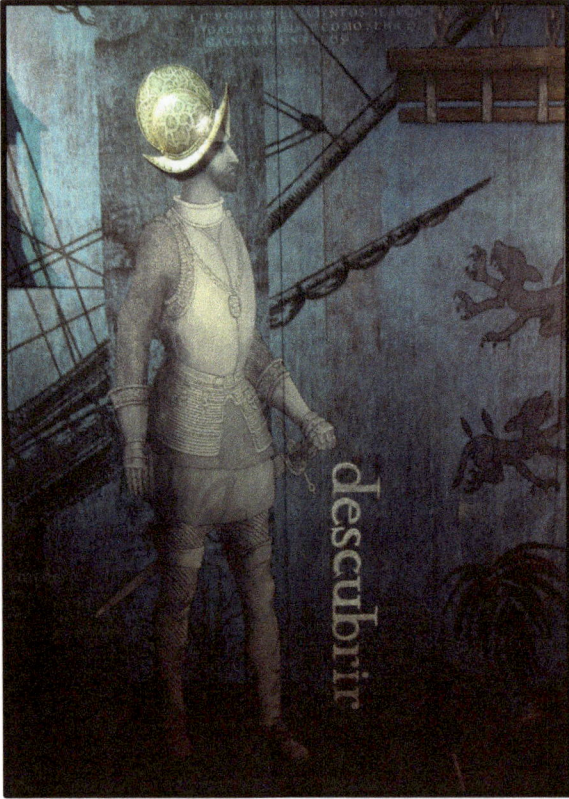

7.4. "Conquistador Español"
Navigation Pavilion, Seville, Spain.

Conclusion

Birth of an Empire

Christopher Columbus was the first of a long line of conquistadors who collectively opened the door to the New World. The giants of the conquest were Hernán Cortés and Francisco Pizarro, but it was the Spanish monarchs—Ferdinand and Isabella, followed by Charles I (Emperor Charles V)—who walked through the door they opened and reaped the return on one of the grandest bets in world history. Over the course of half a century, Spain's rulers promoted exploration and conquest, and then commandeered the acquired lands and expropriated the wealth that lay beneath them.

This work examines the initiation of Spain's American colonial enterprise in the context of strategy and politics, illuminating the motives and logistics of conquest, and the reaction and interaction of native-American peoples with the invaders. It offers novel interpretations of historical events and circumstances and seeks to inspire further investigation.

Fifteenth-century Chinese monetary policy increased the demand for silver and spurred the search for new trade routes to the Orient. Its role in the imagining and undertaking of expeditions by Christopher Columbus and others merits due consideration.

The explorers' own dreams of wealth and power galvanized their endurance and brutality, and their battles with each other and the Crown's authority. In undertaking the conquest of the Aztecs, Cortés escaped the clutches of Cuban governor Diego Velázquez, who tried to stop him; and only belatedly secured the support of King Charles. Ultimately, the king denied him the political power he sought.

Two aspects of collaboration between conquistadors and indigenous people stand out. One is the readiness of many tribal communities to fight with the Spaniards against the tyranny of Aztec and Incan rulers. Cortés and Pizarro leveraged this opportunity in different ways, and with dramatically different consequences. Cortés, with the assistance of disaffected peoples, destroyed the Aztec regime and laid claim to Mexico as a Spanish colony. Pizarro likewise had allies among the Andeans who assisted in the overthrow of the existing Inca leader. But he tried unsuccessfully and at great cost to govern Peru through a succession of puppet Incas.

Indigenous women—Malinche in Mexico and Quispe Sisa in Peru—made fortuitous and vital contributions. They could speak Spanish, and thus enabled communication and offered advice. Their partnerships with Cortés and Pizarro, respectively, do not feature prominently in the traditional narratives; yet their knowledge of local politics, culture, and geography informed the conquistadors' decisions at key intervals.

The Crown's maneuvers were of utmost strategic and tactical importance, especially those under the auspices of King Charles. The *Capitulación de Toledo,* which authorized Pizarro to engage in the conquest of Peru, underwrote Spanish intervention in an Incan civil war. The king's ambiguity regarding the division of territory between Pizarro and his erstwhile cohort, Diego de Almagro, kindled a bloody factional conflict. Order ultimately was restored after the king dispatched the shrewd Pedro de la Gasca, who defeated a secessionist rebellion almost without firing a shot, ending the preeminence of the conquistadors in Spain's nascent American empire.

Appendix I

Francisco Pizarro
with Emperor Charles V

Hand-colored woodcut image of a painting entitled *Entrevista del Emperador Carlos V con Francisco Pizarro antes de partir para la conquista del Perú*, by Angel Lizcano Monedero, 1881.
Northwind Picture Archives/Alamy Stock Photo
Note: Enlarged section showing figure possibly wearing an Incan headdress. Quispe Sisa? (page 274)

Enlarged section showing figure possibly wearing an Incan headdress. Quispe Sisa?

Appendix II

The Capitulation of Toledo

26 July, 1529. Toledo. Royal Charter approving the agreement granted by Charles V to Francisco Pizarro for the conquest and settlement of Peru

[PORRAS BARRENECHEA, Cedulario del Perú. I. pp. XIX-XX y 18-24.] [GARCÍA-GALLO, A. (ed.).

Antología de fuentes del antiguo Derecho. Madrid : 1975. pp.745-750.]

Preamble:
The Queen. Insofar as you, Captain Francisco Pizarro, of Castilla del Oro, in your name and in the name of the venerable Father Hernando de Luque, headmaster and provisor of the Church of Darién, sede vacante, which is lies in the aforementioned Castilla del Oro, and Captain Diego de Almagro, of the City of Panama, have related to us, that you and your aforementioned companions, in your desire to serve us and the greater good and the expansion of our Royal Crown, some five years more or less ago, that having obtained permission and consent from Pedrarias Dávila, governor and general captain of the aforementioned mainland, have taken charge of conquering, discovering, pacifying and settling the aforementioned lands, in the eastern part, at your and your companion's expense, as much as you will be able to do, and constructed to that end two ships and one brigantine on said coast; and that as well in this (to transport the rigging and equipment necessary for said voyage and fleet from Nombre de Dios, which lies on the northern coast, to the opposite southern coast) as in the people and other things necessary for said voyage, and to turn and reconstruct said fleet, you have spent a large sum of gold pieces; and you have gone and done said discovery, where you have endured many perils and travails, due to which the people who went with you left you on a deserted island, with only thirteen men who would not leave you, and that with them and with the aid of other ships and people that were given you by the Captain Diego de Almagro you left said island

and discovered the lands and provinces of Peru and the City of Tumbes; in which you have spent, you and your aforementioned companions, more than thirty thousand gold pieces. Because of the desire you had to serve us, you wished to continue said conquest and settlement at your own expense and of your own will, knowing we would never be obliged to pay or settle the costs you will incur there, beyond what was granted you by this agreement. You have requested and asked for my favor in entrusting you with the conquest of said lands and that I would concede and give my favor under the conditions contained above. Upon which things I have set forth the assent and agreement as follows:

1.   First, I grant you, said Captain Francisco Pizarro license and authorization so that you may continue with the aforementioned discovery, conquest and settlement of said Province of Peru, in our name, in the name of the Royal Crown of Castile and for us, up to two hundred leagues of land along the same coast. Of which two hundred leagues starting at the town which in the language of the aborigines is called Teninpulla, which you later named Santiago, up to the town of Chincha, which stretch of coastline may comprise said distance of two hundred leagues of coastline, more or less.

2.   Idem, I understand you have been faithful in your service to God and to us, and to honor your person and favor you, we promise to make you our governor and captain general of all said Province of Pero and of the lands and towns that at present or in the future may lie in the aforementioned two hundred leagues, until the end of your days, with a yearly salary of seven hundred and twenty-five thousand maravedis, starting on the day when you will set sail from these, our kingdoms to continue with the aforementioned settlement and conquest, the which you will be paid out of the rents and rights belonging to us in said lands which you will settle. Out of which salary you must pay each year a mayor and ten squires and thirty laborers, a medic and an apothecary. The which salary will be payed to you by the officials of said lands.

3.   Furthermore, I grant you the title of our governor of said Province of Peru, and thusly the office of her sheriff, all until the end of your days.

4.   Furthermore, I grant you license, with permission and agreement of our aforementioned officials, to build four fortifications wherever you and our aforementioned officials see fit and necessary to protect and pacify said lands. And I will grant you their possession, for you and for your heirs and successors, one after the other, with a yearly salary of seventy-five thousand maravedis, for each of the aforementioned fortresses that would thus be built. The which you will erect at your own

expense, so that neither we nor the king who will come after us will be obligated to pay you at the time you incur the expense, except five years after completion of the fortification, paying you each of those five years, the fifth part of the expense, from the profits of said lands.

5.   Furthermore, we grant you, to help you with your expenses, ten thousand ducats each year, until the end of your life, from the rents produced by said lands.

6.   Furthermore, it is our wish, considering the good life and doctrine of the aforementioned Hernando de Luque, to put him forward to our Holy Father as bishop for the city of Tumbes, which lies in the province and governorship of Peru, with the limits and diocese that we, in our apostolic authority, will indicate. While the papal bulls for the aforementioned bishopric are underway, we name you universal protector of all the aborigines of the aforementioned province, with a yearly salary of one thousand ducats, payed from our rents from the aforementioned lands, while there are ecclesiastical tithes from which to pay.

7.   Furthermore, insofar as you have requested of us, in your name and in the aforementioned name, I may give you some vassals in the aforementioned lands, and, at present, we will not do so because we do not have full possession of them. It is our with that you receive the twentieth part of all the yearly profits made in the aforementioned lands as long as the amount does not exceed one thousand five hundred ducats: one thousand for you, the aforementioned Captain Pizarro, and five hundred for the aforementioned Diego de Almagro, as long as we see it convenient as an amendment to your service to us and for your works.

8.   Furthermore, we will grant the aforementioned Captain Diego de al Magro the possession of the fortification that lies or may lie in the aforementioned city of Tubmes, which lies in the aforementioned Province of Pero, with a yearly salary of one hundred thousand maravedis, with an additional two hundred thousand maravedis yearly, to help with the expenses, all paid from the rents produced by the aforementioned lands, of which he may avail himself on the date when you, the aforementioned Francisco Pizarro will arrive at the aforementioned lands, even if the aforementioned Captain Almagro stays in Panama wherever he wishes to stay. And we name you nobleman so that you may enjoy the honors and preeminences that nobility is due in all of the indies and overseas islands and mainland.

9.   Furthermore, we order that the estates, lands and plots that you hold in the mainland, known as Castilla del Oro, are given to you and to their residents so that you may possess them, enjoy them, and do with them what you will and see fit, according to what we have conceded and granted

to the residents of the aforementioned mainland. The aborigines and aboriginal servants are entrusted to you. It is our will and our wish and we order that you hold them, enjoy them and avail yourself of them, and that they be not taken from you so long as we will it so.

10. Furthermore, we grant whomever were to settle the aforementioned lands, that henceforth, during six years, the exploitation of gold, provided they pay us a tenth of the gold extracted from the mines, after six years the ninth part, and so on, descending, until a fifth is reached. But gold and other things obtained through salvage or during campaigns or in any other way, they will, of course, pay us a fifth part of all that.

11. Furthermore, we allow the residents of the aforementioned lands, during said six years, and more if we so desire, the free passage all the supplies and provisions for their homes they would take, so long as these are not meant for sale. As for what they, or merchants and traders, would sell, we allow free passage for two years only.

12. Idem, we promise that for a period of ten years, and beyond, unless we order the contrary, we do not impose sales tax or any other kind of tax on the residents of the aforementioned lands.

13. Idem, we grant the aforementioned residents and settlers, to be given by you, the plots and lands fit for their persons, in accordance to what has been done and what is done in the Island of Hispaniola. Likewise, we will give you the power to command, in our name, the aborigines of the aforementioned lands, in keeping with the instructions and ordinances that will be given you.

14. Idem, upon your request, we assign Bartolomé Ruiz as our master navigator for the South Seas...

15. Furthermore, we are happy and pleased that you, the aforementioned Captain Pizarro, while we so desire, will be governor and administrator of the aborigines in our Isla de Flores, which is close to Panama, and that you will enjoy, for yourself and whomever you wish, of all the resources of the aforementioned island, it's lands, plots, hills, trees, mining, pearl hunting, as long as you will be obliged to give us and our officials in Castilla del Oro, every year we wish to have it, two hundred maravedis, plus one fifth of all the gold and pearls that in any way and by any person be extracted in the aforementioned Isla de Flores, without any discount, provided the aforementioned aborigines of the island be employed not in pearl hunting nor mining but rather in farming and exploiting said lands, for provisioning and maintaining your fleet, and whatever other purpose you would have for said lands. And we allow that if you, the aforementioned Francisco Pizarro, once arrived at Castilla del Oro, within the first two months after your arrival, would declare before

our aforementioned governor and the residence judge who be there, that your do not wish to take charge of the aforementioned Isla de Flores, and that the island remain with us, as we possess it currently.

16. Idem, considering how well Bartolomé Ruiz and Cristóbal de Peralta and Pedro de Candía and Domingo de Safaluce and Nicolás de Ribera and Francisco de Cuéllar and Alonso de Molina and Pedro Halcón and García de Gerez and Antón de Carrión and Alonso Brizeño and Martín de Paz and Juan de la Torre have served in said voyage and discovery and because you have requested it of me, it is our wish to give them our favor, thus we hereby declare noblemen any of them who are not members of the nobility in those parts, so that in them and in all of our Indies and overseas islands and mainland they may enjoy the honors and pre-eminences that nobility is due in our Kingdoms; and we declare that those who are members of the nobility be made Knights of the Order of the Golden Spur, given first the information that is required in that case.

17. Idem, we shall grant twenty-five mares and as many horses out of what we have in the Island of Jamaica. And if we do not have them when you ask for them, we will not be bound to their price nor anything else on their account.

18. Furthermore, we grant you three hundred maravedis, to be paid in Castilla del Oro, for the artillery and munitions that you will have to take to the aforementioned Province of Peru, taking proof from our officials at the House of Trade in Seville of the things you bought thusly and at what cost you bought them, including the their interest and exchange; and moreover, I will grant you another two hundred ducats to help with the transport of said artillery and munitions, along with other things of yours, from Nombre de Dios to the aforementioned South Seas.

19. Furthermore we hereby grant you permission to take from these our kingdoms or the Kingdom of Portugal and Islands of Cabo Verde or from wherever you or someone in your name see fit and to transport to the lands under your governorship fifty black slaves, of which at least a third should be female, free of all rights belonging to us, so that if you left all or a part of them in the islands of Hispaniola, Cuba and Santiago, or in Castilla del Oro, or somewhere else, those whom you would thus leave would be lost or adjudicated, and we hereby adjudicate them to our Property and Administration.

20. Furthermore, we will give favor and charity for a hospital to be built in the aforementioned lands, to help care for the poor who may go there, in the amount of one thousand maravedis, taken from the council fines collected in the aforementioned lands.

21. Likewise, upon your request and by the consent of the first settlers of said lands, we hereby grant the hospitals of the aforementioned lands the rights to byproducts from foundries that will be built there, of which we will order our provision to be given as is fit.

22. Furthermore, we hereby order that in the city of Panama, or wherever you order them to reside, there must be a carpenter and a caulker, each receiving a yearly salary of thirty thousand maravedis from the time they begin residing in said city or, as mentioned before, wherever you send them. We will have them be paid by our officers in the aforementioned lands of your governorship when it is of our will and favor.

23. Idem, we will order you to give our provision when it is fit so that in the aforementioned coast of the South Seas you may take whatever ships you may need, with the consent of their owners, to be used in the trips you may have to make to the aforementioned lands, paying the owners of these ships a fair freight, even if others have hired them for other parts.

24. Likewise, we hereby order and defend that from these our Kingdoms no persons travel to the aforementioned lands who have been forbidden to travel to those parts, under the penalties comprised in our Laws, Ordinances and Charters, created by us and by The Catholic Monarchs, nor any jurist or procurer to use their services.

25. We grant you everything that was said, as long as you, the aforementioned Captain Pizarro be obliged to leave these our kingdoms with the ships and rigging and supplies and other things necessary for said voyage, with two hundred and fifty men: of which one hundred and fifty from these kingdoms and the hundred remaining from the islands and mainland of the Ocean Sea; as long as you don't take more than twenty men from the mainland called Castilla del Oro, other than those who were with you on the first and second voyage you made to the aforementioned lands of Peru, because we give these men license to go with you freely. You must do this six months from today's date. And arriving at the aforementioned Castilla del Oro, and passing by Panama, you will have to make said voyage and make said discovery and settlement within the following six months.

26. Idem, with the condition that when you leave these our kingdoms and arrive at the aforementioned Province of Peru you take and keep with you the officers of our estate that were named by us as well as the religious or ecclesiastical person that will be appointed by us to instruct the aborigines and naturals of that province in our Holy Catholic Faith, under whose judgment you and they must conquer, discover and settle said lands. You must pay freight and matalotage and other necessities for these

priests, in accordance with their persons, at your own expense, without giving them anything during the whole of the navigation because of it, the which we charge you with as a service to God and to ourselves, because we would otherwise fear defraudment.

27. Furthermore, you must keep, during the aforementioned pacification, conquest, settlement and treatment of said aborigines, concerning their persons and their assets, our ordinances and instructions which we have made for that purpose and which will be made and handed to you in our Charter and Provision, which we will send you to charge you with said aborigines.

28. And you, the aforementioned Captain Francisco Pizarro, having complied with what is contained in this assent, in everything that befalls you to keep and comply with, we promise you and assure you by our Royal Word that henceforth, we will be in keeping with everything we grant you and we give you and the settlers and the traders of the aforementioned lands our favor. For the execution and compliance of which we will order our necessary particular Charters and Provisions be given to oblige you, the aforementioned Captain Pizarro, first, before a public scrivener, to keep and comply with what is contained in this assent which concerns you, as was stated. Issued in Toledo on July sixth, one thousand five hundred and twenty-nine.

I, the Queen. Endorsed by Juan Vásquez. Sealed by the Count and Doctor Beltrán.

Charter of Obligations of the Conquistador (August 17, 1529):

Let it be known to any who read this charter of obligations that I, Captain Francisco Pizarro state: That insofar as Her Majesty ordered and gave a certain assent and agreement with me regarding the conquest and settlement of the lands and provinces of Peru and the City of Tumbes, which lie in the South Seas, the contents of the aforementioned assent and agreement are the following:... [the preceding text is reproduced]...

Therefore, by this present letter, I, the aforementioned Captain Francisco Pizarro, agree wholeheartedly and commit myself, by my person and my possessions and lands, which I have and will have, to keep and comply with the aforementioned agreement and assent, which as is customary incorporates everything that concerns me, in everything and for everything, in accordance with its contents, and not to go against any part of it, not now nor ever and in no way, which pledge I guarantee by my person and my assets and furthermore with a payment of four million gold ducats to be made to the Property and Administration of Her Highness. To keep and comply with this, I oblige myself and my possessions and lands to justice, so that they may help me keep, maintain and comply, as well as if by definitive sentence, upon my request and by my consent, and I renounce any and all laws in my favor, especially the law and right that states that renouncing laws that be and be made is invalid.

Which was made and given in the city of Toledo on the seventeenth day of August, one thousand five hundred and twenty-nine. Witnesses to these statements were the Licenciate Corral and Rodrigo de Mazuelas and Diego de Castresán, who were present in court. Sealded [Pizarro] with his usual seal, as he does not know how to sign [there are two seals].

———————

Source of Spanish Text: Cervantes Virtual Library
http://www.cervantes virtual.com/bib/historia/CarlosV/9_9.shtml

Translated from original Spanish by Trusted Translations
www.trustedtranslations.com

Bibliography

Anderson, Charles Loftus Grant. *Old Panama and Castilla Del Oro: A Narrative History* [...]. Boston: Page, 1914.

Bancroft, Hubert Howe. *History of Central America,* Vol. 2, *1530-1800.* Vol. 7 of *The Works of Hubert Howe Bancroft.* San Francisco: A.L. Bancroft, 1883.

Bancroft, Hubert Howe. *History of Mexico,* Vol. 1, *1516-1521.* Vol. 9 of *The Works of Hubert Howe Bancroft.* San Francisco: A.L. Bancroft, 1883.

Betanzos, Juan de. *Narrative of the Incas.* Edited and Translated by Roland Hamilton and Dana Buchanan. Austin: University of Texas Press, 1996.

Brooks, Jennifer. "Marriage, Legitimacy, and Intersectional Identities in the Sixteenth Century Spanish Empire" (2016). *History Honors Projects.* https://digitalcommons.macalester.edu/history_honors/21.

Cahill, David. "Advanced Andeans and Backward Europeans: Structure and Agency in the Collapse of the Inca Empire." In *Questioning Collapse: Human Resilience, Ecological Vulnerability, and the Aftermath of Empire,* edited by Patricia McAnany and Norman Yoffee, 207-238. Cambridge: Cambridge University Press, 2010.

Catz, Rebecca. "Columbus in the Azores." *Portuguese Studies*, 6 (1990): 17-23. http://www.jstor.org/stable/41104900.

Cieza de León, Pedro de. *The Discovery and Conquest of Peru: Chronicles of the New World Encounter.* Edited and Translated by Alexandra Parma Cook and Noble David Cook. Durham: Duke University Press, 1998.

Cobo, Bernabé. *History of the Inca Empire.* Translated by Roland Hamilton. Austin: University of Texas Press, 1979.

Collis, Maurice. *Cortés and Montezuma.* New York: New Directions Publishing, September 15, 1999.

Cook, David Noble. *Born to Die: Disease and New World Conquest, 1492-1650.* Cambridge: Cambridge University Press, 1998.

Davenport, Jade, "Spanish Conquistadors and the Looting of Mexican, Peruvian Gold Treasures." *Mining Weekly*, September 7, 2012. https://

www.miningweekly.com/print - version / spanish-conquistadors-and-the-looting-of-mexican-and-peruvian-golden-treasure-2012-09-07.

Davies, R. Trevor. *The Golden Century of Spain, 1501-1621.* London: Macmillan & Co., 1961.

DeBoer, Warren. *Traces Behind the Esmeraldas Shore: Prehistory of the Santiago-Cayapas Region, Ecuador.* Tuscaloosa: University of Alabama Press, 1996.

Díaz del Castillo, Bernal. *The True History of the Conquest of New Spain.* Translated by Alfred Percival Maudsley. Vol. 1. London: The Hakluyt Society, 1908.

Díaz del Castillo, Bernal. *The Memoirs of the Conquistador, Bernal Díaz del Castillo.* Translated by John Ingram Lockhart. Vol. 1. London: J. Hatchard & Son, 1844.

Díaz del Castillo, Bernal. *The History of the Conquest of New Spain.* Edited by Davíd Carrasco. Albuquerque: University of New Mexico Press, 2009.

Diamond, Jared. *Guns, Germs, and Steel: The Fate of Human Societies.* New York: Random House, 2011.

Duncan, David. *Hernando de Soto: A Savage Quest in the Americas.* Norman: University of Oklahoma Press, 1996.

Elliott, John. *Empires of the Atlantic World: Britain and Spain in America, 1492-1830.* New Haven: Yale University Press, 2006.

Enock, C. Reginald. *Ecuador: Its Ancient and Modern History, Topography, and Natural Resources.* London: T.F. Unwin, 1914.

Enrigue, Álvaro. "The Curse of Cortés," *The New York Review of Books* 65, no. 9 (May 24, 2018), https://www.nybooks.com/articles/2018/05/24/mexicocortes/.

Fancourt, Charles St. John. *The History of Yucatan: From Its Discovery to the Close of the Seventeenth Century.* London: John Murray, 1854.

Flickema, Thomas. "The Siege of Cusco." *Revista de Historia de América*, no. 92 (Jul-Dec, 1981): 17-47. http://www.jstor.org/stable/20139433.

Flynn, Dennis O. and Giráldez, Arturo. "Born with a 'Silver Spoon': The Origins of World Trade in 1571." *Journal of World History* 6, no. 2 (Fall 1995): 201-221.

Gamboa, Pedro Sarmiento de. *History of the Incas.* Translated by Sir Clements Markham. Cambridge, Ontario: In Parentheses Publications, Peruvian Series, 2000. http://www.yorku.ca /inpar / sarmiento_markham.pdf

Garcilaso de la Vega, Inca. *The Royal Commentaries of the Inca and the General History of Peru, Abridged.* Edited by Karen Spalding.

Translated by Harold V. Livermore. Indianapolis: Hackett Publishing Company, 2006.

Garr, Arnold K. "Years in Portugal: Emergence of a Grand Idea." *Christopher Columbus: A Latter Day Saint Perspective*, by Arnold K. Garr. Provo: Religious Studies Center, Brigham Young University, 1992. https://rsc.byu.edu/archived/christopher-columbus-latter-day-saint-perspective/years-portugal-emergence-grand-idea.

Gilder Lehrman Institute of American History (online). *History Now.* "Columbus Reports on his First Voyage, 1493." https://www.gilderlehrman.org / history-now / spotlight-primary-source/columbus-reports-his-first-voyage-1493.

Giraldez Rivero, A. "Born with a Silver Spoon: China, American Silver and Global Markets During the Early Modern Period." PhD diss. University of Amsterdam, 1999.

Gómara, Francisco López de. *The Pleasant Historie of the Conquest of the West India* [...]. Translated by Thomas Nicholas. London: Thomas Creede, 1596.

Hancock, Graham. "The Spanish Use of Animals as Weapons of War." *Ancient Origins* (online), October 6, 2013. https://www.ancient-origins.net/ opinion-guest-authors/spanish-use-animals-weapons-war-00898.

Hassig, Ross. "Xicotencatl: Rethinking an Indigenous Mexican Hero." *Estudios de Cultura Náhuatl*, no. 32 (2001): 29-49. http://www.historicas.unam.mx/publicaciones/revistas/nahuatl/pdf/ec n32/627.pdf.

Helps, Arthur. *The Spanish Conquest of America and Its Relation to the History of Slavery and to the Government of Colonies.* Vol. 2. New York: Harper & Bros., 1856.

Helps, Arthur. *The Spanish Conquest in America, and Its Relation to the History of Slavery and to the Government of Colonies.* Edited by M. Oppenheim. Vol. 3. London and New York: John Lane, 1902.

Helps, Arthur. *The Spanish Conquest in America, and Its Relation to the History of Slavery and to the Government of Colonies.* Vol. 4. New York, Harper & Bros., 1868.

Hemming, John. *The Conquest of the Incas.* New York: Harcourt Brace Jovanovich, 1970.

Hill, Roscoe R. "The Office of Adelantado." *Political Science Quarterly* 28, no. 4 (1913): 646-68. doi:10.2307/2141824.

Kamen, Henry. *Empire: How Spain Became A World Power, 1492-1763.* New York: Harper-Collins, 2003.

Kochis, Paul M. *God, Glory and Gold: Journey to the Conquest of the Incas.* Vol. 2, *The Quest.* Minneapolis: Mill City Press, 2013.

Koskenniemi, Martti, "Empire and International Law: The Real Spanish Contribution." *University of Toronto Law Journal* 61, no. 1 (2011): 1-36. https://doi.org/10.3138/utlj.61.1.001.

Kubler, George. "The Behavior of Atahualpa, 1531-1533." *The Hispanic American Historical Review* 25, no. 4 (1945): 413-27. doi:10.2307/2508231.

Leon-Portilla, Miguel. *The Broken Spears: The Aztec Account of the Conquest of Mexico.* Boston: Beacon Press, 1992.

Lepore, Jill. *Encounters in the New World: A History in Documents.* New York: Oxford Press, 2000.

Levy, Buddy. *Conquistador Hernan Cortez, King Montezuma and the Last Stand of the Aztecs.* New York: Bantam, 2008.

Lockhart, James. *Men of Cajamarca.* Austin: University of Texas Press, 1972.

Lynch, John. *Spain 1516-1598: From Nation State to Empire.* London: Wiley-Blackwell, 1998.

MacQuarrie, Kim, *The Last Days of the Incas.* New York: Simon & Shuster, 2007.

Maddison, Angus, *The World Economy: A Millennial Perspective.* Development Center Studies. Paris: OECD, 2001. https://doi.org/10.1787/9789264189980-en.

Markham, Clements R., ed. and trans. *Reports on the Discovery of Peru.* London: Hakluyt Society, 1872. Reprinted, New York: Burt Franklin, 1970 Markham, Clements R., *The Incas of Peru.* New York: Dutton, 1912.

Marley, David. *Wars of the Americas.* Santa Barbara: ABC-CLIO, 1998.

Mavor, William. *History of the Discovery and Settlement to the Present Time of North and South America and of the West Indies.* London: Richard Phillips, 1806.

McCaa, Robert, Aleta Nimlos and Teodoro Hampe- Martínez. "Why Blame Smallpox? The Death of the Inca Huayna Cápac and the Demographic Destruction of Tawantinsuyu (Ancient Peru)." Paper presented at the American Historical Association Annual Meeting, January 8-11, 2004, Washington D.C. http://users.pop.umn.edu/~rmccaa/aha2004/

McEwan, Gordon. *The Incas: New Perspectives.* Santa Barbara: ABC-CLIO, 2006.

Mitchell, Mary Ames. *Crossing the Ocean Sea.* Online: Mary Ames Mitchell, 2015. http://www.crossingtheoceansea.com.

Morgan, Edmund. "Columbus' Confusion About the New World." *Smithsonian,* October 2009. https://www.smithsonianmag.com/travel/columbus-confusion-about-the-new-world-140132422/

Murphy, Robert Cushman. "The Earliest Spanish Advances Southward from Panama along the West Coast of South America." *The Hispanic American Historical Review* 21, no. 1 (1941): 3-28. doi:10.2307/2507517.

Neill, David and Peter Jorgensen, "Climates." In *Catalogue of the Vascular Plants of Ecuador.* Missouri Botanical Garden Press, July 30, 1999. http://www.mobot.org/mobot/research/ecuador/welcome.shtml

Newson, Linda. *Life and Death in Early Colonial Ecuador.* Norman: University of Oklahoma Press, 2005.

Ober, Frederick A. *Pizarro and the Conquest of Peru.* New York: Harper & Brothers, 1906. https://www.heritage-history.com/index.php?c=read&author=ober&book=pizarro

Odling-Smee, Lucy. "Early Gunshot Victim Uncovered," *Nature,* June 20, 2007. doi:10.1038/news070518-8

Olivares, Rafael. *Ñusta: The Inka Love of Francisco Pizarro.* Bergenfield: Xlibris LLC, 2014.

Parker, Geoffrey, *Emperor: A New Life of Charles V.* New Haven: Yale University Press, 2019.

Peck, Douglas. *The Yucatan: From Prehistoric Times to the Great Maya Revolt, A Narrative.* Xlibris, 2005.

Powers, Karen Vieira. *Women in the Crucible of Conquest, 1500-1600.* Albuquerque: University of New Mexico Press, 2005.

Prescott, William H. *History of the Conquest of Mexico and History of the Conquest of Peru.* New York: Modern Library, 1843.

Prescott, William H. *Mexico and the Life of the Conqueror Fernando Cortes.* 2 vols. New York: Peter Fenelon Collier & Son, 1900.

Prescott, William H. *History of the Conquest of Peru.* Vol. 2. New York: Harper & Bros., 1847.

Prescott, William H. *History of the Conquest of Peru.* Partly abridged and revised by Victor W. von Hagen. New York: New American Library, 1961.

Provan, Josh. "Atahualpa's Rook: Chess and Murder During the Conquest of Peru," *Adventures in Historyland,* March 10, 2019. https://adventuresinhistoryland.com/2019/03/10/atahualpas-rook/

Quintana, Manual José. *Lives of Vasco Nunez de Balboa and Francisco Pizarro.* Translated by Margaret Hodson. Edinburgh: William Blackwood, 1832. Reprinted by Kessinger, 2010.

Reséndez, Andrés. *The Other Slavery: The Uncovered Story of Indian Enslavement in America*. Boston: Houghton-Mifflin, 2016.

Restall, Matthew. *When Montezuma Met Cortés: The True Story of the Meeting that Changed History*. New York: Harper Collins, 2018.

Rostworowski, Maria. *Doña Francisca Pizarro, Una Ilustre Mestiza, 1534-1598*. Cuarta edición. Primera edición digital. Lima: Instituto de Estudios Peruanos, Diciembre 2017. https://books.apple.com/ us/ book/do%C3%B1a-francisca-pizarro/id1334482619.

Rowe, John Howland. *Inca Culture at the Time of the Spanish Conquest*. Washington, D.C.: U.S. GPO, 1946.

Sahagún, Bernardino de. *Florentine Codex*. Book 12. *The Conquest of Mexico*. Translated by Arthur J. O. Anderson and Charles E. Dibble. 2nd ed. Rev. Salt Lake City: University of Utah Press, 1975.

Sardone, Sergio. "Forced Loans in the Spanish Empire: The First Requisition of American Treasures in 1523." *Economic History Review*, 72, no. 1 (February 2019): 57-87. https://onlinelibrary. wiley.com/doi/10.1111/ehr.12604

Schwaller, John. *The First Letter from New Spain: The Lost Petition of Cortez and his Company, June 20, 1519*. Austin: University of Texas Press, 2014.

Schwartz, Stuart B., ed. *Victors and Vanquished: Spanish and Nahua Views of the Conquest of Mexico*. Boston: Bedford/St. Martin's, 2000.

Seaman, Rebecca, ed. *Conflict in the Early Americas: Encyclopedia of the Spanish Empire's Aztec, Incan, and Mayan Conquest*. Santa Barbara: ABC-CLIO, 2013.

Silverman, Reuben. "A Kingdom Set Aflame: Diego de Almagro and the Struggle for Spanish Peru." December 26, 2013. https://reuben silverman.wordpress.com/2013/12/26/a-kingdom-set-aflame-diego-de-almagro-and-the-struggle-for-spanish-peru/

Sitchin, Zecharia. *The Lost Realms: Book IV of the Earth Chronicles*. New York: Harper, 1990.

Smith, Adam. *An Inquiry into the Nature and Causes of the Wealth of Nations*. London: Strahan and Cadell, 1776; Ann Arbor: Text Creation Partnership, 2011. http://name.umdl.umich.edu/004861571. 0001.001

Stewart, Paul. "The Battle of Las Salinas, Peru, and its Historians." *The Sixteenth Century Journal* 19, no. 3 (Autumn, 1998): 407-34. doi:10.2307/2540471.

Stirling, Stuart. *Pizarro: Conqueror of the Inca*. Stroud: Sutton, 2005.

Thomas, Hugh. *Rivers of Gold: The Rise of the Spanish Empire from Columbus to Magellan*. New York: Random House, 2003.

Thomas, Hugh. *The Golden Empire*. New York: Random House, 2010.

Varner, John and Jeannette Varner. *Dogs of the Conquest.* Norman: University of Oklahoma Press, 1983.

Varón Gabai, Rafael. *Francisco Pizarro and His Brothers: The Illusion of Power in Sixteenth Century Peru.* Translated by Javier Flores Espinoza. Norman: University of Oklahoma Press, 1997 Ward, Thomas. *Decolonizing Indigeneity: New Approaches to Latin American Literature.* Lexington: Lexington Books, 2016.

Wood, Michael. *Conquistadors.* London: BBC Books, 2010.

Illustration Credits

Google Earth eye alt 8774.93 mi.
Image Landsat/Copernicus
Image IBCAO
Data SIO, NOAA, U.S. Navy, NGA, GEBCO.

Flag of New Spain and the Viceroyalty of Peru
Ningyou. (https:// commons.wikimedia.org / wiki/File:Flag_of_Cross_of_ Burgundy.svg), "Flag of Cross of Burgundy," https://creativecommons.org/ licenses/by-sa/3.0/legalcode

Plus Ultra (Further Beyond) was the personal motto of Emperor Charles V (King Charles 1 of Spain), adopted as Spain's national motto.

Keith Pickering
(https://commons.wikimedia.org / wiki / File: Columbus_first_ voyage.jpg), "Columbus first voyage," https://creativecommons.org/licenses/by-sa/3.0/ legalcode

Keith Pickering
(https://commons.wikimedia.org / wiki / File:Columbus_second_ voyage.jpg), "Columbus second voyage," https://creativecommons.org / licenses / by-sa/3.0/legalcode

Keith Pickering
(https://commons.wikimedia.org / wiki / File:Columbus_ third_ voyage.jpg), "Columbus third voyage," https://creativecommons.org/ licenses/ by-sa/3.0/legalcode

Keith Pickering
(https://commons.wikimedia.org / wiki / File:Columbus_fourth_ voyage.jpg), "Columbus fourth voyage," https://creativecommons.org/licenses/ by-sa/3.0/legalcode

1.5 Balboa's Expedition to the South Sea, 1513 .... **25**
Joanne Thornton
Drawn on map by Natural Earth (naturalearthdata.com), based on the narrative in Charles Loftus Grant Anderson, *Old Panama and Castilla del Oro* (1911) 214-223, and illustration of Eastern Panamanian Chiefdoms in Mary W. Helms, *Ancient Panama: Chiefs in Search of Power* (Austin: University of Texas Press, 1978) 164, Fig. 5.

1.6 Córdoba´s Expedition to Yucatan, 1517 .... **32**
Joanne Thornton
Drawn on map by Natural Earth (naturalearthdata.com), based on "The Expedition under Francisco Hernández de Córdova," in Bernal Díaz del Castillo, *The True History of the Conquest of New Spain*, trans. Alfred Percival Maudslay, M.A. (London: The Hakluyt Society, 1908), lxiii.

1.7 Grijalva's Expedition, 1518 .... **35**
Joanne Thornton
Drawn on map by Natural Earth (naturalearthdata.com), based on "The Expedition under Juan de Grijalva," in Bernal Díaz del Castillo, *The True History of the Conquest of New Spain*, trans. Alfred Percival Maudslay, M.A. (London: The Hakluyt Society, 1908), lxiii.

1.8 Diego Velázquez de Cuéllar **39**
Portrait by Antonio de Herrera y Tordesillas, circa 1625; published in Antwerp, 1728, by Juan Bautista Verdussen. Accessed at https://commons.wikimedia.org /wiki/File:DiegoVelazquezCuellar.jpg, marked as Public Domain.

2.1 Hernán Cortés **42**
Nineteenth century engraving, author unknown. Accessed at https://commons. wikimedia.org/wiki/File:Hernan_Fernando_Cortes.jpg, marked as Public Domain.

2.2 Expedition of Hernán Cortés to Mexico, 1519 .... **45**
Joanne Thornton
Drawn on map by d-maps (https://d-maps.com/carte.php?num_car=1386& lang=en), based on "The Expedition under Hernando Cortés," in Bernal Díaz del Castillo, *The True History of the Conquest of New Spain*, trans. Alfred Percival Maudslay, M.A. (London: The Hakluyt Society, 1908), lxiv. Depiction of approximate area controlled by Aztecs drawn principally from information contained in this image: Giggette (https://commons. wikimedia.org/wiki/File: Territorial_Organization_of_the_Aztec_Empire_1519 .png), "Territorial Organization of the Aztec Empire 1519," https://creative commons .org/licenses /by-sa/3.0/legalcode

2.3 Spanish War Dogs ....…..…...…... **47**
Author unknown. Posted on May 3, 2017 by The Loyal Ming General, World History Amino (https://aminoapps.com/c/world-history/page/blog/spanish-war-dogs/1Pdb_DZC6u1kjQ6V6bGWP2DBLKZxPobYxj)

2.4 La Malinche ....…..…......... **48**
Author unknown. Published by Xavier L. Medellín and Felix Hinz, medellinhistory.com (http://www.medellinhistoria.com / medellin / pbiogH_ Cortes.htm#Malinche)

2.5 Montezuma II ....…..…......... **51**
Painting attributed to Antonio Rodriguez (1636-1691) (https://commons. wikimedia.org / wiki / File:Moctezuma_Xocoyotzin.png) "Moctezuma Xocoyotzin," marked as Public Domain.

2.6 Cortés' March to Tenochtitlán ....…..…...…... **54**
Joanne Thornton
Drawn on map by Natural Earth (naturalearthdata.com), based on the narrative in Hubert Howe Bancroft, *History of Mexico, Vol. I, 1516-1521* (San Francisco: A.L. Bancroft and Company, 1883), 191-283.

2.7 Tenochtitlán in the basin of Mexico, 1519 ....…..… **59**
File:Lago de Texcoco-posclásico.png: Yavidaxiu File:Valley of Mexico c.1519-fr.svg: historicair 13:51, 11 September 2007 (UTC) derivative work: Sémhur (https://commons.wikimedia.org/wiki/File:Basin_of_Mexico_1519_map-en.svg) , https://creativecommons.org/licenses/by-sa/4.0/legalcode

2.8 Escape from Tenochtitlán ....…..…......... **72**
Joanne Thornton
Drawn on map by Natural Earth (naturalearthdata.com), based on the narrative in Hubert Howe Bancroft, *History of Mexico, Vol. I, 1516-1521* (San Francisco: A.L. Bancroft and Company, 1883), 454-475, and image by Yavidaxiu (https://commons.wikimedia.org/wiki/File:Ruta_de_escape_de_los_españoles_h acia_Tlaxcala.svg), "Ruta de escape de los españoles hacia Tlaxcala," https://creativecommons.org/licenses/by-sa/3.0/legalcode

2.9 Capture of Tenochtitlán ....…..…......... **76**
"The Capture of Tenochtitlán," second half of the seventeenth century. Oil on canvas. Jay I. Kislak Collection, Rare Book and Special Collections Division, Library of Congress (096.00.00), www.loc.gov/exhibits/exploring-the-early-americas/ExplorationsandEncounters/conquestpaintings/Assets/object96_t_725. Jpeg

Author unknown. (https://commons.wikimedia.org/wiki/File:Tenochtitlan_y_
Golfo_de_Mexico_1524.jpg), "Tenochtitlan y Golfo de Mexico 1524," marked
as public domain. This map of Tenochtitlan and the coastline of the Gulf of
Mexico is described as having been presented to Cortés as a gift sometime during
1519-1521, and published in 1524, along with Cortés' second letter to Emperor
Charles V (written in 1520), by Fridericum Peypus in Nuremberg. It depicts the
Aztec capital at its height, before its destruction by the Spaniards. See Elizabeth
Hill Boone (2011) "This new world now revealed: Hernán Cortés and the
presentation of Mexico to Europe," *Word & Image*, 27:1, 31-46, DOI: 10.
1080/02666281003771190

Joanne Thornton
Drawn on map by Natural Earth (naturalearthdata.com), based on images by
Bruce C. Ruiz: Hojeda_Map.gif at http://www.bruceruiz.net/PanamaHistory/
alonso_de_ojeda.htm
and Nicuesa_Map.gif at http://www.bruceruiz.net/Panama History/diego_
de_nicuesa.htm

Joanne Thornton
Drawn on d-map images https://d-maps.com/carte.php?num_car=1838&lang=en
(main map) and https://d-maps.com/carte.php?num_car=1410&lang=en (inset).

Joanne Thornton
Drawn using Google Maps (main map coastlines) and d-maps https://d-
maps.com/carte.php?num_car=1410&lang=en (inset).

Antonio de Ulloa (https://commons.wikimedia.org/wiki/File:Andean_raft,_1748.
jpg) "Andean raft, 1748," marked as Public Domain.

Joanne Thornton
Drawn using Google Maps (South American coastline) and d-maps image
https://d-maps.com/carte.php?num_car=31136&lang=en (inset).

"Quispe Sisa (Inés) Yupanqui," artist's rendition of her face. Author unknown.
Accessed at https://www.noblezaseminario.com/MasterE.html?a=213

Joanne Thornton
Google Earth image. Tower locations based on work of scholars including John Hemming and Edward Ranney, *Monuments of the Incas* (Albuquerque: University of New Mexico Press, 1990) and Graziano Gasparini and Luise Margolies, *Inca Architecture*, trans. Patricia J. Lyon (Bloomington: Indiana University Press, 1980), as cited by José Antonio Mazzotti, "The Lightning Bolt Yields to the Rainbow: Indigenous History and Colonial Semiosis in the Royal Commentaries of El Inca Garcilaso de la Vega," in *The Places of History: Regionalism Revisited in Latin America,* ed. Doris Sommer (Durham and London: Duke University Press, 1999), 70-71.

Vitaly Markov
Alamy Stock Photo DMAA39, "Inca Wall in SAQSAYWAMAN Peru South America. Example of polygonal masonry. The famous 32 angles stone in ancient Inca." Used with permission.

Joanne Thornton
Google Earth images used for main illustration and inset.

Don Mammoser
Alamy Stock Photo JBJ25D, "Inca Fortress in Ollantaytambo, Peru. Ollantaytambo was the royal estate of Emperor Pachacuti who conquered the region." Used with permission.

Joanne Thornton
Drawn on enlarged segment of d-maps image https://d-maps.com/carte.php?num_car=31136&lang=en

Joanne Thornton
Google Maps used for enlarged segment of Peru coastline.

Valentin Carderera y Solano creator QS:P170,Q3574278 (https://commons.wikimedia.org/wiki/File:Pedro_de_la_Gasca.jpg), "Pedro de la Gasca," marked as Public Domain.

CarlosVdeHabsburgo (https://commons.wikimedia.org/wiki/File:Conquistador_español.JPG), "Conquistador español," https://creativecommons.org/licenses/by-sa/3.0/legalcode

North Wind Picture Archives
Alamy Stock Photo DE6CYR, "Francisco Pizarro with Holy Roman Emperor
Charles V (Charles I of Spain)," Hand-colored woodcut. Used with permission.

Index